LIFE AFTER DEATH

Understanding Bereavement and Working Through Grief

24 Real Life Stories

Dr Philip Bachelor

HILL OF CONTENT
MELBOURNE

First published in Australia 2002
By Hill of Content Publishing Pty Ltd
86 Bourke Street, Melbourne 3000
Tel: 03 9662 2282
Fax: 03 9662 2527
Email: hocpub@collinsbooks.com.au
Web: http://hillofcontent.bizland.com

Typeset by Midland Typesetters, Maryborough Victoria
Printed by McPherson's Printing Group

National Library cataloguing-in-publication data

Life after death : understanding bereavement and working
through grief : 24 real life stories

ISBN 085572 326 2.

1. Bereavement—Australia. 2. Grief. I. Bachelor, Philip, 2. 1955–.

155.937

Published with the assistance of the
Australasian Cemetries and Crematoria
Association

Contents

Acknowledgements

The contributions of numerous others toward this compilation of bereavement stories are gratefully acknowledged. For introductions to interview participants, I am indebted to several staff, business colleagues, clergy, friends and neighbours.

I have especially appreciated support from Fawkner Crematorium & Memorial Park, and the Australasian Cemeteries & Crematoria Association towards this publication. From Fawkner Crematorium & Memorial Park, I thank chairman Keith Joyce OAM, fellow trustees Henry Curwen-Walker, Keith Evans OAM, Philip Rock, Bruce Robinson, and Rosemary Kerr; general manager Ian Roddick, and grief counsellor Damien Peile. From the Australasian Cemeteries & Crematoria Association, I particularly acknowledge the roles of president Bruce Macumber and executive officer Robyn Smith.

I am also indebted to Dr Neil Lipscombe and Dr Jim Birckhead of Charles Sturt University for guiding me into the field of ethnographic social research. But I am most grateful to my best friend and dear wife, Jan Bachelor, for untiring support through all my endeavours.

To those bereaved individuals (identified by pseudonyms) who allowed me to delve into their personal grief and explore their intimate experiences, beliefs and practices, I express my heartfelt appreciation and sincere thanks for the privilege of sharing such an important part of your lives. I trust that your stories will not only continue to provide meaning and comfort to other mourners, but also understanding and guidance to those who seek to support those who mourn.

Philip Bachelor

Introduction

In this collection of personal stories, diverse mourners share their intimate experiences of bereavement and what their respective losses mean to them.

The stories represent a series of windows into the lives of recently bereaved persons from a range of relationships and ethnicities commonly found throughout Australia. Each case represents a snapshot of personal interpretations of bereavement at a particular point, between two months and five years, since the death of a significant other. Collectively, the cases reveal common and contrasting experiences.

Rather than conforming to any standardised process, we each grieve differently in different circumstances. No two persons grieve the same way over the same loss, nor does one grieve identically over separate losses. Variable factors influencing the way we grieve include our emotional bond with the decedent (ie. deceased person), circumstances of the death, our religious beliefs, nationality, gender, age, personality, socio-economic status, previous and subsequent life experiences, and social support.

While some individuals seek to avoid confronting the reality and inevitability of bereavement, this renders them unprepared to cope with their own personal grief, and leaves them of little consolation to other mourners in need of support. From studies involving thousands of bereaved Australians, I have learned that the overwhelming majority just want to be listened to and understood. Most mourners would love to be understood by their family members and close friends, rather than by some specifically trained expert. Nevertheless, professional counselling is an option where knowledgeable, supportive friends and family members are not able to provide required empathy and support.

In this collection of stories, adult mourners speak of the life, death and funeral of someone with whom they have shared a very close bond. Many also discuss personal values of visiting the respective grave or memorial toward accommodating bereavement within their altered life.

Interviews, from which the case studies were derived, mostly took place within private homes; though some were conducted within a public cemetery, and others elsewhere convenient to specific interviewees.

Each person interviewed formally consented to his or her story being tape-recorded. In each case, the presence of a tape recorder was quickly ignored and so did not impede natural flow of conversation. Most interviews involved one-on-one discussions between a single mourner and myself. As well, three married couples participated, and three mourners had the comfort of a close friend or family member present. In a further two cases, the daughters of non-Australian widows assisted with interpreting to and from their mothers' first language.

Main interviews ranged in duration from less than one hour to over three hours. Some participants were quite composed, objective and pragmatic. Other interviews involved highly emotional outpourings. In several cases, home visits included guided tours to show me how the mourners now live, and to see photographs and other memorabilia of the deceased.

A transcript was made of each tape recording and these were then edited, deleting unnecessary or irrelevant discussion, including my own questions and any superfluous repetitions. Actual names of interviewees, several places and organizations, and some other identifying factors were substituted. Some broken speech was reconstructed where this enhanced clarity of expression. In each case, editing resulted in a condensed draft case study report.

These draft reports were then presented to respective mourners, or their representatives, to validate accurate portrayal of expressed words and feelings. Participants were asked to suggest any corrections, additions or deletions to their respective case study. Most were completely satisfied with the first draft. Only two interviewees suggested minor alterations.

The following comments were typical verbatim responses to the draft case studies:

> *'There's nothing I would change. I mean, that's what I said. It's just my words.'*
> (40-year-old Italian Catholic son)

> *'It's very accurate. I thought it was very good. My daughter also read it and she also thought it was very good.'*
> (66-year-old Maltese Catholic husband)

> *'It was really funny reading what I said. My husband also had a laugh, because he read it too. I said, "Do I really sound like that?" And he said, "That's exactly you; that's just how you sound".'*
> (35-year-old Australian non-religious grand-daughter)

Some interviewees had not previously related much, if any, detail of their personal experiences to anyone else, nor even clarified their perspectives of grief for themselves. In several such cases, participants or their partners reported that the interview experiences and review of resultant case studies had provided considerable cathartic value.

> *'The interview reads well and is as [my friend] spoke, so we both agreed that it reflects accurately how he responded to your questions. I must tell you that after the actual interview, [he] was*

surprised at how much he had been able to feel again and welcomed the opportunity. It was very therapeutic for him.'
(Companion of 51-year-old Australian non-religious husband)

'It was really helpful to read what you wrote. I got the feeling you really understood how we felt. It was really interesting to read what we went through; and I think it's helped me somehow to get over it more.'
(60-year-old Australian non-religious grandmother)

In presenting these personal stories, I seek to offer readers insights into the reality of bereavement. I have endeavoured to convey a deep understanding of the ways in which some mourners reason, feel, and see things. And I sincerely hope that this compilation will help extend and broaden common understanding of contemporary bereavement and the needs of those who mourn.

Greater social awareness of the phenomenon of bereavement is essential, not only to those endeavouring to give meaning to their own grief, but also among those who seek to empathise and lend support to those who mourn.

Cemetery Visitation

On an average day, around 90 000 mourners attend cemeteries throughout Australia. Less than a quarter of these visits relate to funeral participation; most visits are to the grave of a close family member. We mainly visit to help control our personal grief.

Bereavement has been recognized for some time as the most psychologically and socially significant life event that most of us ever experience. But the role of the cemetery in the management of personal grief has, until recently, remained an oversight from bereavement research.

Urban memorial parks are among the most visited places in Australia. They are virtual hives of activity with recently bereaved persons of diverse cultural backgrounds. Some sites, hosting over two million annual visitors, are more popular than major tourist attractions. Within a national population of virtually 20 million, around 33 million visits are made to Australia's 2 300 cemeteries each year.

Cemetery visitation is a most significant bereavement behavioural activity, and for millions of bereaved Australians of various social and cultural backgrounds, a crucial component of satisfactorily working through grief.

Why people flock to cemeteries, who visits, when, what they do there, and what it means to them, are some of the questions recently answered through complementary quantitative and qualitative sociocultural studies involving thousands of visitors

to cemeteries throughout Australia. The research was conducted in association with Charles Sturt University's Johnstone
Centre for Social and Biophysical Environmental Research,
and with the support of the Australasian Cemeteries and Crematoria Association.

These studies opened a new dimension to understanding
the phenomenon of bereavement. As well as extending our
understanding of grief control and bereavement behaviour, the
findings offer the cemeteries industry, in particular, intimate
knowledge of its various clients and their personal needs. This
provides a basis for planning improved facilities and services,
offering the potential to help ease the grief of literally
hundreds of thousands of mourners each year, throughout
Australia.

Frequency of visitation relates to the strength of emotional
bond to the decedent, duration of bereavement, family ethnic-
ity and choice of burial or cremation. Some 41% of those who
do visit a cemetery attend at least once each week. Frequent
visitors typically include those attending a grave, particularly
of their own child, spouse or parent, and those of Greek
Orthodox and Italian Catholic families. Conversely, very in-
frequent visitors typically include those attending a cremation
memorial, particularly of a grandparent or friend, and those of
Anglo-Australian Protestant and non-religious families.

Parents' graves and memorials are the subject of 38% of all
visits, spouses' 30%, children's 11%, and grandparents' 6%.
Even though more of us have deceased grandparents than other
close relatives, the commitment to visiting graves of grandparents is much less than to those with whom we share a greater
emotional bond. The greater the bond: the greater the grief.
The greater the grief: the greater the frequency and duration of
cemetery visits. Altogether, just over 95% of cemetery visits are
made to graves and memorials of relatives, and almost 5% to
those of friends. Just two out of each thousand visitors attend for
other reasons, including heritage interests and leisure pursuits.

Australian cemetery visitors may be identified by faith as: 44% Roman Catholic, 18% Anglican, 13% Orthodox, 11% other Protestant denominations, 2% of non-Christian religions, and 12% of no religion. Nationalities by which families identify themselves are: 49% Australian, 17% Italian, 9% Greek, 7% British, and 18% all others. Naturally, the specific ethnic mix of visitors varies between individual cemeteries.

Families opting for cremation are much less likely to visit a cemetery than are those that choose burial. And those who do visit a cremation memorial typically attend much less frequently and for a much shorter duration than do those visiting a grave.

Commemorative visitation abates rapidly soon after the funeral, so that more than one fifth of all visits occur within the first year. The median interval between the respective funeral and a cemetery visit is less than four years. Abatement of visitation frequency is most evident within weeks or months of the death and funeral, but in some cases occurs a year or more later. Most mourners find that abatement of cemetery visitation correlates to subsiding intensity of emotions of grief.

Customary pre-bereavement practises of giving gifts on personal and public anniversaries and religious festivals (including birthdays, Mothers Day, Fathers Day, Christmas and Easter) are commonly substituted after death with placing flowers, greeting cards and other symbolic gifts at the grave or memorial site. Symbolic giving expresses continuing love, which, for many mourners, is crucial towards maintaining an important social bond, and helps mitigate emotions of loss, particularly at times of specific personal remembrance.

For millions of Australians, the cemetery provides an essential place of focus. For many, it is the only place where vital communication with the decedent may occur on important occasions.

The most common gravesite activities, and those undertaken by the majority of visitors, involve placing flowers, maintaining the grave or memorial, and talking to the decedent.

As placement of flowers represents a gift, maintenance of the site represents continuing care for a decedent. Talking to a decedent at the grave or memorial site is also popular across various faiths and relationships, though usually requires some personal concept of an afterlife. Common gravesite 'conversations' include renewal of acquaintance by saying hello, assuring decedents that they are missed and not forgotten, and updating them on recent and current events. Visitors of some faiths may also request divine intercession on behalf of other family members.

Moderately common, and perhaps secondary, activities include crying and praying. Crying is more common during early stages of grief, among females, and particularly those of Italian and Greek origin. Prayer is a moderately common practise among some religious visitors.

Other gravesite activities include performing various religious rites, kissing the memorial, feasting or drinking with the decedent, placing mementos and other gifts on the grave, standing silently at the memorial site, talking with other mourners, and conjuring up images of the decedent.

Across cultures, significant differences are evident between the sexes in their typical emotional and behavioural responses to bereavement. Females visit in much greater numbers and stay longer than do males. Females are also more likely than males to bring flowers, place mementos, maintain gravesites, and socialize with other mourners.

Very few children have reason to visit cemeteries, as the incidence of death among significant others is something that increases with age. So the median age of cemetery visitors, at 56, is over twenty years older than the average Australian.

To literally millions of bereaved Australians, the cemetery allows potentially stressful obligations to be expressed and resolved. A sense of being in a decedent's presence can provide some control over the common early-bereavement anguish of separation and loss. Visiting the cemetery commonly provides appreciable solace and a strong sense of personal well-being.

Intensity of grief, and of other associated emotions, including sadness, guilt, loss, loneliness and anger, generally decreases rapidly after the funeral, or following a specific turning point, and continues to subside progressively in most regular visitors.

However, not all bereaved persons visit a cemetery. Major reasons include the remains not being interred in a cemetery, inability to travel to the cemetery, repression of grief, religious restrictions, and no perception of any need to visit.

To most mourners, however, the cemetery holds great personal significance, including cultural, social, heritage and remembrance values. But a sense of sacredness is the most commonly held value. While it may not be as sacred as the church to everyone, the cemetery is at least a place to be venerated, even by most non-religious mourners.

Many visitors value opportunities that the cemetery provides for continuation of cultural traditions. To this end, cultural segregation of traditional funereal and commemorative activities is particularly important to many persons of diverse backgrounds. Yet this choice has become less available in modern cemeteries developed within the homogenizing concepts of non-denominationalism or multiculturalism.

For many mourners, cemeteries are venues of important social support and assistance towards grief mitigation, through mutual sharing of personal bereavement experiences with other visitors. Valuable friendships develop among truly empathetic mourners of specific cultural and social groups, within their dedicated cemetery areas. To many mourners, particularly mothers and non-English-speaking immigrants, peer support is considered more helpful than professional counselling.

Cemetery heritage value is recognised more by those with a greater concept of Australian family heritage. Heritage may be considered a residual value, in that it is what remains, and may become more apparent, as the primary emotional and spiritual values of a functional cemetery abate over time.

Within the cemetery, a memorial proclaims the significance of the life of a decedent, and may hold several short and long term values to visitors, including providing a focal point for remembrance, facilitating cultural or personal expression, fulfilling the decedent's wishes, symbolising the decedent, identifying the location of the remains, and recording family histories.

Leaving a grave unmarked, or scattering cremated remains, can be convenient to some mourners, particularly in the short term. But these actions are also found to hinder grief resolution, and to evoke emotions of distress, among those for whom identification of a point of focus and/or historical recording are particularly important. The existence of a permanent memorial, even if not regularly visited, plays a part in the control of grief by most mourners.

In the following real-life case studies, socially and culturally diverse mourners relate their own experiences in their own words. They share insights into their family backgrounds, faiths, and experiences of death, values of funerals, subsequent adjustments, commemorative activities, and individual values of personal memorials in natural control of grief.

Death of a Child

Different Person Now

Donna is a functional manager within a large government service organization. She was the third child born to a Melbourne Catholic couple just on 27 years ago. Her brother was ten, and her sister six years old, when Donna was born. She had a Catholic schooling and married in the Church two and a half years ago. Her husband is from an Italian family.

'I've had a very good life in a lot of ways. But I had an alcoholic father, and my mother had a couple of nervous breakdowns when I was around seven or eight. I didn't know what was happening at the time, but as I've gotten older it's become clear what happened and we've spoken about it.'

'It was a very hard life. I can remember being very young and praying: "If you make Dad stop drinking, I promise I'll be good. I'll do this for you. I'll come back to church, I promise. I'll go every Sunday for the rest of my life". I didn't fulfil my end of the bargain, but I've been lucky. Dad hasn't had a drink in five years. He's an amazing man now. I love him, you know. So we've been touched by some good things; but unfortunately, probably by just by as many bad things as well.'

'My brother told my parents, when I was seven and he was seventeen, that he was homosexual. We're talking about a time when you just did not do that kind of thing. And he also turned to drugs at the time. It was a very, very difficult time for my parents. It never made me think any less of my brother; I just adored him. I didn't know about the drug problem until I was a bit older.'

'As I got older, my brother told me things that happened to him when he was seventeen. He was very confused about what to do about these feelings that he had and the first person he went to tell was a priest: a family friend of ours. At the time this priest basically told him that he was excommunicated—he couldn't do that: it's wrong—to get out of here and ignore his feelings. And I think from that moment I had a hell of a lot of questions. I think that was it for me; I was finding the Catholic religion very hypocritical. You know, I just look at it and tear my hair out sometimes. Sometimes I wish I was Anglican.'

Donna's brother died three weeks after her wedding. 'He had been an HIV patient for about twelve or thirteen years, and had done really well. He got really sick about two years before he passed away; that was when he developed full-blown AIDS. He was an absolutely amazing person, my brother. We were so close, even though he was ten years older than I was. He just idolised me from the day I was born, so of course I loved him. We were extremely close through my entire life, and especially when he was diagnosed with HIV; I would have been only twelve or thirteen at the time.'

'Being homosexual, he opened me to a whole different world that I never knew existed. But he didn't tell anyone in the family for two years. So—poor thing—he went through it all on his own.'

'He was an amazing person. He ran a house for people with AIDS whose families disowned them and problems like that. Unfortunately that happens. And I met this amazing group of people through him. Unfortunately most of them have passed on now.'

'My husband and I are very lucky. We've always been a very close couple, but we had to deal with my brother's death so quickly after our marriage. I wouldn't have blamed him if he had said, "Stop this; I'm out of here. I want an annulment".

But he supported me through all of that and I treated him terribly—I really did—and he put up with it all.'

'Then I fell pregnant six months after that, and I thought maybe that was God's way of giving me a new start and bringing me some happiness—and she did. Natalie was a blessing: our little surprise. I stopped working prior to having Natalie. I went on maternity leave and didn't think I would've gone back; I was really enjoying being at home. She was fine and healthy and great: a normal child. I had a bad pregnancy and not a pleasant birth, but she was beautiful: a very healthy child. Everything was going along wonderfully.'

'Then she came down with a fever in November, when she was five months old, and couldn't shake the fever. After a week of fever and ongoing doctor visits we ended up taking her to the Children's Hospital. They admitted her with a suspected urinary tract infection, but that turned out not to be the case. Then she was diagnosed as having glandular fever, which they say occurs very often in young children.'

'She was in hospital for about four weeks and wasn't getting any better. The doctors didn't really have any answers, but nobody thought there was any major thing wrong with her. We just thought everything would be OK eventually. But then, one day out of the blue, she started to bleed from her mouth and her bottom—and that was it!'

'That was on a Saturday and unfortunately, with the way the hospitals are run these days, she couldn't have a bone-marrow test until the Monday. So she bled over the weekend, and then on the Monday had the bone-marrow test done. They suspected it might have been leukaemia, which is quite rare in children that young; she was almost seven months old.'

'When they sat down with us on the Monday night—three days before Christmas—it wasn't leukaemia; and we were pretty relieved about that. We thought that was pretty good. But unfortunately, they weren't smiling. She had a very rare blood disorder. There's only been half a dozen cases known in

Australia and it's a disease that they don't really know a lot about. She died thirteen days later.'

'We thought that Natalie was our crack at happiness. But to lose her then certainly raised a lot of questions like, "Why the hell is this happening to me? This can't happen now; she was meant to be here. She was my happiness; she was meant to help me get through the rest of my life". Then she got taken away as well. Oh, it's a very, very difficult time: a very difficult time.'

'Since Natalie passed away, I've met people that have lost their child suddenly through SIDS and I've seen other people that have lost children that were sick from the day they were born. We're a little bit in between. We really only had thirteen days to get used to the idea that she probably wasn't going to make it—and that was right over Christmas. It was pretty awful: a pretty horrible Christmas Day last year, and pretty horrible New Year's Day. She passed away on the third of January.'

'Right up until the fever, she was perfectly healthy and a beautiful little baby. There's a photo of her at the gravesite and you wouldn't even believe that she could possibly get sick—and that's only two weeks before she did. So it's very frustrating—very frustrating—to have such a rare disease and no research done in Australia. Yeah; it's pretty horrible.'

'When they tried to explain that she had this disease we just sat there completely baffled by everything they said. We didn't understand any of it; and there was no time. Because she was already so sick, chemotherapy started right then. We didn't have any time to think about it or discuss what we wanted. There was no choice in anything. It was just like: this is what's happening and it's happening now and that's it.'

'She was lying in her cot sleeping and real sick. When they left the room, I looked at my husband and said, "We're going to lose her"; and he said, "I know". I think that was probably out of fear that we said that. Then over the next couple of days, I think we tried to talk ourselves out of it when they started the chemotherapy.'

'I remember sitting there on New Year's Eve looking at her, and it came the New Year and I looked at him and said, "Yeah; happy New Year. This is great".'

'They had her on a lot of medication, because I didn't want her in any pain obviously. So she was sleeping a fair bit and she had all these tubes in her body. I can't even describe how many, but I couldn't hold her. She just had to lie there—and that's just awful to think I couldn't even hold her. About midnight we tried so hard to talk ourselves into the fact that she was going to get better. But then around nine or ten o'clock in the morning on New Year's Day, she just took this really bad turn for the worse; and then she only lasted another two days.'

'The hospital staff kept telling us that everything would be OK, because they'd just treated a little girl with the disease and she was OK. I don't think they really realised until the night she passed away that there was no chance at all, so we still lived in hope all that time. I don't think we really had much time to prepare at all.'

'We knew nothing about the disease and there was no reading material or anything they could give us. It was horrible. It was Christmas and New Year time, so there was no social work department: they were on holidays. There was no priest: they were also on holidays. And the doctors had no idea what she really had. Only one doctor in the whole hospital had even heard of the disease.'

'They put her on the resuscitator machine and that was horrible. They kicked us out because they wanted to look at her. And when we came back in they had already tubed her without even asking us; but they felt that's what they had to do. I don't really carry much anger towards the hospital about the whole thing, because I just don't think they knew what to do.'

'Because she was tubed, she started to blow up; she looked awful. She was very jaundiced and very swollen, because her liver and spleen had swollen. Her face started to swell and she just didn't look like Natalie. I think that's when we started to realise how bad things really were, because everything was just changing before our very eyes.'

'Around eleven o'clock in the morning, I asked the doctor: "Is she going to make it? I need to know". And he said, "There's still a chance". I said, "If she's not going to make it, let's end it now; let's just do what we have to do", because it was awful.'

'Then about six o'clock, I called the professor in again from the intensive care section and I said, "Look, she's changing more and more. Is she going to make it or not?" And he said, "She's not going to make it". I said, "You told me six hours ago there was a chance". And he said, "Well, I'm telling you now there's not".'

'I asked what our options were and he said, "You can leave her on the resuscitator and she might last another day or two, or you can take her off it and she could last thirty seconds or thirty minutes, but not much longer than that".'

'So we obviously had a very big decision to make. I asked, "What would happen if we left her on?" And he said, "Well, besides you getting more time with her, she's not going to get any better; she'll just get sicker and sicker".'

'We decided we didn't want that to happen to her, so we told them to take her off the resuscitator. We were very lucky; she died in our arms. You know, we got to hold her while she passed away and that's something we're very grateful for. At least we were given that opportunity.'

'You know, if there was any sign of hope then it would obviously be a completely different story. But if there was absolutely no chance, then I didn't want her to suffer any longer. We were very fortunate, because we didn't just hold her, we actually bathed her and dressed her; many people don't have that opportunity. I'm not one for seeing people after they pass away. I was there when my brother passed away and we spent three or four hours with him after that; but I didn't want to view him again.'

'I think that if Natalie had looked more like herself, then maybe I might have said goodbye again; but I didn't want to remember her like that. I surround myself in photos of her when she was well, and try really hard not to think of her in hospital.'

'We got nothing from the hospital, you know. The nurse that looked after her was beautiful and gave us her footprints, her handprints and a poem. But then we were sent on our way with: "I'm very sorry that this has happened. We'll take care of her. See you later".'

'I've spoken to a lot of bereaved parents now. You're faced with so many decisions to make so quickly, you know. Those next two days were just so bad; the next day would probably be the worst day of my life. My husband and I were literally screaming at each other, because we wanted completely different things and we had no one and nothing to help us make any decisions. We had no guidance: nothing.'

'Hospitals like the Children's—unfortunately they lose children all the time in there—should be equipped with some sort of pamphlet, you know: even just a pamphlet. Maybe a lot of people would say that's the last thing you want when walking out after just losing your child: you don't want something shoved in your face. But my Mum and Dad were there. You've usually got someone else there: it's not just you and your husband. They could even approach them and say, "Look; they might not want to hear this right now, but here's a little pamphlet for them. They've got a lot of decisions to make in the next couple of days. This tells you some different options they've got and some things that could help". We had to know what we wanted by the next day when our funeral director came.'

'My first grandfather—my Mum's dad—died when I was five. That was a very big loss as I was close to him at the time. Then my grandmother—his wife—passed away when I was fourteen. Probably five years ago now, my Dad's parents tragically passed away within 21 days of each other, so that was horrible. They were both sick and everyone knew it would be quick, but I don't think anyone realised it was going to be that quick. They were great people; all of them were really great people.'

'The only way that my brother's death helped when we lost Natalie was that we knew who to contact for funeral arrangements. I still remember with my brother I was devastated; I just wanted to die. We were just newly married and I don't know how my marriage got through that first couple of months. It really affected my life, you know. It affected my relationship with my new husband and it affected my work. I couldn't go to work, you know. It was shocking.'

'When he passed away, I honestly thought that was going to be the worst loss I'd ever have to experience. But I'm sure my brother wouldn't mind me saying that it's just not in the same realm as losing a child. There is nothing to compare to losing your own child; there's absolutely no comparison.'

'I adored my brother and I miss him, but when I speak about him I can still smile and laugh. He had a life. He was 34 years old—way too young—but he had a life and he lived life to the fullest. He was a great person who created opportunities for himself. But you don't expect to lose a child; it's never a possibility. I knew that I was going to lose my brother at some stage. There's no cure, so obviously I was going to lose him, but when it happened that didn't make it any easier; I was still devastated for months.'

'Natalie's funeral was very important to me. We had a family friend that's a priest, who understands all my views and opinions; he did our wedding and my brother's funeral. I wanted some certain things done in the service. I wanted the priest to stand up there and yell at God for me; that was really important to me. I didn't want anyone telling me that she was in a better place or that this has happened for a reason. It was very important that I got my point across to him and he was pretty good, because he did it for me; so I was pretty rapt.'

'We asked the priest to do the eulogy; but overall the rest of the funeral arrangements were pretty much left up to me. Now unfortunately, I've had a bit of experience of this. With my brother I did all the booklets and the service and everything for him. So I chose all the music, readings and the poem. I arranged the entire service. I don't think I was all there on that day. It was bizarre sitting there and actually writing out my daughter's service; it was pretty weird. But it was the most beautiful service; I couldn't have been happier.'

'My husband carried her coffin out, and that's always quite emotional: seeing a man with a little white coffin. There was a great turnout: nine-hundred-odd people. We asked for a private burial. I would've liked it even a little bit more private than it was, but my husband's family is Italian and they take immediate family to include cousins and second cousins and third cousins. We just had close friends and families at the burial and I'm really glad. I still wish it was smaller, but it was fine at the time.'

'The funeral was very, very important: very important. And I wanted it to be really, really sad. I wanted everyone to be howling, because they should be, because it's my little baby. A lot of those people had never met her, so it was important that everyone walked away feeling like they'd known her; that's why we had a fairly lengthy type of eulogy. Even though she was only seven months, we tried to make it like everyone could share part of her life; that was very important. And it was very important that I had lots of flowers. That was something else everyone is so different on; we wanted donations for the Children's Hospital, but I wanted donations and flowers.'

'The initial period after she died was just the worst time. It's a very, very difficult time. During this time, while we were organising the funeral, my husband said to me, "I've come up with the reason why this has happened". I said, "OK, let me hear it".'

'Now, I don't know how I feel about this, but it comforts him. He feels that my brother had a bit of a hand in taking her, because he never had a child and wasn't ever going to have a child, but he loved children. And he feels like he actually had a hand in taking Natalie, and he's sort of looking at us saying, "You know, I'm sorry; but this was my chance at having my child".'

'Well, you know, I just think that if my brother's done that, then I reckon he's a bit of a selfish bastard and I'll lay him out when I see him. But that made my husband feel better. I don't know if he still feels the same; this was two days after it happened and I think he desperately needed to find a reason why. At the time, that was the best answer for him. Whereas, I think I could ask why until the day I die, and I don't think I'll ever know. Religion is a funny thing.'

'It was very important that we christened Natalie, especially as my husband is Italian; he's a lot more religious than I am. The reason she made it to six months without being baptised was probably me, more than anything else—oh; and the fact that she didn't fit into her christening dress. But when she got very sick—you know; you do turn. I can remember saying, "We need a priest; we need one here now!" It was quite important to me that she didn't pass away without being baptised. It's not like I thought she wouldn't have gone to heaven or she wouldn't be looked after. I mean she's a tiny little baby, of course she would; but it was sort of important.'

'We actually jumped on a plane straight after her funeral and flew up to Queensland for three weeks. In retrospect, I can't believe I did that; but I desperately needed to. I was very run down at the time and we just wanted to run away and bury our heads. We lost her in January and I went back to work in February. It's coming up to the anniversary of when she got sick, so I'm going to have a couple of months off. I just think I need a bit of a break.'

'Mum and Dad are still going strong. I don't know how when they've lost a son and a grand-daughter now; and they've both lost both their parents as well. So it's pretty hard. My sister's married and has three beautiful, fantastic children who I love and adore. I'm really close to them—especially to her 7-year-old daughter; we have a really special relationship.'

'Emotionally, people tell you there's a pattern for grieving. They tell you: "You're going to be really upset initially" and, "Oh; you'll probably get angry" and, "You'll probably go through this phase and that phase", you know. Maybe they're right; I don't know. But I don't really take notice of that; I just go with how I feel at the time. With my brother, I tried denial and found that it just didn't work. I tried keeping it all in saying, "Sure, I'm fine". But with Natalie, I knew I had to grieve properly and just let it all out.'

'I think on every level I'm a completely different person now since Natalie's death. I am nowhere near the same person I used to be. Emotionally, it just completely changes you; all your priorities are different. I've always been a fairly emotional person anyway; that's my nature.'

'It's affected me in the sense that I couldn't look at other children—which is pretty awful—but I'm getting better. It's ten months down the track, and I'm just finding now that I can look at other children. It's quite difficult, because I have several friends that had children at the same time as me, so their children are exactly the same age as what Natalie should be. I made sure that I saw them soon after Natalie passed away; because I thought the longer I leave it, the harder it will be. So I just tortured myself and saw them. It almost killed me and I didn't hide it. I mean, these are very dear friends that I've known all my life who have these children, so I didn't feel I had to hide anything—which is very good.'

'I don't try and suppress my feelings. In a lot of ways I'm probably stronger now, because it just makes you harder to be hurt. It makes you very cynical and a little bitter sometimes, but I try not to be too bitter, because I don't want to end up bitter and old.'

'A lot of people can't tell others how they feel; I feel sad for them. I've been able to express my feelings, but I only have a couple of people that I'll really confide in. That's changed a lot. People let you down, including really close friends. My best friend in the whole world hasn't spoken to me since it happened; she's never called to see how I am or anything. That's very disappointing. I don't wish my best friend any harm, but I never want to see her again. I've proven I can do without her. For all she knows I could be in a mental institution—which you get so close to.'

'It's just awful what you have to put up with from other people. When I first went back to work, some people came up and said, "I heard about Natalie and I'm so sorry" and, "It's just terrible and I just wish you to know I'm thinking of you". To those people you say, "Thank you". That's all you expect; you just want to know that people were thinking of you and that they're thinking of her.'

'But then other people just ignore the fact and say, "Oh; hi. It's nice to see you're back at work. Bye". And they walk off and you think, "You must know; can't you at least tell me you're sorry". Initially, that really hurts you; and then you learn.'

'So people do let you down. In some ways it weakens you emotionally, but in other ways it strengthens you as well. It's usually either black or white. I have never felt so black and so white at the same time; there's no grey. You don't ever feel in-between any more.'

'I've been really lucky. I work for the government and they're very understanding; my boss is great. So I'm very fortunate in that way, but I know of another mother who lost her job, because she physically and emotionally couldn't go back to work after it happened.'

'Having Natalie changed us a lot; it's not just her death that changed us. It wasn't a planned pregnancy; having her really changed us. And through losing her you take it out on each other: definitely. I can't express my feelings to Mum; but I do with my husband, so we tend to take it out on each other at really strange times just when we think things are going OK. It's easier to take it out on each other, because we're the only two people in the world who really know how each other feels.'

'But it's difficult in the sense that everyone grieves differently. Just because I was her Mum and he was her Dad doesn't mean that we're grieving in the same way. I found that I went through real anger. I hated everything and everyone—and God. How could this happen to me? At the same time, he was still just crying and sad. He couldn't understand why I was so angry. So you go through these different phases differently. I can certainly understand how couples break up; it would just be so easy.'

'It's very difficult when you've got different views, especially in a large family. I know another mother from the cemetery whose child died at only four days old, and her husband's way of coping is to ignore the fact that the child was ever born. They've got two other children; but to him the third one never existed. I don't know how their marriage will ever survive, because her heart's breaking. I mean, he did exist—maybe only for four days—but especially for the mother. Mothers carry them and give birth. You know, I think what's so tragic is that it affects so many people so differently.'

'At one stage, we got that close to breaking up. I just looked at him and said, "We're coping with this badly together. Can you imagine what it would be like if on top of this we decided to split up as well?"'

'I think in our case it's made us stronger because we do communicate; we do try and share the grief. My husband can cry in front of me and knows that he's comfortable in doing that. I try to be strong for him, but more often he has to be strong for me.'

'The old religion is a bit of a strange thing. When you lose someone you love—probably especially a child—you do your best to look for answers. With my brother, there were a couple of obvious answers. With Natalie, there's nothing. There's nothing: no answer anyone can give me as to why I don't have my daughter here now. And I try so hard to tell myself she's in a better place, but part of me says, "Well, hang on; to me, the best place is with her Mum and Dad". I don't care what anyone says—I don't care how good heaven is, or how good God is—nothing can beat being with her parents, you know.'

'I still hate God; I always have and always will. But I'm not like some people who say, "There can't be a God. How could a God take away children?" Part of me feels that way, but I have to believe. I have to believe that God is with her. But as long as my brother's with her and she's with the other kids I don't really care too much. But you have to believe that there is a nice place for her: that she's OK, she's not sick, that she's better. And you have to believe that you're going to see them again; that is really important.'

'I've called God some pretty bad names, and most of the time I get pretty angry about him and continue to hate him; but I'm pretty sure he'd understand that. He must surely be looking down and saying, "I've taken this woman's child from her; she's got every right to be angry". I think I've got every right to be angry with anyone I want to be angry at really.'

'You go through suicidal tendencies when you lose a child. The pulling that you feel to be with them is so very strong. You think, "I shouldn't be here; I should be with them". I think at some stage we've probably all considered that. I had to justify to myself why I am still here and she is there.'

'So I have to believe there's a God. I have to believe he's looking after her. And I have to believe that he will let me be with her again no matter what I say about him in between time. It's really important that I believe that way, but it's very hard. For my husband it's not hard to believe, because he's always believed. But I've been too angry to believe. It has changed my faith, but it doesn't stop me from calling him names.'

'Having her in the children's part of the cemetery really

helps; I don't think it's a burial. I think burials are just the hardest part of it all. I hate burials: hate them. I found it very difficult to walk away after she'd been put down. To me that is so final. It was just like, "she's gone now"—and that was awful. But at the hospital, we probably had as much time as we could've had.'

'I had a dream not long ago where she actually spoke to me. It was very important to me to know that she'd met Mark, the son of one of the other mums at the cemetery. I can remember saying in the dream, "Do you know Mark; are you with Mark?" And she said, "Yes; yes". I mean she didn't speak—she's only seven months old—but she spoke to me in the dream, which is great.'

'At the time, Mark's mum was really struggling; and I must have been thinking about that, because I said, "I've got to know if Mark is OK; I've got to tell his mum". And she said, "Yeah, Mark is fine; we're together and we're both OK". She didn't say, we're both really happy or we're both great; she just said, "We're fine; we're OK". That was good. I like that wording. She told me she was only OK. I want her to be OK, but I don't want her to be too happy without me. I want her to miss me, but not crying because she misses me.'

'I think she's in heaven. I don't know where it is or what it is, but there's certainly a place and she's certainly there; and she'd be making everyone else smiling and happy like she made us.'

'The night Natalie passed away some family members actually said, "Don't worry; you'll have another baby". But what has having another baby got to do with losing Natalie? It's got nothing to do with it! Yeah; we probably will have another baby, but it will be another baby. It will be my second child, who will have an older sister who just happens to not be here, that's all.'

'I think there are different situations; if you have a miscarriage or a stillborn—especially if you haven't had other children—I think it's probably fairly important to have another child fairly quickly. In a sense this would be a replacement, because you never fulfilled the role of becoming a mother in the physical sense. But not so when you've had a child with you and got to know their own personality and everything about them—what makes them laugh and what makes them cry—and they know that you're their mum.'

'As time has gone on people probably piss me off more in that sense. Some people say, "Well it's been ten months now; maybe you should think about having another child"—like: "What are you still crying for?"'

'Most people don't know someone that's lost a child, or if they do, it's often a stillborn or a miscarriage. Not many people know children that have passed away at seven or eight months, or two or three years. They just fumble for words and yap on, trying to make you feel better. But usually what happens is I just say, "Yeah, yeah; no worries". Then I'll hang up and ring one of the other mums from the cemetery and say, "You wouldn't believe what this idiot just said to me". So we have big bitch sessions about all the silly things people say to us. We could write a book on all the stupid things people say.'

'When the funeral director came around to see us we still did not know what we were going to do. I didn't know there were private cemeteries and public cemeteries. I don't know if I'm naive, but I only thought of where my brother and my grandparents are buried. This is where we've always come, so I didn't think of any other cemetery. But I had no idea the children's area existed. I wanted to buy a plot for us—thinking that was really the only option we had—but my husband didn't want a bar of it. He said, "No! I'm too young. We're too young to buy a plot". I said, "We're too young? Our daughter's seven months old and just passed away. How young is young?" So I was ready to do that, but he just wouldn't. And in retrospect I'm glad, because we might never have found out about the children's area.'

'I thought of cremating her and keeping her with us. I didn't really want to do that; I just thought that it was the only option we had, but he would not have a bar of that either: "No way!" Then—thank God—when we sat down with the funeral directors, they said, "There's a couple of special children's sections".'

'They offered to check out the one that they thought was best and to get back to us. And I'm telling you, you don't know just how much it means to us now. It was a blessing; it's one of the few good things. If she can't be with me, then I am just so relieved that she's in that area with all the other children. I can speak on behalf of probably fifteen different sets of parents that I've met down there; it brings us all so much comfort to know they're all together: it really does.'

'It is really important to me that the cemetery staff know that I come here for comfort. I don't believe she's here—although she may be in body. I do feel a spiritual thing, but I don't feel it about my brother; I hardly visit my brother. I suppose that's just one of the differences you find. I can talk to her anytime I want. I can feel her anytime I want; and I can smell her anytime I want. I don't have to be at the cemetery to do it.'

'I feel really sad for the people who feel that they have to come to the cemetery every day, because this is where they are. I don't feel that way. I come here because it brings me comfort, because the area is just beautiful and because I like to have fresh flowers there all the time as a sign of respect. That's why I come, because it is in a sense where she lives—and I like her garden area to be the best. I want it always to look great. That's very, very important to me.'

'I couldn't think of any place I'd rather her be than at the cemetery; I absolutely love the area. I have never seen any other children's sections before—fortunately I've never had to go to any other children's funerals, so I don't know what other cemeteries offer—but where she is, is the most wonderful, beautiful area. The area is very, very important to me. I think this is probably hard to get across to people who haven't lost children.'

'I was closer to my brother than anyone in the whole world, but I still know that there's a difference between having my brother buried here and having my daughter buried here. I've got different requirements, or different needs. I mean I'll spend ten minutes when I go to visit my brother, and I visit him only on special occasions now. I go and see him on birthdays and at Christmas, and he's just over the road and I'm here all the time; I still don't go across there.'

'But if I'm anywhere this side of town and I'm in the middle of work, I'll never drive past the gates without driving in: never, ever. I wouldn't care how short I was for time; I could never drive past.'

'It's a very different area in that it certainly brings the parents a lot of peace and a lot of comfort. And I know cemeteries are probably meant to do that anyway, but I find it a lot more in that area. There's just something really nice about being there and I think the area itself is lovely. It really is great for the parents.'

'I think that anyone who goes around destroying property in a cemetery should be shot. I can't believe there's people out there who do the things that happen. At the children's section, there are lots of toys and other articles left on graves. We all know we're running a risk in leaving anything there. I've never left anything of vital importance: something that couldn't be replaced. I would never do that, because there are idiots out there and people who don't have respect and could damage or take things. So to me it's quite sacred in that sense.'

'It's also sacred in that the area as a whole does affect me: especially Natalie's plot; that is sacred. I'm very fussy about how it looks and how it's looked after. It's important to me that the gardeners in the area have respect.'

'I just think that that you should respect and honour the dead. I think that it's a very sacred area, but you don't have to be religious to respect or understand people's grief or situation. I think that all people should understand that this is sacred ground and that if you come in you come to visit someone and pay your respects. But I know different people view respect differently and that's a problem in the cemetery. Some people think it shows a lack of respect to leave so many things around. I suppose to everyone it's different: it's in the eye of the beholder.'

'This is our family cemetery, and my husband and I will be here one day. I hate to hear on the news that many cemeteries are filling up and they have to look at changing things and moving things; I can't stand that idea. Hopefully I'll be gone before anything like that ever happens. I hate the thought that anyone would ever touch Natalie. I'll end up here for sure one day. I want to be where she is; that's very important to me.'

'Mum gets really worried about me being here on my own, but I don't. I feel a great sense of peace when I'm here, especially when I'm on my own. I don't care if there are gardeners around.'

'I don't feel close to God, and I don't feel especially close to Natalie. If anything, I probably feel much closer to her at home—and we've moved from the house she lived in. But I have my little nightly routine, where I kiss her photo goodnight and that sort of stuff. Sometimes I'll sleep with some of her clothing or something, if I'm feeling like I really need to feel her. That's different to a lot of people.'

'A lot of people at the cemetery feel like that's where they have to be to see them, feel them, or be with them. I don't feel that way; I feel like she's with me all the time. At the cemetery, it's more a respect thing.'

'I come down to the cemetery because it makes me feel really good, and because I can arrange her flowers. Everybody always tells me how beautiful her area is: "Gee; you do your flowers nicely". That makes me feel really good, because I can't mother her any more; there's no mothering left. I can't feed her. I can't change her. I can't hold her; and I can't stop her from crying. I can't do any of that. All I can do is trim her grass and do her flowers; so I'm more than happy to make sure that I do that, because here is my outlet for mothering.'

'It's more than: "I've got to be here because she's here". It's more like: "this is the place where I can do things for her". So it's very important to me that I am able to do those things for her, you know: very important.'

'I don't have big conversations with her. I always say hello to her and give her photo and her angel a kiss, but I don't really have full-on conversations. I tend to talk to her more at home and at night, rather than at the cemetery.'

'On her grave there's a cross in the ground. It's a beautiful pink cross with her name, her photo and an angel sitting on the top of it. I've also got a couple of windmills and little things—bees or something—and she's got a plastic Big Bird that I bought. Big Bird was her favourite thing, and so that sort of sits there just in front of her vases on the ground. Other people have given her everything else.'

'We're now looking at putting a monument there, but I love her cross. A lot of people I know feel that it would be nice if we could just leave the crosses there, because there's something about babies and just having a simple cross that just seems right; but at the same time, I'm very happy with what we've chosen for a monument. So yeah; it is important to me to have a final monument to her. The cross does feel a little bit temporary.'

'The loss of a loved one is horrible no matter who it is, but I know that the loss of a child is worse than losing my brother. I understand the cemetery has to treat everyone as being in the same position. The last thing you can do is say, "Well, they lost their child and you only lost your husband". I mean, you can't do that to people, but I think visitors to the children's area have special needs, because we do visit there longer. We're there a lot longer than other people who go and visit, just do the flowers, say a prayer and leave.'

'When I got there today, one of the other mums was laying

on her rug reading a book and making an afternoon of it. You know, it's a very different visit than when you go and see your grandparents, your brother or anyone else; you're there for a lot longer. So it's very important to us that the area does look beautiful. And the parents are very funny about people walking on the actual graves. They understand they've got to be mowed, so obviously that's not a problem, but walking on them is really offensive to a lot of people.'

'I visit with my husband every weekend—usually on a Sunday. And I try and visit during the middle of the week—usually on a Wednesday. I like to come around again on either a Monday or a Thursday just to make sure the flowers are still looking fresh and that everything looks OK. I've visited three times this week. It varies, but it's probably no more than three times a week and certainly no less than once a week. I've got a bit of a routine.'

'When we come together we stop first at the florist. And when we get to the cemetery we always get the rug out and put it on the ground. All the flowers get taken out of the vase and the good ones separated from the bad. The two of us do our flowers together and that probably takes about an hour. I'm pretty fussy; I've become a little bit of a flower arranger since all this has happened and a bit fussy about how it looks. We know the gardeners do the borders and everything, but it gives us great satisfaction in trimming back all the little bits of grass, you know. My husband will go to the canteen and get a cup of coffee and come back.'

'As I met some of the other mothers, I started to come a little bit more. I like coming on my own. I love coming with my husband—that's very important to me—but I probably like it just as much to come and spend time here on my own.'

'When I come by myself I do pretty much the same: get the rug out and usually have a snooze. I probably spend longer when I'm here by myself, but it depends. I spend an absolute minimum of an hour and sometimes over two. Once, it was five hours; but that was a bit of a strange day—or different. I was very upset and couldn't go into work that day.'

'Usually, I come here crying and leave feeling better. On this day, I woke up and was really upset, so I wanted to come down and just spend some time with her. I came on my own—about ten o'clock in the morning—and threw the rug down. I bought some flowers on the way and did her flowers and went and got a cup of tea from the canteen and was sitting down. And then another couple came and we were having a bit of a chat. He started to talk about his religious beliefs; so religion was a big topic that day. Then a few other mothers came and everyone just sort of sprinkled through, so I just stayed chatting to them all and it was really nice. I felt heaps better when they were here.'

'Religion can be a fairly big topic. It's not something I really like to talk about a lot, because I think everyone has different beliefs, and you can't judge people on what they believe. Some people there don't believe in anything, and I understand that; but don't tell me not to believe. Don't tell me there's nothing, because I can't believe that.'

'A lot of our conversations are what you'd call "bitch sessions", if you overheard us. They're just about all the stupid things that people say to us and how our families make us feel and stupid things our best friends say. It's really good to have that outlet, because otherwise it could fester. So the lack of understanding is one of the big things we talk about.'

'There's one woman there that I don't like to speak to as much. Her daughter was born sick and also passed away in the Children's Hospital—at roughly the same time, but the year before—and she just focuses on her daughter's illness. When she sees me she wants to discuss what ward Natalie was in and what doctors she had and that sort of stuff. I can talk about it now, but it always hurts. She's always talking about that and I find that she brings me down. I've actually turned around the car and gone to see someone else or gone to the canteen when I've seen her car.'

'I suppose emotionally it has probably become a little bit easier to visit now. The first couple of times we pulled up I just shook my head thinking, "I can't believe what I am doing here. This can't be my life". I still feel it even when I'm driving out; I'm still in disbelief for sure. I'm still in shock; I still can't believe it. But I'm coming around emotionally I suppose. It's probably a little bit easier and it makes me feel better too, and that's important.'

'I'm looking forward to summer and being able to come and spend some good times. The last month has been really hard; visits have had to be a lot shorter with all the wind and the rain and everything. But I'm probably going to spend more time there in summer than I have up to date. I'm having some time off work and I can definitely see me spending more time lengthwise.'

'So many people say, "As time goes on you won't feel the need to go there as often"—and I know older parts of the cemetery get visited less—but at this stage I find that hard to imagine. I can't really see what time is going to do in this sense to me. I can't see how that will change. It's very, very important to me that when I have another child they understand the importance of this place. It's very, very important to me that they understand that they have an older sister. But I understand that maybe if I have another child they might have cricket and football and maybe my time might be a little bit more restricted.'

Where Only You Can Go

Paul was born in rural Victoria 37 years ago. He has four older sisters and considers himself the spoilt baby of the family. 'It's a great position to be in really. We were brought up in a Baptist family with both our parents heavily involved in the church. I ended up doing the normal teenage thing of throwing that all out and then returning to it, but in a slightly different shape than it was given to me as a child.'

Paul and Jane have been married for eleven years. 'I was on a dairy farm we owned when our daughter died. That was nearly three years ago. Now I'm a university lecturer and we have a six-month old son. I think my Christian-based faith has served me reasonably well through the death of our child—never well enough, but it has served to help somehow through the crisis.'

'We attended church regularly for the first couple of years of our marriage, but neither of us go these days. She'd like to go more than I would. I think that occurred partly from having lived in the country. It's difficult to find a church with more than twelve people and a dog in a small country community with most of the people over 65; so it happened naturally. We attempted to find a country church, but it just didn't happen and then we came back to the city and haven't got involved again.'

'Jessica was our first child. We lost her at 39 weeks gestation. She was an IVF child; so was our new boy. And although there was a secret wish to have another girl, I think we're lucky that we had a boy. He's very much his own little individual now. He hasn't filled Jessica's shoes, and I think that's been nice for both Jessica and our memory of her, or our attempted memories that we've tried to build. Now we have our son, and I think that's good.'

'With Jessica, the pregnancy went terrifically well. The child was healthy, but she was always very quiet in the uterus. So when she died, neither my wife nor I assumed anything was wrong. We were probably naive, even though we'd been through quite a lead-time to have a child. You live in a sort of naive vacuum that everything will be all right. It's amazing: the human capacity to create that sort of sense of security. I mean, even with the second pregnancy, I think we did feel very insecure; but it didn't take long to feel secure at times. So we oscillate now. And most of the people we know who have been through a similar experience are somewhat the same. They go between complete fear and insecurity to feeling quite secure about the child.'

'After two years of trying to conceive naturally, we were on the IVF program for two years before Jessica was conceived. Friends of ours went through a coroner's inquest on the death of their child; and during the inquest the obstetrician stated that, "No child is more valuable than another child". And I guess from our perspective that's true, but it's also false. I think that in reality, the replacement of that child—and replacement sounds horrible—is far more difficult for people who have been through IVF, or have had trouble conceiving.'

'And it's not just the child you lose when a child dies; it's also the lifestyle that you imagine with that child that disappears as well. So it has far greater consequences. I think that's possibly where infant death is very different from the death of a parent or an older person.'

'Your lifestyle doesn't necessarily change a lot when your 80-year-old mother or father dies; whereas our lifestyle was turned upside down. We had created it in a new way through those nine months. We knew how it might be—and then it wasn't. So I think there is a sense in which IVF is very costly in that way—not financially—because if you lose a child after IVF it's very difficult to rebuild your life again from that position. And we know people going through it now.'

'With Jessica's death there was no warning at all. On the Monday night she was fairly quiet. We were going through the birth centre for the delivery and they taught me to listen to the heartbeat. So I could hear the heart beating away: quite well, as far as I was concerned. So we went to sleep with a fair degree of confidence. She'd often been very still for long periods of time; it was just her nature I think.'

'But on Tuesday morning she was still quiet and Jane decided to go to the local hospital—we were living in the country—and they couldn't find a heartbeat. So that was the first indication we had. Then, at about eleven o'clock, we had an ultrasound and discovered that she was—that her heart had stopped—and she was dead.'

'For Jane it was an instant response. She was just wrecked. But for the first fifteen minutes, I don't think I really knew what had happened, whereas Jane seemed to know straight away. At that point, all I could think about was her—her pain—the fact that she was just distraught.'

'And it wasn't until we got home an hour and a half later—because it's a forty-minute drive to the hospital—and I think it was actually ringing someone and saying that she'd died, that it hit me. I can remember just staring out the window across the farm and not being able to breathe: almost hyperventilating. At that point Jane had her father support me. And I think that's the way it has been since then: each needing support at different times. But we've both lost our way at times.'

'That initial reaction was just shock. And for weeks we both felt fairly numb. I guess this is where the background of faith comes into it. I think that through that period of numbness, we did have a sense in which there was an understanding of being still—of just letting time take it's course—and we'd be better.'

'It wasn't until six or eight weeks later that we actually felt absolutely terrible again. I think that we knew our life was a mess. But there's a sense in which you're just numb—and thank heavens you are, because I don't think you'd deal with it all at once. But then after that, it gets raw again and people stop visiting as much.'

'At the ultrasound, when they found she had died, we wished we had asked what sex the baby was. That's about the only regret we have through that, because we had to make decisions. We were lucky enough, I suppose, to have an obstetrician there. Jane had private backup as well as the birth centre; and that slowed everything down.'

'Jane said, "I just want to get this done. I can't deal with this". She said, "I want to have a Caesar". And he said, "No. Come up tomorrow morning to the hospital". So we stayed with Mum that night and went to the hospital the next morning.'

'So she died on Tuesday, we ended up at the medical centre on the Wednesday morning and it was actually the Thursday before Jessica was delivered. So Jane had this for two days. We wish we had known that she was a girl at that point; but I guess we got the surprise that she was a girl when she was stillborn.'

'I think the birth was really difficult for Jane. Being a midwife she knew what was coming. Before Jessica was actually delivered the birth seemed futile. But she was delivered in the kindest possible way where Jane felt in control of the situation. I felt like I was contributing to her pain and the midwife and the obstetrician were actually involved in a sympathetic way. But once she was delivered, there was a sense in which bringing her into the world still happened. And if anyone went through the same thing, I'd say to go that way: never just say, "Cut this baby out" or "Pull this baby out". She was born—although still—she was warm. And you know, there was a sense in which life was still there—even though it wasn't.'

'So I think those two days after the ultrasound were incredibly valuable although they were hard. It was hard to go to sleep at night knowing that we were going to sleep with a dead baby. And it was hard to think of Jane carrying a dead baby. We got time to read the SANDS book; we got time to think about what we wanted for the service. We had to have that time. Most people we've talked to since didn't get that time and are still suffering. Whereas, I think that we moved along fairly quickly, because we had that time; so it's incredibly fortunate.'

'And I think the delivery was really important to us, even though she wasn't with us—but that's not the right thing to say, because I think we both felt like she was with us for about six or eight hours. I think that's associated with her getting colder—her body naturally getting colder. There was a point at which we felt she'd had enough. We kept her over the Thursday night in the room. But I think we knew the next morning that there was no point in staying any longer.'

'We have photographs. The hospital did a little memorial book and Jane's father took black and white shots, which are actually terrific. Because Jessica died two days before, she'd lost a little bit of skin around her eye and a bit on her arms. We didn't see that when she was dressed. The black and white makes this all softer than the colour photos.'

'I think we said goodbye as much as we could. I think we felt like she was leaving us through the night. You know I keep saying this, but we were lucky. We'd had a midwife with us on the same shift—for three shifts—and she was just wonderful. We actually put Jessica in her arms, rather than just have her wheeled out. That was a very difficult thing to do. Jane talks about wanting to turn around and run back; but I think I accepted then that Jessica had passed it. Blood was starting to come out of her nose and there was a sense in which she needed to be put somewhere and not touched again. Touching her was starting to upset her whole physical being, or what was left of it.'

'My father died in a car accident when I was fifteen. I was at home by myself when the police came to the door, and that was our first knowledge of it. Mum was actually arranging flowers in the church.'

'But I think, for me, the shock of Jessica's death really taught me what bereavement was. I wasn't very close to my father, so in a sense it was a change in our family life; but for me in some ways it was probably a change for the better. It was a little bit more solid and easier to deal with our family after his death. So if someone asks me what it was, or if I knew anything about grief at that stage, I don't think I did really. I knew things had changed and I knew it was different.'

'I wasn't involved in any of Dad's funeral arrangements. I was the youngest of five; the girls probably arranged it and did all they had to do. I can remember having half a sleeping tablet poked down my throat on the first night. My Grandmother was saying, "Oh, you have to take it; you have to take it". I thought it was a terrible thing, because I had terrible dreams in response to that sleeping tablet. But it was interesting the way people wanted to take over and not have us feel as much.'

'My stepfather died six years ago, and I was involved then. I actually did the service for his funeral. I was probably closer to him than I was to my father. But once again, his death didn't change my life. So it's hard to say there was an impact then, because our life was very separate from him and Mum, in the sense that they lived in their house and Jane and I were continuing our life as normal.'

'Grief is a place where only you can go; I don't think anyone goes with you. I know there are faith concepts that come into it, but in terms of everything we understand easily, it tends to be a really lonely place. I never felt that after Dad died. Whereas, after Jessica died—even though I'd never met her— that feeling was very intense and the physical concept of death was real. I couldn't breathe; and I experienced all those things that you read about grief, whereas none of that occurred with my father. My concern then was for my mother—and it was easy—whereas, with Jessica's death my concern was for my wife. But there was also a sense in which I was more intimately involved with Jessica.'

'Jessica died on the Tuesday; the birth was on Thursday—around 7.30 in the evening—and we kept her with us until the next morning. We left the medical centre around 10.30 that morning, and the funeral was on the following Monday. She was born three year's ago—on our wedding anniversary. The world's a very strange place.'

'She was buried at our local cemetery, where we lived; it's just a small country one. We were lucky—look, I keep saying this, because we really were—when I compare us to other people who went through a similar thing and just have so many regrets. We don't have those sorts of things to regret, so it was really important for us to say we're lucky in that way.'

'I was at Bible College for three years and met a good friend of mine who is now the minister of an Anglican Church. He actually came straight to the hospital when he heard and spent some time with us then. So we asked him to do the service and he did. So having someone who knew what we'd been through—who knew us and actually saw Jessica—made the service all that much better. Now I realise that's a sort of really privileged position and most people don't have that option; but in the service he certainly managed to bring Jessica to life with the people that were there.'

'Over those couple of days that we got time to think, we decided that we wanted pictures of her in the entrance there. So I guess we made it really hard for people. We wanted people to know that she was there, and we made sure that they did know. And I think that's been good ever since, because people have this picture of our little girl. In fact, we do have one friend who came to the church and had to go back to the car, because she couldn't cope with being confronted by the pictures; whereas we just felt that was really important.'

'Now that I think back, the day itself was really important to me. I'm very much a pragmatist. I knew she was dead. I knew she was dead before the funeral; it wasn't as though I needed the funeral to tell me she was dead. I needed the funeral for other people to know that she had been alive. That's what I needed the funeral for; and that's what it did, I think.'

'Jane and I probably spent three or four hours just talking about the service and then my friend the minister and I spent more time talking about it. Again we were lucky. We had a choice of two funeral directors and we chose the right one; they were just really sympathetic and understanding about it. Also Jane's mother—and this is a contradiction in her—wrote a poem; and so did Jane's Dad, the night that Jessica was delivered. And they were used in the service. It just fitted together really well and made us feel that they were representations of the fact that: yes, she was dead, but she'd been alive. And they said it really well. I mean, it's something that Jane and I couldn't do then, and still can't do—write that sort of thing.'

'I look back now, on the day that I carried the coffin and all these things we're scared of doing, and they were really important, you know. I don't know how others handle it, but the coffin was between Jane and me—just in the back seat of the funeral car—just put on one of those fold-down arms. I guess all that was good, because we got to take her away: no one else did so.'

'I had the sense in which most questions after the death were directed to me about Jane. And at that time I didn't feel betrayal or anything like that. In a way I still don't, but when someone asks, the question would be, "How is Jane coping?"'

'The family was better than that. I think we were really lucky with the family support and the honesty we had from our family—especially my side of the family, who'd been exposed to a lot. We've had a couple of divorces in the family; my father died when I was fifteen; my grandparents died the year before. So we've had a lot of having to deal with things not going right, whereas Jane's side of the family weren't exposed to that as much. So for them, it was a bit more difficult.'

'Jane's mother has trouble talking about it still, especially to me. I don't think she's ever actually talked directly to me about the death of Jessica. So I didn't feel left out by people, but the orientation was certainly towards Jane's grief. I still felt supported on the whole, especially by family and a couple of close friends.'

'It's funny: now that we've had our son, I do feel a sense of having got to know Jessica as a person. I've got a comparison now. He was incredibly boisterous in the womb, but she was really quiet. Appearance wise, they are very similar. So although he's a boy, I guess we have some idea of how Jessica's features might have matured. So I have more of an image of what she'd be like now than I did before. I think before he was born I really struggled to have an image of her. And I think that was one of the hardest things for us, that we couldn't develop an image.'

'I have a stronger belief in a sense of heaven than I ever had before. In fact, I was probably one of those Christian people who could almost think that heaven didn't exist. Now I have to believe it exists, otherwise I think it's all pointless. I couldn't describe it for you, but I think in most ways she's more whole than we are now; but I couldn't describe what that means.'

'I guess I see Jessica being looked after. It's too easy to say it's an old man with a white beard; and that's not the impression I have any more. But when you're bought up with that so much, it's hard to get rid of it. I really just have an image of her being looked after and cared for and held really, really well—and that's all I have. She exists still, but not for us: not now anyway.'

'I expect to be reunited with her one day. In fact, I think it would be wrong not to see that sort of unity completed. I still see us as a family and Jessica's still part of it; she's just not with us. So I think the family will be together one day. And I guess I need to think that I will see Jane holding her; I need to think that.'

'I don't necessarily cry more now, but I am more emotional. The most recent experience would be this morning. On the news there was a mother with a cerebral palsy child who'd got a walking frame designed for cerebral palsy kids. And when she said what it had meant to her that's when I nearly cried. That happens a lot now—more than ever—and it's still happening. It often just takes a comment by a parent to have that effect. I guess I have a better understanding of the loss that parents suffer; I think I do. So I'm definitely more emotional, but not necessarily to the point of tears; and I don't know whether that's a conditioning thing or that it just doesn't happen.'

'I think that Jane and I understand each other's frailties more than we did before Jessica was stillborn, but I also think a lot of that had occurred through the process of IVF. I mean, it's a horrible way to put it, but IVF prepares you for stillbirth in a way, because you have lots of little ones: you have embryos. Of course, not many people ever see their embryo. Well, with IVF you get to see them, and you get to have an incredible level of expectation that is often destroyed. So I guess we were used to seeing each other's reactions: our weaknesses and strengths, in those situations.'

'It's hard now to go back to what we were like before that, because it's seven years ago now since we started the process of trying to have a child. It's hard to say what we were like before that period of time, because it's been a slow process of change for both of us. I think the best description would be that we are just very comfortable gloves for each other now, and that gives us the warmth and security to keep going. And I don't think we can imagine doing that without each other. We probably have more arguments now that we've got our son than we had before, but that's more because kids have this capacity to make you feel short on patience and on the edge. But our relationship is very secure in each other's presence and I guess that's developed over seven years.'

'At 37, I tend to just accept that people are like they are and I try and take my mother-in-law for the strengths she has. She has trouble talking about death and emotional things, you know. It's upset Jane occasionally, but I think she sees that as the way that her Mum is and she sees the good things. I think it's taught us to do that more.'

'The only problem we have at the moment is that when Jessica died, I guess it created a separation with Jane's sister-in-law—who had a child only a few weeks before, and they've had other children—but that was occurring anyway because of IVF. We had an expectation that Jessica would include us in that club—the baby club—and we lost that inclusion I suppose. In fact we had a bigger wrench between us. My interpretation is that we belonged to a small group already: that of IVF parents. We moved into a smaller one: of still-birth. But then we really found that it was actually smaller still: it was stillbirth and IVF. So it changed our relationships more with other people rather than with family, except for that sister-in-law.'

'It's difficult to say what IVF is like. When an embryo is implanted, you have a high degree of confidence, and it's only experience that tells you that really only ten per cent of those are going to take. But no matter how much experience you have the expectation is still high. I guess we went through that quite a few times, though not as much as most people do. I don't think there's any doubt that those incidents are more than disappointments. They are mini-griefs. And they grow in intensity depending on how many failures you've had. You get better at dealing with them, but you're also weaker. As I said earlier, it's hard to put a value on a baby, but a baby born through IVF needs special treatment to make sure they get there alive.'

'I think the process of IVF and then stillbirth puts conclusions to things. The evangelical faith tends to bring you up as a person who believes in an interventionist sort of God: a God who jumps in and fixes problems. Now that's the immature view of God; and I've had to change that, otherwise there could be no concept that there was anything bigger than we are, because I couldn't believe that there could be a God that could allow these things to happen intentionally, without jumping in to fix them up.'

'So I guess the faith I have now says that we don't have this interventionist God, but I haven't quite put together what this God is. I don't know and I'm not as worried about that as I used to be. I just think I have a stronger concept of the idea of relationships with people, and I think that indicates that I have a stronger idea of a relationship with this God. I don't quite know what shape that relationship will take, or should take, in time. I just don't believe that he jumps in and out of history like I used to.'

'On reflection, I guess that when we went through that six or eight week period I was talking about earlier, I really felt there was a God, because I have no other description. I could feel far more a sense of presence and a sense of peace about that. But I guess the scientific part of me says, "Oh, my goodness; it's just hormones and all the rest of it helping you deal with grief". But you know, I still try and hold onto that period as something really valuable.'

'Then when we moved back to the city, I decided to actually go through a period of spiritual guidance with a Christian-based organization. And through that I discovered that the concept of God I had developed through that period of time was one where I still felt—it's very difficult to explain—that there was a separation between me and God; and I couldn't seem to get rid of that.'

'So I wanted to feel a sense of intimacy; and I could when I was in grief, because maybe all my reservations were broken down by the physical and emotional wreck you are when that's occurring. I think, once I felt that I was back in control to some degree, I could rebuild these separations. I don't know; I just can't seem to get rid of them. So my relationship has changed, but I can't really say how. I don't know whether I ever had one; I'm probably still in the same boat. So that's a historical thing that changed slightly during grief, but I don't know why. I realise that doesn't make any sense, but I can't really make sense of it all.'

'The cemetery is in an ideal location for Jessica, because of the life we imagined her leading. Some cows walk within five or ten feet of her grave and there are some trees with koalas in them. It's right in the middle of a pastoral environment and I guess that fits into my concept of where she would have been living. Even though I don't think she lives there, it's my concept of where she would have been living. It makes sense that she's in that location. Whereas, if she was in the city, I'd probably find that wrong.'

'It's a mixed cemetery; there's a lawn section and then there are monuments. Jessica is buried in the lawn section; it's got a sloping concrete bit where the plaques are facing either way for graves on both sides. She has a small gold plaque.'

'To me, the cemetery doesn't hold much significance. Jane finds it more important than I do. We were thinking about this, because we are moving back to the country. We've actually bought a farm again, in the same district. I guess the importance of it is that I couldn't move anywhere else in Victoria or interstate. We thought about other areas, but when it came to the crunch, I needed to be close to the cemetery. But I know I won't go there a lot. I'll go when Jane wants me to, basically. I wouldn't plan to go there on my own. We haven't had picnics there or things like that. I know some people do really spend a lot of time at the gravesite.'

'For me, when I go with Jane, the only thing I do feel is that it helps her loss—but not my loss—because for her it is an emotional place. I mean she'll normally cry there. For me it's reminding me of those days when she was like that all the time. I guess I've seen it enough now to know that it has to happen, and it will pass, and it will come back again. And that's fine; it's quite healthy. It's only if you stay there for three years or something that you've got a problem. I have no problem with the idea of her crying.'

'I think I have a different view of the cemetery to a lot of people; but maybe a lot of males are the same. For me, it's a location where we buried our daughter. And it's important that she was buried in that location: that the cemetery fitted what I imagined being our life and her life together. It was in the middle of the country and that's important. But in terms of it bringing things back to me, or heightening emotional responses, it doesn't. To Jane it certainly does; but it's one of the things though, it's not necessarily the only thing. Other things would be seeing a child of similar age or something like that on TV.'

'We've probably only ever gone twice specifically to visit Jessica's grave. Jane just really needed to go, so we drove down specifically to go. And then we'd only be there maybe five or ten minutes. It takes about two and a half hours or so to get there. It was important to be able to go there for her first anniversary, but it was not as important when we went there for the second anniversary; that had nowhere near the same importance.'

'We tend to try and down-play Mothers and Fathers Days; we got used to that during the IVF program. It might be different now that our son's been born, but it was difficult on those days, because of the advertising leading up to it. We had quite a few years of Mothers Day and Fathers Day coming and us feeling, "Oh, well; it's lucky that some people can celebrate it, I suppose. But we're not in that position".'

'I have two sisters and good friends who live in the area, so we mainly call in to Jessica's grave when we are visiting somebody. I think there's a sense in which Jane always wants to go to the cemetery and I don't. She will sometimes go on her own or we'll go together or she'll go with a friend.'

'Before we moved back to Melbourne, she would tend to go regularly. At the start, she went very regularly and then it dropped off. Even Jane would say that there was a sense in which she couldn't let Jessica go. It was important that as a mother, she could go and be there.'

'In that sense, when you think about sprinkling ashes across the sea or something like that, neither of us could've done that. The location is important. And I think that is indicative of the fact that I couldn't go to the other side of the state to live, because that would be too far from the location. I don't necessarily want to be there often, but I need to know that I could be there. I need to be able to go and see the small plaque.'

'Over the last twelve months, I've probably been four times: once on the anniversary and then a few times recently— probably because we've been in the area making arrangements to move. Very early on I wouldn't have found myself there at all unless Jane wanted me to go; whereas she would've been there almost daily at the start, and then it broke down quite quickly to weekly and then less. I just don't believe that's where she is. I don't see it as a rite of passage or anything like that for me to be there. It doesn't help me get anywhere and it doesn't remind me of Jessica; I have enough ways to do that.'

'I don't think either of us prays, or talks to Jessica, when we are there. I tend to look at the cows across the fence and say, "Well if she's got to be anywhere I suppose this is it". We talk a little bit, but not a lot: sometimes about what she would have been doing. But the cemetery's not the place that prompts that discussion; that happens pretty naturally in lots of instances.'

'When I visit, I walk up and shine the plaque with my hanky, and basically that's about it. We've got a small cylinder for flowers and, because we can't be there regularly, we tend to change silk flowers once every few months. We get plenty of nice silk flowers; we won't take live ones, because we just don't want dead-looking flowers.'

'We sometimes only stay for two minutes if it's blowing a gale: sometimes ten, but no longer. Even on her first anniversary, when we let go a balloon with her name on it—and did a couple of other things—it still would have been only fifteen minutes.'

'Because I mainly visit at Jane's prompts, I just respond to her need to go. It's not important for me personally; it's more that I go to support Jane. It's not something that I have to do. And I have no perception of guilt about it: none at all.'

The Price for Being Human

Beryl is sixty years old and was 'brought up a Presbyterian', though she has had no church affiliation since her 'younger days'. Both she and her 62-year-old husband, Kevin, were born in Melbourne of Australian parents. They have three married daughters: aged 40, 38 and 26. Beryl did not have any paid employment while the children were at home as Kevin kept her 'quite comfortable'. However, she started a job three years ago at a local club 'just to fill in time, and thoroughly enjoyed mixing with people'.

Kevin was 'christened Church of England' and attended church until he was 'around twelve or fourteen, but says he could be termed 'non-religious and non-conforming'. To Kevin: 'Religion doesn't matter. It's just not a problem.' He was a self-employed tradesman for 38 years, until two and a half years ago. He now works part-time as a courier.

Five years ago Beryl and Kevin were devastated by the accidental death of their 4-year-old grandson. Robert was their eldest daughter's second son; he had a 7-year-old brother and two cousins.

Beryl recalls: 'He was a dear little boy: very cheeky. We've got very, very good memories of him: excellent memories. If you could have seen him you would laugh too. "You old bitch", he'd say and run straight out that door with me after him, "Don't you smacka me". And he'd take off with me after him many, many times. I have never smacked my other three grand-children, but Robert: on average, four times a day. I loved him dearly. But I think he loved his grandfather a little bit more than me.'

'Kevin would go up and have a shower, and the next minute Robert would be in the shower with him: "Me, Pa; Me with you Pa." We had a lot to do with him as we do with our other grandchildren, but we particularly had a lot to do with this little fellow. He had a couple of little setbacks; he couldn't hear properly and he used to talk a bit funny.'

Kevin and Beryl were staying at a holiday resort with friends. There were eight children between the four families staying together. Beryl recalls: 'The day he was killed, Kevin and I were minding him and that's what made it hard for us, because we had to ring his mother and tell her to come to the hospital, because he was gone. Only a quarter-of-an-hour before the dear little fellow had the accident I whopped him three times. He just went over and went "Bop!" to this poor little girl. He was a cheeky little devil, he really was; but he was also just adorable.'

Beryl spoke of Robert's accident: 'All he wanted that day was one of those horse-drawn carriage rides. So Kevin put him on and stood by the kerb. He thought, "I won't put him up top there; it's not safe. I'll put him inside". So Kevin did put him inside and I went off shopping. Halfway around, Robert decided he'd leave the seat and lean on the door. Now he was a very little boy, but as he leant on the door it opened—fortunately there were witnesses—and as it opened he went out with it, and then he came back. If he had let go when he was out, the cart wouldn't have run over him. But when he came back in he dropped.'

Kevin added: 'The cart bloke was an ex-ambulance officer. He jumped down immediately, realised the little bloke was gone and gave him mouth-to-mouth and brought him back. He resuscitated him on the spot.'

Beryl felt sure that 'he was brought back to life a couple of times'. 'When I came out of the shop', Beryl said, 'and looked on the ground, there he was lying there. I said to my daughter, "That's Robert! Go and get your father". So she went and got Dad. But it was too late. As the ambulance didn't stop people said, "He's alive". And I really thought he was alive; honest to God I thought he was alive. I really believed that when the ambulance didn't stop he'd be all right. Later I asked my daughter, "Why didn't they ask for his organs?" She said, "Mum, there were no organs left".

'When he was lying on the ground they wouldn't let me near him. But when we did see him in the hospital it was just as if he was asleep: weak as a kitten. It was just awful. But we went back to the caravan and did what we had to do. The police even offered to drive us all home to Melbourne.'

Kevin said, 'they wanted to keep Beryl in the local hospital for shock. They didn't want me to take her. I had to virtually stand over them and say, "Well I'm sorry, but she's not stopping here. Jesus! I've got one crowd following the bloody ambulance over to that town and the other crowd's gone back up the river to get the kids. I just can't leave her here".'

Kevin felt that he 'sort of had to bully the family into doing what had to be done. One of us had to be on the ball. We lost him on the Sunday and we didn't get him to town until the Wednesday. The autopsy was done there. The length of time all this was taking was really dragging on people. Luckily we got him and could bury him on the Friday. But it looked like going over the weekend and into the next week, and that was starting to impact heavily on people.'

Kevin also spoke of the death of his mother seventeen years earlier. 'We hadn't had a close relationship and I wasn't in any bereavement really of any description when my mother died. I didn't grieve, because our relationship had long since finished in that regard. She was still my mother. I buried her and did everything I should have done, but she said she didn't want me.

She'd say, "I'm going to leave it to the church". I said, "Well that's fine. Leave it to the church; but let them bury you too". Then I think the pennies might have dropped. She was a bitch; she was a funny lady.'

'She'd been ill for a long time. We got a surprise, or I suppose it was a shock, when she did die. Although she hadn't been well for a long time, she just fell dead in the street. That came out of the blue. But it wasn't totally unexpected. I mean you would've expected it at any time, because she wasn't a well person. I think my father dying when I was eighteen was a bigger shock. That was definitely a shock; though I didn't agree with my father a lot. But it was nothing like the grandkid, you know. Phew!'

'It's taken all this time to get a bit easier', Beryl said, 'and then I had two more close deaths: my Mum and uncle. But they weren't at all so hard. I nursed Mum for months and it wasn't even hard. Mum died about two years ago. Her boyfriend of 52 years—who I called my uncle—died six weeks earlier; he had cancer. But it wasn't hard, because Robert had made us better people. I'll always say that and I'm sure Kevin would too; but Robert's death has made me, in particular, a much better person. When my Mum and uncle went, I was so much stronger. I even said words for my uncle at the funeral; that's what a stronger person it has made me.' Kevin interjected: 'It makes a person different. I wouldn't say better; I'd say different.' Beryl reiterated, 'I think it made us better people.'

Beryl continued: 'We definitely grieved for Robert. With Mum it was a relief; with my uncle it was certainly a relief. To watch somebody die is terrible. But with Robert there was no reason why. They told me in the hospital—other than not being well, as she'd had a heart complaint—that Mum died of a broken heart. I said, "Oh, come on. She's 82 years old". But she did die of a broken heart: she really did. The only last sensible thing she said was, "He promised he wouldn't leave me". That proved to me that she fretted away; she just died.'

Kevin agreed, 'She did, and she didn't realise she'd lost him probably in the first three weeks. She was well in dementia; we couldn't even take her to the funeral. We put her in hospital when Uncle was in the hospice, because we couldn't handle him at his place and Beryl's mother at her place.'

Kevin had known Beryl's mother and uncle for forty years. 'I had expected the two of them to go around the same time. I said for a long time, "It's going to be a race". It didn't really impact on either of us heavily. There was a sense of loss. We had our grieving period and the grieving period was evident. But it was so much shorter, because we were grieving more while they were here than when they left. I felt that they were two people who required grieving for; I really felt sad for them.'

Beryl said, 'When my mother was cremated the funeral director strongly advised me to, "Get it over and done with" by placing the ashes the next day or so. But I let it go for nearly a month. Oh, it was terrible; their advice was so sound. Putting Mum's ashes into the grave affected me months later more so than her death and funeral did. That I would never do again; I would do it immediately.'

'However, Beryl's uncle was a Catholic and we buried him', advised Kevin. 'I said, "He was brought up a Catholic and he's going to go down as a Catholic too".'

During Robert's church service, Beryl did not notice other people present. 'I asked Kevin, "Why didn't the people come? He was only a little boy, Kevin. Why didn't people come?" Yet honestly, they were falling out of the rafters; but far as I was concerned there wasn't a soul there.'

Kevin disagreed with his other grandchildren being prevented from attending their brother and cousin's funeral. 'They were wrong in not letting the children go to the funeral service and nothing would change my mind about that. It might only be a very small way of helping, but it's still got to be there. It doesn't matter how old or young they are. We had Robert's brother with us when we had an open casket at the funeral home the night before. He didn't want to go in; he was only seven. I took him aside and said, "Now look. You'd better go and see him. This will be your last possible chance of ever seeing him, because tomorrow he's closed down and he is put away and that's it". I let him go for a couple of minutes. Then I went in and came back out again and then he said, "I want to go in".

Beryl recalled: 'We did say to the minister, "Now we don't want this too religious; you know we're not religious people". And he said, "OK, that's fine, but don't you make it too sad and hard for me, because I've got to stand up there".' Kevin added that the minister had a reasonably long association with the family. 'He taught our children and had already conducted two weddings. He was certainly feeling for the family. He came out and sat up in the bedroom for a couple of hours and spoke to us: he was fine.'

Beryl said, 'He did a little bit of religion: very little, but what he did was perfect. We chose little bits of music that Robert loved. We all clapped our hands together and that helped us more.' Kevin agreed. 'That helped the whole family. There was a tape recording of his favourite little piece of music that he used to jump around with. All the family there had to jump around and clap our hands and we'd all fall down. Nobody else in the church got the benefit of it, because they didn't realise what it was all about. They just sat there, probably dumb-founded.

Beryl found comfort in the period leading up to the funeral. 'But the funeral day was a blur. I fainted outside the church and then sat in the car out of the way.' To Kevin, 'the funeral was 'just a hell-of-a-day finishing off a hell-of-a-week.'

According to Kevin, 'Robert's parents were straining at the bit a little, and all this put extra strain on their relationship.' He considered, 'It would make or break them. So far, they've returned now to where they were. They tolerate each other, but

it still wouldn't surprise me to see them bust up. There was a
night that certain things were said, and—well, I copped the
blame. It was as if I wasn't blaming myself enough at the
time—which I was. I still do. It was thoughtless, but he more or
less straight out blamed me. But we got over that and it was
never brought up again.'

Kevin insisted: 'I would never have got in the same street if
I had known there was a problem with the horse and bloody
cart. I've always been safety conscious. We've never had work
accidents: kid accidents, any accidents. And we've been boating
for thirty years of our lives. We can't get heaps of cotton wool
and wrap our kids in it and say, "No, you can't do that; it looks
dangerous". You cannot do it. If something happens—well
that's the price we pay for being human.'

Beryl feels that she has 'always been a bit of a softie. I
suppose, I'm not as cranky now. I accept things better. Once,
I would absolutely flare up and particularly call Kevin everything. We just laugh now. "You silly old thing", he'll say to me
and we'll get on with it now. We've learnt about what's most
important in life. Now we just say, "Come on", and we'll have
a laugh and go and do what we've got to do. Over the last
twelve months I suppose we've laughed a little bit more, but
not up until then.'

Kevin did not fully agree. 'I'd say we don't laugh as much as
we used to at all; I don't anyway, though I try. Outwardly,
people wouldn't know. People get a surprise when they hear
about it. Somebody else might tell them and they might like to
ask, but they're more embarrassed to ask than I am to tell them.
But I don't go around saying, "Hey, do you want to listen to
this?" Therefore we tend to disguise our emotions. I'm more
emotional now than ever; I cry easily now. I would cry more
now than I would laugh. I laugh a little bit, but I probably laugh
at different things now. Things that used to seem funny don't
seem quite as funny. I couldn't be specific, but that's how I feel.
I became a totally different person and I still am.'

'I get upset when we hear of kids. I can look at adults and can hear about bad things that have happened to them and I don't emote in any way at all, but not so with little kids. When I heard that those two little kids got killed on the railway line there, a few years ago—Boy! Did that break me up? I had to stop the car; I was bawling my eyes out.'

'But strangely, the people I thought about were the grand-parents. I felt terribly upset for the kids, but you can't be upset for dead people, because they're dead; they're beyond being upset for. Let's face it, grieving is for the living; funerals are for the living. But the grandparents—I thought, really I should make an effort and go and see them. But then I couldn't; now I could. Today I could go, but three years ago I couldn't. I would have been in a worse state than they would, probably. So I couldn't physically go and do it. They're the differences I've noticed.'

'Friends of ours lost their son in his early twenties and I found out one night through a phone call. I said to Beryl, "I'm going over to see them"—this was long before we lost Robert—and then I thought to myself, "No. No, I won't. I might feel as though I'm barging in".'

'But after losing Robert, the first thing I'd do now is go straight down to their place, whoever it is. It doesn't matter whether I'd seen them in twelve days, twelve years, or whatever; I would go and see them; because I learned that people coming to see us when we lost Robert helped us tremendously. When Beryl said that there was nobody at the 4-year-old's funeral, there were 400 people and she asked, "Where is everybody?"

Beryl agreed with Kevin that, 'When you're really grieving, people are very important. I love the people that came. I don't know how many hundreds we had through, but I only cooked one meal. People just kept bringing food; it was unbelievable. Our daughter and son-in-law came and stayed with us; they just couldn't go home.'

Beryl considered, 'Another thing that made life easier for Robert's mother and me were the flowers. I had them everywhere and that was a great comfort. Every day my little grand-daughter and I would go around and water them and we'd talk about the person that gave me this one and that; it was lovely. We buried him on the Friday and on the Sunday, his mother brought a lady in who picked flowers from every bunch and pressed them. So we all got pressed flowers: framed.'

'Little things that people do are so important. One of his mother's friends gave me a little gift. It was simply a bit of wood wrapped up as a present with a bow on it and it said, "This is a gift from me to you. You can't give me anything in return; I'm not here. But if you're feeling down, you think about me. Pick it up and look at me and love me through this gift". And it was good. It didn't have the gift of life: just written words. That's all it was: a piece of wood. But unfortunately, we were robbed two years ago and it was taken. I didn't care about the diamonds, but they took this too.'

'I do normal things now; I'm well on the way to being on top of it. It is behind me now; but it will never, ever be gone. Every day I have a little think of him some way or another. It might be just some little thought of Robert that flashes through my mind. I'm OK now, but three years ago I'd be hopeless; I'd have to sit down and I'd cry. Many a time I rang Kevin up and said he'd have to come home.'

'I found one of the best things that helped me was when our daughter and son-in-law asked us to go to the funeral director's Christmas seminar a year after he died. It was the best thing I'd done. Those experts put me on track, because I really thought that I was going mental; but I wasn't of course. Then I started to think: the next time someone asks me, "How are you going Beryl?" I'm going to say, "Fantastic!" And that was my turning point; it honestly was.'

Kevin recalls that his grieving was different from Beryl's. 'When I did grieve, it was heavier because I couldn't grieve early. After it all happened, the policeman was sitting there talking to me and I was crying my eyes out with him. The old cop was no better, because he had grandkids; and as he said, "He had to do the job". He said to me, "I thought I had the original ice-man, the day it all happened. You were so in control of everything".'

'But so far as I was concerned, I couldn't do anything else; there was no one else who could stand with me or was stable. One of us had to stand up and that's all it amounted to. They were all falling over—understandably though: completely understandably. They were literally lying on the floor. Even the other son-in-law was useless. Of course, I continued in that vein right through until after the funeral. So I had a week of being held in abeyance or limbo, and then it came onto me during the next week.'

'I think we went back to work on the Monday. We said, "Well, come on; we've got to get going again". It started to impact on me in the second week and it impacted pretty hard. I'd say the third week was when I really went into heavy grief. So much so that a friend of ours who was in the army said, "You don't look good and you're not talking good". And I wasn't good either.'

'Anyway, he asked, "Have you spoken to anybody?" And I said, "No". So he gave me the name and address of a bloke somewhere and said there's an appointment there for you. It was a shrink they use for their own army people in similar circumstances, but the appointment got mixed up and he wasn't there. Anyway he rang me that night and spoke to me a little bit and he apologised profusely for the mess up. He phoned again a few days later and said, "It sounds as though you're fine". And I felt I was. Just the fact that I'd made the effort to see someone had helped.'

'Some people say, "It couldn't possibly be as bad as losing one of your own". But I would defy anybody to tell me the difference between losing one of your own or a grandchild. It's been five years now. The grieving was reasonably heavy for three years, but slowly and surely you come out of it. I'd say I've been in good control now for well over twelve months.'

'I look at things totally different now. Once I'd stand and argue with someone. Now I just say, "Well you must be right", or something like that, and walk away and leave it. I just couldn't be bothered. But I suppose age might have something to do with that too.'

Beryl says that she appreciates the grandchildren bringing Robert's name up and talking about him. 'I'm very pleased with that. They have never forgotten him and we laugh about the funny little things he did and we're fine.' Kevin commented that their youngest daughter is now pregnant. 'A few weeks back, the kids turned around and said to Beryl, "That'll make it even. There'll be four of us again". So another one's coming back to take the place of the one that's gone; that pleases us too.'

Beryl considers: 'While I am not really religious, when it came to the nitty-gritty of Robert's funeral, I particularly wanted him buried from a church. I must have gone back a bit. I would never say that I don't really believe in God, but I had my doubts there for a while; now it doesn't worry me. When people used to say, "They only take the best", or whatever, that really got up my nose.'

Kevin recalled when: 'The kids were all here one night and I said, "Well, let's all think about the future, as this proves you never know. I think everyone wanted him to go into a nice quiet little area, not into a big commercialised cemetery. So I said, "Let's go out of town and have a look". And as soon as we walked through the gates, I said, "This is it". We worked out that we needed four plots to accommodate our family and maybe one or two of the grandkids. So now it's there and all of this was brought about purely and simply. I wouldn't have done it if Beryl's mother and uncle had died first; I wouldn't have even thought of it. But with the little bloke dying, I just looked at life a little bit differently.'

The thing I thought of was, none of us had made provision down the track for when we're going to die. And it all came together; it had to be done that day. So I asked, "Well how many plots do we need?" Then I went out and I purchased four plots. At that time, Beryl's mother and uncle would have been in their early- and mid-seventies. They were very relieved, because they knew the cemetery they were going to.'

'I say I'm not religious', said Beryl, 'but some little things really get to me. And many Catholic people said to me at the time, "There is a hereafter Beryl". And I said to Kevin, "There's got to be a hereafter". And that's one thing that kept me going, because I knew he was at the hereafter; and that's how I felt. When I go up to the cemetery I know that he's not by himself any more. My Mum and uncle are buried there now and then there are two graves and then Robert's. The two middle ones are ours. I believe that he's not by himself, and that makes me happy.'

'I think this earth is so complicated that there's got to be a peaceful hereafter; that's how I look at it. At first, I used to worry about him being up at the cemetery by himself, particularly when it rained. I hated it when it rained. But then I started to think: "You're somewhere else now with other people". And he isn't by himself: definitely. My uncle is with him and so is my Mum. That's how I comfort myself. I don't think about whether it's true or not. Kevin always says to me, "If it helps you, think that way".'

However, for himself, Kevin holds a more pragmatic view: 'I believe he is six feet under the ground and that's it.' Both Beryl and Kevin respect each other's perspective.

'At the gravesite', Beryl says, 'I always sit for at least two or three minutes to just think about Robert. Then I get some water, clean out the vases and put the flowers in. Then I give his headstone a kiss and I come home. If I'm really upset, I'll just stand there. But it's been a long time now since I've been really upset. I just say hello to Mum and my uncle, and put some flowers there; that never upsets me. But I never, ever go away without giving Robert's headstone a kiss. The time I spend there all depends—on a good day I'll stay five or ten minutes—depending on how long it takes to do the flowers. On a bad day I'm there and out. But as I said, it's been a while since it's been a bad day; because I now go when I want to go not when I think I should.'

'We place flowers every time. On special occasions we put windmills; so if flowers are not there he has always got his windmills. His brother also put a balloon there in our football club colours. If we go to the Show, his brother will always get a blow-up toy and we tie it onto the grave and it stays there till I pick it up and take it home. At Easter time we take him Easter eggs; at Christmas time we put angels on it. He's always got an angel on his grave. It is a very cute little cemetery and it's very easy to visit. You see lots of people visiting: obviously looking at the old graves. I always feel as if I'm going home.'

These days, Kevin usually visits with Beryl. 'I just carry the water. I pull the dead stuff out and tidy up: just the normal type of thing. I don't speak to anybody. I put an odd flower here and there, but Beryl usually does the flowers; there's nothing else to do.'

Beryl felt that: 'The grave was not finished until the stone monument was constructed about eighteen months ago to replace the temporary wooden cross. As soon as that was done we went together and I said, "He's at rest now; nobody else can hurt him". When I go to the cemetery I'm inclined to say hello to Mum and my uncle, but something pulls me to Robert every time and that's where I stand. That's what I get out of going there now. Before I got nothing; it upset me. But now I get rest. Now I visit perhaps every six weeks or so.'

The headstone meant less to Kevin. 'I knew who was there and I knew what the wooden cross was for; I didn't feel that it was unfinished as it was; but I place no importance on the cemetery. Both my mother and father were cremated and there are no ashes, no plots: nothing. That's what they wanted; that's what they got. But with Robert, I found it hard to walk in and out of the cemetery early on. I can walk in and out of there now with no worries.'

'I would have gone more in the last six months than in the previous four and a half years: between six and eight times. I'll go up on birthdays, including my own, because he can't come to my birthday; so I have to go up and see him. I tend to go at Christmas, birthdays and Easter and those types of things. I want to go on days that I want to go. I don't feel obliged to go; I just feel as though I want to go. But I have been known to be driving that way and just pull off the road and go to the cemetery for no reason.'

Beryl mentioned that their second daughter nearly stopped going, even at Christmas. 'Because she just thinks up a migraine'. To this Kevin added that their eldest daughter (Robert's mother) can't go at all. 'Because as soon as she goes there all the bad memories come rushing back to her and she's upset for days; so she handles it by staying away.'

On the odd occasion that Kevin visits the cemetery by himself, he doesn't take any flowers. 'I'm not like that. When I'm going, away I go, there and then: that's it. I only stay a couple of minutes. I was doing that early in the piece, but haven't done it for a long time now.'

Beryl suggested to Kevin, 'You'd be stressed out by the time you got home'. To which he replied, 'Yes, I used to stress something shocking; it really knocked me around. And when I stopped just dropping into the place, I improved quicker. I could have quite easily said, "That's it; I'm not going any more". That's how it was stressing me. But I was determined not to let it stress me to the point that I wouldn't go. I was going to beat it; it wasn't going to beat me. And I did beat it: totally. But that was the mad time. I suppose, had I given in then and said, "That's it, I'm not coming again", I'd have gone back now and probably been OK, because time has elapsed. Time is a healer.'

'Beryl recalled being told at a bereavement seminar that even time doesn't help some people, but she was similarly adamant: 'It certainly helped us. Time has definitely helped us.'

Beryl remembered that, 'In the early days, we'd go on special occasions and always bump into one of the family. We wouldn't all go together and we'd more or less like pass in the dark. It's not that we weren't talking to each other: we were, but we'd just say hello and they'd go their way and we'd go our way. That was the early days; but then it became easier.'

Kevin observed that family members soon learnt the visitation patterns of each other and intentionally avoided visiting during what was likely to be someone else's personal time. 'We didn't work it out together, but we all tended to know. We didn't want to encroach on each other's grief. On Christmas Day, we go up there early in the morning and his parents go up later.'

Beryl added: 'We know who's been by the flowers.' And Kevin noted that 'Robert's other grandparents go up regularly: about every fortnight. They're a lot older than we are. His other aunty goes up a fair bit too.'

Beryl has observed change in her own need to visit over time. 'In the beginning I went because I had to. I felt as if I had to, because it was the right thing to do. But now I go because I want to and it's much nicer. Early on I visited very, very frequently; and now less frequently—not for the lack of love for him, it's just that you've got to get on with your life. The personal need to be there is not as great. I feel I'm very important to my family and my grandchildren that are alive, and I've got to keep going for them.'

During earlier visits, Beryl found Kevin's presence to be a necessary comfort. 'He'd just stand there and that's all I needed. He knew that's all I needed.' Kevin said, 'I'd stand probably three metres back from the grave and let her potter and have her cry and do what she wanted to do; I'd get the water and that kind of thing. Well now I don't have to stand back. I only stood back because she needed it more than I did.' Beryl agreed.

Kevin continued: 'Although I was pretty heavy and grim on it, Beryl needed it. She needed the cemetery at the time: badly. But I needed to not be there. I'd dried up by the time I got there. I should have stopped driving there, because I was starting to get dangerous. I wouldn't stop crying. The crying went on for two and a half years; I was a mess. But once I came away again, I'd come good pretty quick. I drove slower home than I went there. But I did get better, I must admit.'

Eventually, Kevin became concerned at what he considered to be excessive compulsive visiting behaviour on Beryl's part. 'It got to the stage where I thought I had to make her look at the amount of times she was going. She jumped up and down at me when I did say it. I forget the exact words I used at the time— but it was pretty cute phraseology—to imply to her that maybe she was going too often. And she was; she admitted later on that she was.' Beryl agreed, but added, 'I took no notice at the time; I did what I wanted'.

Kevin continued: 'I said to her, "You know he's not going to fly up out of the grave and say, hello Nanna; here I am". Another person we know used to go every day and that's what her husband said to her. Their son got killed in a car accident; he was only 21. I don't think the father has even been to the cemetery since the funeral; that was ten years ago. He won't talk about it, like it just didn't happen, except that his son is not there.'

'I feel that going to the cemetery does you good, because you know that's where they are. That's why you're going to the bloody place; if they weren't there you wouldn't go. I felt that for Beryl, it was becoming a compulsion: "I've got to go; I'm relied upon". Beryl is a little bit that way, you know, though she may not admit it. But I didn't want to get to the stage of going to the cemetery like that: "I've got to go, because I'll be relied on to be there". I thought that would have been extremely unhealthy, not only for her, but also for me too. But anyway, she broke out of it herself and worked her way through it.'

Beryl responded, 'I've got to admit that I used to go to the cemetery—not too much, but I used to go every day or every second day—and I used get so uptight. There was no sense to it. So then I said to Kevin one day, "That's it; I'm going when I feel like it". I'm sure he was pleased when I told him that. So now I do go when I feel like it and when I go I don't even get upset, because I want to be there.'

Kevin added: 'This was when I said to her, "Have a think; just have a think about what you're doing".' Beryl continued: 'And that's when I started to get myself into control. I worked out that this little fella was not going to come out and say, "Don't worry Nanna", so I broke out of it'.

Beryl now feels a sense of peace within the cemetery. 'Not always so, but lately I feel peaceful; but I definitely don't think of God. I'm quite happy to be there now, because to me he is in his final resting-place. I think about just him and me. I really don't think about anybody else. I don't think about his mother or his father's sadness; I just think of him and me. Going to the cemetery now is my time. I like my time; that's important to me.'

Kevin's visitation emotions have also modified. 'I've come away sadder than I've gone there in the past, but now I can walk away and not look back. Once I used to drive around the corner so we'd go past again, but we don't need to do that now.'

Beryl concluded: 'This is the first time I've really broken down in months and months. I can relax in front of some people. It wasn't hard for me to talk to you about it and I didn't care about crying in front of you. That makes it easy for me, so I don't hide it. But we don't cry as much as we used to.'

Kevin feels similarly: 'That's right. It only flashes back to us now. But we keep going, because we know we'll clear ourselves again, and I don't care when I cry now. If something happens, I'll cry. You know what they say: "Grown men don't cry". Well that's crap! And I must admit it took this to bring that out of me.'

In God's Hands

Mahmoud was born 52 years ago. He immigrated to Australia at the age of 23. 'The year after I came, I brought all my family here. We come from Cyprus; we are Turkish. We are Muslim.'

Mahmoud worked as an electronics technician with a communications firm for several years before operating his own repair shop for a short while. Thirteen years ago, he suffered back and arm injuries in a car accident; he has not worked since. 'I am now on a pension.'

His 47-year-old wife Pinar is also Turkish. She commenced work at the same firm the year Mahmoud arrived. 'I married Pinar three years after I came and we had three children: a son and two daughters. One of my girls is now 21, and one sixteen. My son was 23 years old, but he passed away fourteen months ago.'

Ali died in a motorcycle accident. The previous day (which was also his mother's birthday), Ali's girlfriend had given birth to a baby boy. 'His son was born on Sunday and he died on Monday. He was a good boy and he used to go to work, and he was doing his apprenticeship. It was his last year to finish his apprenticeship.'

'They say he was riding a bike with his friend—two separate bikes. Suddenly his friend stopped and he looked behind to see what happened to his friend and he lost his control. I was overseas when he died. My wife rang me and I came to his funeral. I took a plane Tuesday morning and I came Thursday morning. His funeral was on Friday.'

'I lost lots of relatives. When I was three, I lost my father in Cyprus; but I was too young to remember. My mother remarried and all my family is here in Australia. When I was in my country, my young brother died; he was three and a half years old. I lost my grandmother in Australia; she's buried in this cemetery.'

'Ali was in a freezer three or four days, and they were doing that operation and checking, you know. But in my country, if someone dies—say he dies in the morning, they bury him lunchtime.'

'Friday morning, we went to the mosque and prepared for the funeral. First they wash his body and they put him into a white cloth, in a coffin. But we don't bury our kids in that; we keep the coffin. We just take them out of the coffin. But in the mosque, we put him in a coffin and keep him all day at the mosque. It was on Friday: a special day for Muslims on Fridays. After praying in the mosque, everybody comes out.'

'Anyway, we put him down on the mosque and everybody comes out after they pray. And we pray for him again. We take him to the cemetery. And after that, take him out from the coffin putting him down into the ground and we cover him with wood. I mean, he lies under the wood; and the Hoca reads the Koran. Then we stay there; he reads more—mostly part of the Koran—we pray and we put flowers on top. We go home and have three nights grieving and crying for him. After the three nights, forty or fifty days pass and then people cry for him.'

'We believe everybody will be going when their time comes up. I don't know what will cause a death—accident, or age, or sickness—only God knows. Nobody else knows. We believe when your time comes up, you go.'

'It's not really changed the family—a bit, but not much. Our daughters, they're really upset. They go to his grave, you know;

but they are still in shock. Fourteen months passed, but they are still in shock. But it had an effect on me and we changed a lot, you know. We can't enjoy any more and we are not going out much. We are not going to parties, and we are not going to weddings. We don't feel like going. We just stay at home. We have a room and we have his pictures in the room; we just go in and, you know, sit there.'

Eight months before his own death, Ali's best friend also died in a motorcycle accident. At the time, the two young men's parents did not know each other, but have since developed a strong relationship. 'Yeah, we met first at the cemetery, and then we met at a restaurant. We are best family friends now; we visit each other and just talk, you know. We try to give us a bit of comfort, you know.'

From meetings at the cemetery, Mahmoud and Pinar have befriended members of several other families that they consider to have experienced greater tragedies than their own. 'You know, once we stop and talk to people, we find there are two boys, and one was sick and one had an accident. They're both buried in the same grave: brothers. One was sick; he died the same day his brother had an accident, and he died too. One is 25 and one is 22. So when we see that, I say, "Gee; we lost one and they've lost two".'

Pinar produced from her handbag a laminated Turkish-language newspaper clipping featuring some eight young people from Turkish families, all of whom were recently buried in the cemetery. 'All the kids here died in one year's time. These two were walking on the footpath, and one drunk went on the footpath with a car and he killed them. Another one—he's thirteen—sitting on a bicycle—he was crossing the road, and someone hit him and killed him.'

'The poor boy we talked to yesterday—young boy—his sisters died. He's a very good boy, you know. He's friendly, and always he says, "Hello; how are you?" He told me that they died from an accident. And his father is an ambulance man and his mother was a nurse. They rang his father and said, "There's an accident". And he was with his ambulance, and he was going to pick them up and said, "Oh, gee; my two daughters—and they both are twins". So when we learn these, you know, we are getting a little bit of relief. We're saying we are worse, but some people are more worse, you know.'

Mahmoud says he and Pinar see their grandson and Ali's girlfriend quite regularly. 'She's not Turkish, but she's good, you know. I see my grandson; she brings him to us every couple of days, you know. So far, we've got a strong relationship; but I don't know in the future.'

'I always remember him, you know. Even now he's in my mind; I can see him anywhere and everywhere. He's a spirit now. I believe he's a spirit—always with us. He's coming around, and most of the times we feel he is with us, because we saw things we didn't expect. So he is with us, you know, all the time. Two times, at twelve o'clock, the lights in the car came on. No one touched the lights. The doors were locked and the lights came on, without the switch on. The switch was off, but the lights on. And when he used to drive the car he put the seat like this when he was driving. You know, we found his seat like that. And we feel things; like sometimes his son comes and he's looking there, and I'd be looking there too and see nothing, but he just starts laughing like this, you know. I feel him then, you know; I sense him.'

Ali was buried in an Islamic section of a public cemetery. To Pinar, the cemetery is now more important to her than her house is: 'Because every day I go there.'

A modern 'European-style' granite monument now covers Ali's grave. 'You know, in our country, they put memorials on the graves, but they don't close the top; they just leave soil on top and they plant on top of them.'

'In visiting him and praying for him, we feel like he's next to us. While we're visiting we feel close to God too, because we're praying for him there, you know. We are closer to God when we go to the mosque and pray. We really feel like close to him then.'

Pinar maintains a personal record of monthly interments at the current Islamic area of the cemetery, including details of decedents. According to Mahmoud: 'As soon as she sees someone digging the grave she goes and talks to them and asks them. We just go in and meet each other and talk, and she writes it in the book.'

Both parents consider the cemetery to be a peaceful place. 'There's no fear; it's just peaceful, you know. All the people have broken hearts. Any people that come over there, they've lost a son: children, father, mother or a family friend. It's the same problem.'

Pinar insists on visiting and staying at the cemetery on her own. 'People even told me, you know, "Don't go over yourself". I said, "No, I go; I'm not scared". I don't care now if I live or die; I don't care.' Mahmoud concurs. 'It doesn't matter; time comes and your time comes up. It's in God's hands.'

'What my wife does—every day she goes to cemetery and she has a little recorder, which is someone reading the Koran. She puts that on for our son, but also she puts that on for all the whole area. Because speaking on the cassette she has most of the names of the people there; and after that, sayings for everybody.'

'It is very important to be there, especially on Fridays. I come every Friday and sometimes on Sundays or Saturdays. I feel very sad, and I feel I'm going to visit my son. But it shouldn't be like that, you know; he should be alive. I feel terrible, you know: same as my wife. I go twice a week—or maybe three times a week—not every day. But what she feels, I feel the same. I go and I pray for him. I fix his flowers. I take him some flowers sometimes. We never really keep his grave without flowers, you know. Always we have flowers.'

'There are Turkish special days, two times every year. One of them is after the fasting—end of the Ramadan. And two months after that, we have another special day. And we come on those special days and we visit the cemetery.'

Pinar visits her son's grave every day. 'Sometimes, two times a day. In the morning, I stay there for two hours; then I go home. And if I'm feeling his death, I come back again. It makes me feel much better. I talk to him, you know, about everything. I tell him I miss him.' Pinar reports that, sometimes, she stays at the cemetery for up to six hours at a time.

Mahmoud visits both with Pinar and by himself. 'But I won't stay long. Most of the times I'm visiting with my wife, so I stay there about an hour. Then I sit there, because when we go together, she's not comfortable with me. I said to her, "Why don't you stay with him as much as you want?" So she stays on and she talks to him. When it's raining she stays in the car; she goes there, but she stays in the car.'

As well as placing flowers and praying, Pinar also spends her time looking at other graves. 'In the summer I put water on his grave and a few friends' graves. I fix the flowers, you know. I look everywhere. Sometimes I go to the Christian part and talk to people and put water on graves. I talk to ladies there, you know.'

You Just Never Know

Lynda was born in Melbourne 33 years ago. She has been married for eleven years. 'My husband was a plasterer for years, but is now a warehouse manager. His work is quite hectic and busy.' Lynda is now a 'full-time mum' to their 8-year-old son.

'I was brought up in a Catholic family and I went to a state school; my husband was brought up in the Church of England. I used to go to church regularly, but once I got married the priorities changed. Weekends are now with the family and my husband. But the thing is, it doesn't worry him whether I go to church or not; he's quite easy about it. I mean, both our children were baptised. So he's pretty easygoing; he's not really strict. He doesn't say, "You can't do this" or "You can't do that". I'm pretty lucky like that. He used to come to church when I'd go; and I think his family approved when we christened our kids Catholics.'

Almost two years ago, Lynda's second son, Timothy, died at the age of thirteen and a half months. 'He was diagnosed with this illness at eight weeks of age, so he had a struggle all his life. He had a lot of tests and he needed a liver transplant. Then he passed away just before Christmas. The condition he had was quite rare, so it made it really hard to know how to treat it. He was a very happy little boy; it never showed that he was as sick as he was.'

'We didn't know from the outset that he was so seriously ill. The doctor gave us a positive outlook, because he was just so different to other children with his condition; he was the opposite. So they never thought that he would get so ill that he would actually pass away. The doctors were surprised at just how quickly he deteriorated in the last few months of his life. That was pretty hard to take. The worst part was that I wasn't there for him, because he was in the Intensive Care Unit, and a mix-up with the nursing staff sort of tore us apart a bit. It's very hard to take when it's your child.'

'It was only a week before he passed away that we knew he was in such a serious condition. Because a week before, he was at my son's birthday and he was as happy as anything. You wouldn't think that in a week he could go downhill so quickly. He went into hospital for a routine biopsy and he was supposed to come home the day after, but he didn't. He just deteriorated overnight and passed away within two days. Never once did we think that he wouldn't be here in two days time. I think that's the hardest part to take.'

'I spent a few hours with him after he passed away in Intensive Care. We also had a couple of close family come and see him and say goodbye. I held him for a couple of hours. There were things that I now wish I had done that I didn't do then: things like bathing him. But at the time, because of the shock of what's happened, you don't think about it.'

'My husband's father died when Timothy was a week old. But luckily, he just got to see him and then he passed away two days later. It was a rush out of hospital and over to see him. We didn't think he would actually see him alive; we weren't sure. So I think the whole pregnancy was a bit up in the air: a bit of a nervous thing. It was pretty hard with Timothy. It was just constant doctor visits and hospital visits. I didn't have time for my husband and my other child as well; it wasn't easy.'

'To lose a child and to lose a father-in-law are two different things; they're both different cases really. Timothy was home with us, so he was part of our family. Even though my husband's Dad was part of our family, he wasn't actually living with us. So it was hard, but I think it's a different sort of thing. I mean, a child is part of you. He was born to us and we brought him up.'

'Timothy's funeral was very rushed, because he passed away on the twenty-first of December. It was very close to Christmas, and just the worst day of our lives. We were so rushed in getting things organised; we didn't know what we wanted. I mean, we didn't really have a chance to look around. So I said to the funeral director, "I want him where all the kids are, not where adults are, and I want him beautiful".'

'We had his funeral two days later. There wasn't time for people to come from interstate, because of public holidays. I wish I had more time with him. I would have liked to stay until he was covered up, but I couldn't. We were rushed into the cars, and people were all around. I think I was very angry in some ways. People turned up for his funeral that couldn't be bothered when he was alive. I'll never accept that.'

Timothy was buried in the current children's section of a large suburban cemetery. Lynda hopes that he is now in heaven with all the other kids. 'I have to think that way, but I can't say any more than that. I had a little bit to do with planning the funeral, but not much. The main things to me were that he had a white coffin and I just wanted him with the kids. My husband did a bit more, and Timothy's godmother and a good friend of mine organised it. Their brother was a funeral director at the time and that made it a lot easier, because she also knew Timothy very well.'

'We had a church service at the Catholic church where he was christened. We had a photo of Timothy sitting on top of his coffin, so that everyone could see what a lovely boy he was. The church was packed; it was full of people—not that I can remember much of the day. I wasn't always there I guess. During the funeral itself, my husband was pulled at one end and I was being dragged the other end, whereas we wanted to be together and we couldn't be.'

'We had two viewings: one on the Sunday—the day after he passed away—and then again on the Monday. They were only for very close friends and family, because I didn't want everyone to see him. I just told them that I wanted to see him for the last time, before he was buried. I would have liked to hold him again. I was told the pros and cons; I could if I wanted to, but then things could happen if I did hold him. I would have liked to dress him too. There are little things that I didn't get a chance to do and they're regrets that I guess I'll always have. I didn't mention it at the time. I think when you're in such a shock, you need to be told the things that you can do, because you don't really think about it at the time.'

'I'm happy with the way the funeral service went; it was a very pretty service. I guess that did help me a bit in my grief—but I just never expected it to happen. The funeral was another part that I suppose we had to get through; we didn't have a choice. I mean, what could you do with him otherwise? If there was another alternative, I'm sure I would've considered it. But I knew that's what happens when someone dies—you have to bury them—and I had to accept it. There was no choice about it.'

'My other son has had a hard time, especially at school. Of course all the other kids have got brothers and sisters and he no longer has; he's only got himself. People just don't realise—even though he's only eight years old now—how much he understands, even with the funeral. Compared to other kids, he's a lot older for his age because of what he's gone through. He's grown up a lot, I guess. In losing his brother, his whole world fell apart.'

'It helped pull us close together. We make a point of spending time together now, whereas before, we used to just get on with our hectic lifestyle. Now we do make a point of spending more time together and we appreciate that time, because now we know that you just never know what's going to happen tomorrow.'

'My parents are always there for us. They know how difficult it is to be with other kids Timothy's age and they're always only a phone call away. My parents only live across the road, so they're very close; my husband's family live further away. I think, in some ways, they're distancing themselves a bit more.'

'I'm a Catholic, but I don't really practise it that much. I don't go to church every Sunday. I've lost a lot of my faith since I lost my little boy. My husband's the same as me. He's just not practising; he doesn't go to church now. I think, like me, he's lost a lot of his faith since we lost our little boy.'

'I used to go to church a fair bit when I was younger, but when Timothy died—I just feel things differently. I think, well if there is a God, then why do they take a child so young? They could've taken us. We've already lived some of our lives, whereas Timothy hasn't; he's just too young. I'll never accept it. I want to know why they took him. I mean, he's only a child after all. Yeah; I've lost a lot of my faith. I've spoken to priests and they seem to understand, but they always wonder why too. They always find it very hard doing funerals for kids. I just can't accept it.'

'I still go to church occasionally; it just depends. Sometimes I have the urge: I really want to go. If I feel a bit down in the dumps, then I go. Or if I just feel like going, I do. I go a lot less since I've been married. I guess, sometimes you've got better things to do than to go to church. I know that's the wrong attitude to have, but your time is so precious these days; you just try and get so much done in a day that it becomes impossible.'

'But Timothy's situation made me really question my belief. I'll always wonder why. I just don't think he should be taken from us so young. My husband tends to agree with me; he won't accept it. He'll never accept it, because he keeps saying, "If there is a God, they wouldn't have taken him from us". That's just the way we see it.'

'People always say things happen for a reason, but I'd like to know the reason. Are we being punished or why? People write in sympathy cards: "Things happen for a reason" or "They only take the best". Well why do they take the best? I think those people need to actually go through it themselves to understand what it's really like to lose your child. I mean unless you go through it, you can assume, but you never know the pain a parent goes through. But I really wouldn't wish what I'm going through on anyone.'

'It's coming up to two years, but some days it just seems like yesterday. It was his birthday on Sunday, so I had a bad week—but just to get through every day is such a struggle sometimes—and people forgot his birthday and that tore me apart. I made my intentions clear from the start. As soon as he passed away, I said I wanted him included in everything. I don't want his name forgotten or anything like that. I want his name put on cards, because as far as I'm concerned he's still part of our family and he won't be forgotten.'

'I see people differently now. You learn who your real friends are; you learn to trust fewer people. I guess I am emotionally a different person altogether. You make different friends. I laugh a lot less. Important occasions don't mean much to me any more. Christmas and birthdays are just no big deal any more—Easter and Mother's Day. It just doesn't feel the same any more. People get on with their lives as if nothing has happened, whereas to me, it's the opposite. It's a different life altogether now. I just see things differently, and I've learnt to appreciate life a lot more with what I've got.'

'For the first twelve months, I was very emotional. Now I still do get emotional, but it depends on what sort of a day I'm having. I mean, I can have a couple of great days for no reason and I can have a couple of bad days, where he's constantly on my mind and I wish I could hold him. When I'm around other babies, it all comes flooding back, even though it's nearly two years. If I hold a baby I just wish it was him and everything will come back—his illness and his funeral—it just seems like yesterday. Then I'll have a couple of bad days, or a couple of bad weeks.'

'When people say they understand, I get angry: because they don't understand. They've got no idea what it's like to lose a child, no matter how much they read in books, or what they've been trained to do. As far as I'm concerned, unless it's their own child, they'll never understand.'

'It would be hard no matter what age the child is that you've lost. But I think people handle their emotions differently. Lots of people bottle it up and don't speak; they don't do a thing. Whereas, I guess I'm the opposite. I'm very open and I tell people how I feel. If I want to cry, I'll cry and no one will tell me otherwise. That's just me; I'm an emotional person. I guess people's emotions are all different. It's got a lot to do with their upbringing and where they've come from, especially men who get told not to cry. "You're not an adult if you cry". But you shouldn't be afraid to talk about things.'

'It's coming up to two years now, and I guess I can talk about it a lot more without crying so much. For the first twelve months, every time I spoke I'd burst into tears. Whereas, now, I can talk about him to anyone. I still burst out crying at times, but I guess I can talk about him a lot more without getting so upset. I still have to accept it I guess.'

'To me, the cemetery is a place where you can pay your respects to family and friends. It's a special place where you can come and put fresh flowers and see family and loved ones. We've made a lot of friends there and we all look after each other's children there. To us, it's a special place and we try and make it as pretty as possible. The children's area is very, very important to us mums. If our kids were just buried here and there in a general adults' area, it just wouldn't be the same. We wouldn't have that bond that we've developed. I guess we all hope that our kids are all playing together. I think we all try to see it that way.'

'Oh, I've seen counsellors; I've spoken to counsellors and they seem to understand what you're going through. But in talking to other mums that have lost kids, we've developed a great bond, because we're all going through the same thing. In some ways, it's more helpful than talking to a counsellor who's gone through textbooks, but hasn't gone through our emotions and how hard it is. So yes, a lot of us mums have become quite close. Other people just wouldn't understand us; they'd think we've gone nuts.'

'In the past, I've found some people at the cemetery to be quite rude. I don't think we're informed enough about what's happening, but I really like what they've done recently. I'm very happy with the way it is now. I guess everyone's got faults; no one's perfect. I know every person's job is hard, and I accept that and if I can help in any way, I'm more than happy to.'

'I just feel that sometimes they should understand people's feelings a lot more, especially when it's a child that's concerned. I think they should be a bit more lenient, because with the parent losing a child it's very hard. I think that if people want to have a few more flowers or other items on the grave they should understand that, within reason. I've got a lot of friends that come and visit Timothy and they'd love to leave flowers, but they get heartbroken when they see the extra flower vases removed; it shouldn't happen.'

'Some people are very friendly and very helpful; half the gardeners are terrific. When they laid the grass I was very grateful. And I showed them how grateful I was, because I really appreciated what they did. Overall, they're pretty good, but they do have their faults and I just think they need to understand people's feelings a bit better and be a bit more lenient. I think they need to talk to people more, and not just do things and let the parents find out afterwards.'

'I know the cemetery people have got a hard job ahead of themselves, especially in the kids' section; people do have a lot of items there. I guess I try and see both sides of it; I try not to have too much if I can help it, but then when family take things there, you can't say: "Don't".'

'I visit the cemetery regularly. I have to come and see him; I have to look after him. I make sure his flowers are pretty and that his headstone's maintained. I have to do something. I can't do anything for him at home, so I have to come and just talk to him. People might think I'm being silly. But quite frankly, I don't care what people think. That's my child there and this is the last thing I can do for him.'

'For the first twelve months after he died I came to the cemetery every day. Now it's every second day, or sometimes every third day. I try to see him every day or every second day. I just have to come and see him even if it's only for five minutes. I'll pop in and say hello to him. I water his grass and maintain it, and I try and make it as pretty as I can. I change his flowers and make sure nothing's broken or taken.'

'I'm just his Mum. It's my motherly instinct to look after him and to make sure everything's well maintained and pretty, just as if he was at home where I could look after him. That mother/child bond will always be there. I mean, I gave birth to him and I've got to do what I can for him, and for myself.'

'The cemetery is only fifteen minutes drive from home. I park near his grave there. I check his flowers: check the water, and I cut the grass. I keep everything in my car boot: like scissors for the flowers and to cut the grass. I fertilise the lawn, clean the headstone and put pretty windmills on there. I try and make it as pretty as I can.'

'If the grass is really dry, we go and water other graves or just remove dead flowers. And we just help the gardeners in any way we can. I mean, we know their job is enormous—looking after the kids' graves with all the windmills—and we appreciate that, so we try and help as much as we can. At times, we don't like the things that they do, or get told to do by various people. It's a kids' section and we try as much as we can, I guess.'

'If it were a cold and wet rainy day, I would stay there probably five or ten minutes; but if it's a warm day, I can spend hours there. Once I'm there, I just find it hard to go home. I can sit there in the sun and just be with him for hours. A lot of times, I organise other mothers to be there, so we can be together and have a chat. But we're also there with our kids and that means the world to us; we're sure they know that we're there. If I'm on my own, I spend the time specifically with Timothy, but if I'm with other mums, we just get together in the sun and we sit there and just talk and talk to our kids. It's mainly mums, because most dads work. We usually have a coffee there and a talk.'

'My husband makes a point of coming on the weekends; but he can't come every weekend, because of the hours he's at work, so he finds that very hard. When he does come—after he finishes work—he feels rushed; he can't spend enough time there. You can spend hours and you don't realise how quickly the time goes. My other son comes on weekends and on days off school; he loves to come. He talks to his brother and brings toys, or makes pictures for him, which I put on his headstone. He always talks about his brother; he misses him a lot.'

'When my husband and my son are there, we do the same things. My husband knows what I always do; he quite understands and he respects my feelings. He does help me, but because I know what to do, it's easier if I just do it. He does try to help if he can. He gets the water. He normally fills the containers up and waters the grave for me. He's pretty good, but he mainly leaves it to me to do. I just like to be there.'

'On the way to the cemetery, I feel happy that I'm going to see him. I just can't wait to come and say hello to him. But when I'm leaving I do feel sad. I know I have to go home and get on with life and do what I have to do at home. I'd like to spend a lot more time if I could, but I guess we have to get things done. I wish he was a bit closer to me, but I'm pretty lucky that it's only just a short drive from home.'

'At times, when I'm there I feel happy. But I have bad days when I'm really sad and I just wish I could take him home with me. But most times, I feel happy just that he knows I'm there. When I get there his windmills start turning. To me, that means that he knows I'm there. I just feel he knows that I'm there and he knows that I'm looking after his area. But I do have bad days; I can go there and just cry. I suppose I'll just never accept that he's gone.'

'I do find it a bit easier to visit these days. I'll always come and see him a lot. I mean, that's my son there, and until they bury me, I'll always come frequently. I'll always make sure that it's maintained and looked after, and he's got fresh flowers.'

Time's a Healer

Max was born in Melbourne almost 64 years ago. 'I was in the motor trade for 44 years. I worked for the same company all my life. I had had other positions through the company at varying times, but I guess the most recent would be that of service manager. I retired nearly four years ago now.'

Margaret was also born in Melbourne 64 years ago. She had been a secretary in a small business and then did part-time sales work. 'It's been about ten years now, since I've gone out to work. The family's grown up and gone now. We had two daughters, two years apart. We've now got one daughter living nearby, and we've got two grandchildren. We belonged to the Methodist Church, but it's the Uniting Church now.'

Max and Margaret's 38-year-old daughter, Lorraine, was killed three years ago when her car left the road, not far from her country home.

'She'd only ever wanted to be a schoolteacher from when she was a little girl', said Margaret. 'When she went to kindergarten and primary school, she'd come home and do work on the blackboard and in books, and be a teacher. That's all she ever wanted to do. And she was an excellent schoolteacher, held in high regard. Lorraine married at twenty, but wasn't able to have any children; she lost several. She liked sports and she loved all animals. She always did very much more than was required of her.'

Max added: 'As well as enjoying the sports, she was a very keen horsewoman; she loved her horses. She lived out of town, on a nice property of about three and a half acres. She had plenty of room to move with the animals and so forth. As Margaret said, she was very highly regarded in her teaching life. She'd studied and had two degrees. You know, she thoroughly enjoyed the teaching aspect. She loved the kids and the kids loved her.'

'Just the day before was my birthday, and the family were together. We had dinner together at our younger daughter's. Little did we know that 24 hours later Lorraine would be gone. But I've always been thankful that we'd had that opportunity to all be together so soon before the accident.'

Prior to Lorraine's death, Margaret and Max had both lost parents and grandparents. Max's father had passed away 'around 28 years ago', and his mother, 'about six years ago'. Margaret's father died 'twenty years ago', but she lost her mother 'only last year'.

'I think in the case of our parents, both our fathers were ill and we knew that they were going to go, so we were somewhat prepared for that. Our mothers both lived to ripe old ages. My Mum was 89, and I think Margaret's Mum was 92. So I guess we were very sorry at the time they did go, but having lived to that age you can't be too sad, because they'd had great innings. Whereas, with our daughter, that was totally unexpected and came as a real bolt from the blue. So I think our parents going didn't prepare us in any shape or form for Lorraine going.'

Margaret said: 'With our fathers, it was a happy release for them. All we wanted for them was peace; they'd both had bowel cancer and were very ill. And our mothers had got to the stage where they'd had enough. They didn't want to live any more; they said they'd had their lives. And in the case of my mother, well she would've willingly given her life and would rather it had been her taken than her grand-daughter, of course.'

With some input from John and their younger daughter, Margaret planned the funeral service herself. 'Well you have to have something as a farewell and a memorial to the person, and to let the people who want to come and pay respects to Lorraine herself, and also to other members of the family. I think the funeral and the way things went was really helpful at the time, because it's something to work to. I sat down and wrote out the service and typed it out. It's important that you put into it what you want to go into it, and don't leave it to other people to do, because I think you'd be sorry later.'

'We couldn't have had anybody better than the man we had to conduct the service. We met with our minister and sat down with him. I gave him all that I'd written out, which he was grateful for, and he made other suggestions as well.'

Max felt that: 'The service was a great tribute to Lorraine—that so many people attended, from old to quite young. A number of children that she'd taught came along, and I thought that was a wonderful tribute. There were perhaps about 350 people there in all, and everything went very well.'

Max found that his period of deepest grief lasted twelve months or more. 'During that time I'd still expect the telephone to ring, and those sorts of things. Different things trigger off emotional times. It's just time. Like the old adage: time's a healer.' Margaret added, 'And you have to keep busy always: and we do.'

Margaret and Max believe that Lorraine is now in heaven. 'It's just what I've always thought', said Margaret, 'that that's where anybody deserving would go. Otherwise, if you just think everything's finalised and gone, then what's the meaning of your life? And you like to think, hopefully, they've met up with everybody else in the family.'

Max agreed. 'I mean, that's our faith. And I guess that if there is a heaven, then Lorraine would certainly be there and, as Margaret said, she would meet up with other members of the family that have gone before. We expect to meet up with her in the future, hopefully.'

'At the time', Margaret recalls, 'we seemed a lot different. We were a lot more impatient with each other and we certainly didn't laugh much. Then I remember someone saying to me, after quite some time, that it was the first time they'd seen me smile. We find we're smiling more now.'

Max agreed with Margaret. 'She didn't become introverted, but she certainly had changed in her personality a bit. I don't say for the worse, but just differently. And she was reluctant to go and meet people. In my case, being a member of a service club at the time tended to help me get out and get amongst the fellows. I guess it tended to, not bring me out, but certainly keep me involved with others. So certainly, you do have a personality change; there's no question about that. I tended to become a little more sceptical, maybe. I don't know.'

Lorraine was cremated and her remains were interred at the base of a 'family rose' at the local cemetery. The arrangement provides for three future placements, if required. Margaret and Max expect that they will eventually occupy two of the remaining places.

Margaret supposes, 'It's just the way we've always known. That's where most people, or their remains, go. I know a lot of people don't; they have their ashes scattered or they're kept at home. But all the other members of our family have been buried or cremated at this cemetery. So we've got that plot now, for four of us. We talked with our other daughter about that and she agreed also that it would be for the four of us. It is nice to be able to go, particularly living where we do; it's not too far. We planted some little freesia bulbs in the plot as well, because they're nice and we all like those. They look nice and they smell nice as well, but we wouldn't put anything in that would disturb the look of the place.'

Margaret continued: 'About the cemetery, grounds staff are the people we mainly come in contact with, and I think they're very good. They go about their jobs unobtrusively and yet they are approachable, and I think that's very important. And they keep the grounds in excellent condition, which is very nice for people like us to see that it's cared for and clean. It would be terrible to go to somewhere and feel that they didn't care about the place. I don't know a lot about cemeteries—I've been to a few others—but this one has always been very well maintained. I think it's good, having seen other cemeteries where it hasn't been as good.'

According to Max, 'You never, ever forget those that have gone, but I guess the cemetery gives you an opportunity to go and remember them on the special occasions, such as birthdays and the like. We go up fairly often and just remember. I guess we remember more than anything else.' Margaret added, 'And we make sure everything looks nice and tidy; we take any weeds away. We always visit together. These days we visit once a month.'

Max continued: 'In the very early stages, we would have visited more frequently when family and friends might have wanted to go. So we may have gone a little more frequently in the first few months, I guess.' Margaret added, 'We don't need to go all the time, you know; and our younger daughter doesn't like to go at all. She'll go if we want her to come with us, but she doesn't really like it and won't go on her own.' Max concurred: 'Yes, she's not keen on going at all'.

Margaret continued: 'The children have been up with us and they'll come again. Oh, we just go sometimes.' Max added, 'Well we do, but we would certainly be there on Lorraine's birthday. We both went on Fathers Day as a special sort of day—along with a million others.'

'When we visit', said Margaret, 'we always take a bag with us with scissors, a gardening knife and a container of water. If there's any dead flowers left in those little vases that the cemetery provides, we throw them in the bin, or in the bag and bring them home; and when we take flowers, we put water in the vases and place the flowers around. We weed the bed and around it. We have a look at the others—some of the other memorials nearby. Sometimes, if we've got water, we top up some of those people's flowers too.'

'We generally just remember', said Max. 'We don't pray—not openly, I guess—though I have said the odd personal prayer while we were there. I don't know whether Margaret does, but we privately remember.'

Margaret confirmed, 'Yes, I do pray, but not only at the cemetery. And I have also found myself talking to Lorraine when I'm there, but not all the time. I think Lorraine would feel like we do: that we wouldn't want the family coming up all the time. I'd rather they got on with their own lives. You can remember without going to the cemetery of course; and that's what our other daughter thinks. But I wouldn't like to think that they wouldn't come and keep the place neat and look after it for us and the rest of the family.'

'We drive to the cemetery together and spend about half an hour at Lorraine's spot', Margaret said. 'Sometimes we visit the other members as well after that, but not always. Sometimes we go to everybody, and sometimes we don't.'

Max added: 'We never sit down; we just stand silently, I guess. There is a seat not far away. But we just stand silently, having done our little chores and maybe attended to a couple of others nearby, as Margaret said; then we drive off.'

Margaret feels 'just sadness and loss' when she visits Lorraine's memorial. 'The cemetery is nice, but I don't feel any sense of peace with her. With my father and mother I do, but not with my daughter. I've always thought that it was the worst thing that could happen to anybody: to lose a child in the family, no matter what age.'

Max feels similarly about visiting the cemetery. 'I don't feel any closer to God than Margaret does. On odd occasions, I think I feel close to Lorraine, but not all the time. Generally, it's a sense of sadness. As Margaret said, nobody would want to lose a child. So I guess we—or at least I—just feel very sad.'

Margaret added: 'I don't get as upset now. I suppose you'd say I find it easier to visit these days.'

Max concurred: 'I'd pretty much agree with Margaret's comments there. We don't feel perhaps quite as emotional as we did, but it's different. At the beginning, we were going through a real grieving process, which tends to reduce somewhat I suppose; but to a lesser degree I still have that grieving experience.'

Death of a Sibling

Unique Individual

Naomi was the first of four children born to a Melbourne Jewish family. She is now 37 years old, has never married, and currently lives in a unit on her own. She has managed her own consultancy business for about five years. Naomi is not a member of a synagogue, but does attend about twice a year.

'I am not orthodox, but would consider that we're traditional. That is, it's in our heart. We observe to the best of our ability the high holidays, which just involves going to synagogue, family meals, and things like that. I certainly go to synagogue on two of the holiest days: the Day of Atonement and New Year.'

'My mother would do the same; my father is less observant. I think there are a number of reasons why he doesn't really go to synagogue, but we share the spirit of it. It's the family—it's the getting together—it's a time of remembering those who are no longer with us—that makes us all get together and try to be some kind of observing Jews at very important times in the Jewish calendar.'

One of Naomi's two brothers took his own life eight months ago. 'Simon was thirty years old; he was also single. He had been working most recently on a part-time basis, helping my parents in their family business. He was a young, energetic, passionate man: creative, artistic, beautiful and generous. He was just a beautiful human being.'

'He was very secretive—no: not secretive. But I don't think he was able—for whatever his own reasons—to talk to us openly and honestly about what was truly going on in his mind. He had self-diagnosed himself as schizophrenic. He probably had a fear of discussing openly with us and with people in the medical profession what was going on, for fear of being put into an institution or of sedation. You know how certain sectors of the community deal with mental disorder or mental illness in a lot of cases. And he really didn't believe he was unwell. But I would never have believed that five years later that's what would have come out of this situation.'

Simon died in his car, of carbon monoxide inhalation. 'He got the information from the Internet. We found a multitude of pages from the Internet on ways and means of dying.'

'If it was going to happen, I think we would've all been more prepared—or at least better understood—if it had happened two or three years ago, because of his mental state. He was more ill then; his bipolar mood swings were far more obvious, because of more erratic behaviour. I guess on reflection you think: "Shit! Why now, when things appeared to be worse two or three years ago? Why now, when they seem to be calming down or reaching some kind of balance?" He seemed to be coping with life better now—in what he showed us externally—than he was two or three years ago.'

'There were no indications that he may have been contemplating taking his life. We were concerned, but he had a conversation with Mum and he reassured her that he never would. But he wasn't happy, because he said the medication suppressed his creative field. He couldn't create his music; he couldn't create art. He had little interest in the sort of things that were his life before he became ill; and that in itself caused him the unhappiness that he kept to himself a lot. We always feared that depression, but we didn't think it was going to happen, because he assured Mum it wouldn't.'

'I really think that we are fortunate. Apart from having been fortunate to have known, loved, and had him in our physical life, I think that we are really fortunate that he was beautiful in his death—in his passing. The note that he left behind for all of us was beautiful; it just expressed his love for the family. He said, "I'm sorry that my life has come to this. This is not the way I want my life to be. I don't want to cause you pain. I want you to be able to get on with your lives". So he left us as beautifully as he could in his situation, to leave us as little pain as humanely possible. He went in the kindest, most gentle way, as opposed to something like jumping off a bridge.'

'Dad found him, and Mum and I were two seconds behind. It was like, "I chose to do this for myself. I chose to go quietly: as peacefully as I could. I've chosen to do this and I don't want you to have to worry about where I am or what I've done". The police report gets closed; it's not like he was never found or he had a revolting end. Do you know what I mean? All of this follows through from the nature of the person that we knew and love; and I think in some ways that's why we're allowed to be a little bit more peaceful.'

'My grandmother died twelve years ago, and my grandfather nine years ago. I was absolutely devastated and traumatised by my grandmother's death. I don't know whether it was just because it was the first real important death that I'd experienced. I think it's a combination of that and other circumstances. I had really devoted a lot of my time to visiting them and I was really just lost—absolutely lost without her—and totally devastated. She was also a beautiful woman.'

'My grandfather's death probably didn't devastate me as much. I guess I was surprised that he survived as long as he did without my grandmother, because they'd been married for so many years. I was probably more prepared for his death; I was less prepared for my grandmother's death. I mean, I knew that she was old and unwell and had probably given up the will to live for a long time, but I was definitely not prepared for her death at the time that she died. I didn't expect that phone call to say come to the hospital.'

'I think when we got the call we presumed it was my grand-father, because he had a weak heart and he was unwell; they were both in hospital at the time. When Mum and Dad called to say that it was actually my grandmother, I just went quite berserk. I was the last one to see her alive. I'd been to visit her and I told her that Mum would be in tomorrow: to eat and be a good girl; and "What can I bring you in tomorrow?" They hadn't lost any of their senses in anyway. So I think that it was a shock and I was very traumatised by that.'

'My grandfather's death was more in the course of nature I guess. He was old; he'd been sick. He'd had major surgery that we didn't think he'd survive, but he survived many years, including three years without her that none of us ever believed that he would. But he was sick in hospital and we really were anticipating his death.'

'I also had a very close girlfriend who died pretty suddenly of cancer four years ago, but she wasn't as close to me as my grandparents were. It was unexpected, but my life had changed; we weren't as close. She wasn't actually living in Melbourne at the time and hadn't been for a while. But I don't think I was as traumatised by that; I'm not quite sure why.'

'But Simon's death was totally, totally different. I believe that nothing can ever prepare you for the loss, be they sick or healthy. It is just such a shock to the system, particularly I guess the circumstances of Simon's death: the fact that he took his own life. And I guess for all of us it was just a total shock. He had been unwell; he'd been properly diagnosed as being bipolar and had been suffering with a bit of depression, but that had been going on for about five years.'

'Normally, we'd have a service in the chapel, or the little sort of synagogue at the cemetery, and then the burial. We specifi-cally requested that the service not be held in the chapel. There are separate orthodox and liberal Jewish cemeteries. Cremation is not actually the Jewish way, but some Jews do get cremated. They go in the liberal area. So do some that are buried who may marry a Jew, but they don't convert. They may have lived a Jewish life, but they can't be buried in the orthodox part.'

'Normally, the service is held in the chapel with the coffin present and various prayers and possibly a eulogy are read. And then the family and the other mourners follow the coffin in a procession out of the chapel to the gravesite. We specifically requested that if possible we have a graveside funeral rather than the traditional one. That was permitted. I believe it is something that is entirely up to the rabbi conducting the service.'

'It was totally emotional. We just did not want, if at all possible, to be in that situation. The chapel is very cold and very depressing in itself. In the chapel the immediate family—the immediate mourners—would have to sit on small stools on display in front of everybody. And the coffin is in the chapel just covered with a black cloth, and the rabbi says various prayers and it's all sort of there in your face. The mourners sit as they would in a synagogue: ladies on one side and men on the other.'

'And then the coffin is wheeled to the grave. It's quite a procedure—a noisy procession. It's quite a traumatic thing, and it can be worse the greater the distance that you have to walk from the chapel. And now that the cemetery's filling up, the distance between the grave and chapel seemed like a two-hour walk to me.'

'So we decided as a family that if we couldn't have a grave-side funeral, we'd probably go to the liberal side or to another cemetery where we could've had music and done whatever we wanted to do. We would've possibly gone through the proce-dure of finding a rabbi who would've allowed it, once we'd found out that it is possible. A lot of people don't know that it's possible, so they don't request it. And a lot of people won't break with tradition. So that's the way it was done.'

'I certainly remember arriving there and walking from the entrance—which is near the chapel—with a number of people holding us up—to the gravesite, where the funeral took place. As much as I really tried to listen to what the rabbi was saying, part of it was done in Hebrew. He is a very gentle gentleman. I think he said some English words, but in my own mind, I just really wasn't there. I vaguely remember it, but it was almost as though we were in a space of our own and it felt like there were hundreds of people around us. I know because I was told that there were a lot of people, but I really don't remember the service or his words. I do remember standing there; I know that I was at my brother's funeral, but –.'

'We have a special Jewish burial organization: the Chevra Kadisha. And the man came and it was all arranged from home. We didn't even have to leave the house. The man that organises it is just such a wonderful caring person.'

'At Jewish funerals you don't bring flowers and the coffin is a simple pine box. The idea is that you come in with nothing and you go away with nothing. Jewish people get buried as soon as possible. If a person dies in the morning you'll usually find the funeral is by that afternoon. Simon died in the evening and there was to be a coroner's inquest. Quite often in cases like this they ask for autopsies. Autopsies are against the Jewish belief. We got around that; there are very few cases that don't get around it. The Chevra Kadisha usually handles avoiding the autopsy; that's something that the family, under normal circumstances, doesn't have to get involved with.'

'I remember one case where a family had to get involved to stop an autopsy, because there was nobody with her when she died. She was a young girl and both her parents were deceased, and she was an only child. A neighbour who happened to be a friend, or somebody who lived in the street, was walking past her house in the morning. He saw her on her front doorstep, and she was already dead.'

'I know that there was quite a procedure and a process to avoid the autopsy. There was quite a delay in the funeral, because there was nobody with her; there were no circumstances that anybody could find. They had to try and find a doctor who could substantiate the fact that she was a serious asthmatic, to avoid going through an autopsy; otherwise there was nothing that could be done. And I think from memory that's what happened. They actually found a doctor, but it was quite a problem because she didn't go to see a regular doctor. But it hadn't been long before that, that she'd had a major asthma attack and ended up in hospital on a respirator. So proof of that, plus some doctor that had seen her on the odd occasion, was enough. But under normal circumstances, it is something that the family does not have to get involved with. It is usually handled by Chevra Kadisha and doctors. It's just totally against the law.'

'Being an organ donor was against the law for a long time. I don't think it stands with the orthodox, but there is now a Jewish registry. They ask in the Jewish news media for people to become a donor. In Judaism, if a person is injured—let's say they lose a limb—then that limb is actually buried in a grave in the cemetery; and when they die the rest of the body goes in the same grave.'

'Simon's funeral was held in the early afternoon of the next day. We were lucky in that it was a beautiful sunny day, which made it just that little bit more bearable. The coffin is usually covered with a black cloth and there was a Star of David in the centre. The Star of David was embroidered in white, and it was just so bright—so bright. It was amazing.'

'It was a new rabbi at the synagogue and he didn't even know us; we met him just before the funeral. We spoke with him briefly and we asked him not to hold a eulogy, because he didn't know Simon. It seemed very superficial for a rabbi to come along and make up a speech about him. I said that if everybody who would be there knew him then it wouldn't be necessary to tell them how good he was, because they already knew.'

'At his funeral, I wasn't in denial that he had passed away, so I don't think I needed it to concrete in my mind that this was a reality. I don't believe there was anything really peaceful—maybe there was, a little bit. Maybe when somebody passes away then a process has to begin. I think it's something that you dread, so once it's over you're relieved when that part of the process is done; it's something you don't have to talk about or worry about any more. I think the only thing the funeral did for me was let me say, "Well it's done; it's done now". It is a definite finalisation.'

'Jewish funerals are pretty basic: very, very simple. There are no flowers: no decoration. You get there and the hole's been dug and the soil is there to the left—or to the right—with the shovels there.'

'The coffin is lowered by the gravediggers; and then it is the deed of the family to put in the first shovels of soil. There is always a small envelope of Jerusalem soil; and that gets scattered on the coffin first. The men do that; it is not really acceptable for women, but when we discussed it with the rabbi, I asked if it is actually against the law or whether it's just one of those things that isn't done. He said, "If you want to you can". It was actually quite interesting, because I did. I got my sister and we just held the shovel together and picked it up.'

'For us it was important. My Dad had to do it and my other brother had to do it; there was no way that Mum could've done it. I just think it was important for us that we do it too, as long as it wasn't against the law.'

'And it was actually quite interesting, because I went to get the shovel and my uncle tried to shove me away and said, "What are you doing?" And I sort of said, "Excuse me; I'm allowed". But most women wouldn't want to do it. The woman has a different role in the Jewish religion. The woman is the house-maker and the provider and the keeper of the children, and all of the nice traditional women's roles; and that is not one. But yes, we did that.'

'I last saw Simon at some stage during the week before he died; it would've been within the week. I know that a lot of people see the funeral as a time to say goodbye, but for me it wasn't; it wasn't a goodbye. It's not the way I look at it, in any way.'

'The day of the funeral, Mum and Dad didn't open their shop at all; they just put a notice in the door. They didn't even open the shop the day after. People were very sympathetic; many of them knew Simon. I didn't go back to my business for two weeks. At that stage I had two other business partners; they were very understanding and my clients were too.'

'I was always an emotional person, but I definitely cry more now than I used to. I love laughter just as much as I did before, though sometimes I find that it's harder to laugh. I think I take life a little bit more seriously now than I did before—and you look at people differently. For me, to go out and laugh just feels so good. I love those laughter moments; I treasure them. They go from head to toe, because they are just the absolute extreme from the real pain that I'm feeling. And that pain is with me every day, every minute; it just doesn't go away.'

'I think the people who know me well definitely notice that change in me; and I think other people who are either too quick to judge or only think they know me, probably look at me differently. In some ways, I know that I am more emotionally vulnerable and weaker than I was. I could in some ways be broken far easier; but in other ways—be it business and within myself—I think I'm a lot stronger than I was.'

'I'm a little less tolerant and a little less patient than I used to be. Some people who don't really know me well or who are a bad judge of character could easily presume that I am hardened by it: whereas I'm not. I don't believe I'm hardened at all; I'm just a little bit more determined. You know, I've got a little bit of his passion inside me, and I just don't want people to walk over me or use and manipulate me.'

'I've become less tolerant of trivial situations, because they're just not important, but much more tolerant in serious situations, because they are important. He was a very understanding, people's person; and in his memory, I guess I find myself being more tolerant of people that I may not have been tolerant of before, out of respect for his memory. But it's not a conscious thing.'

'I think, in our family, we are all incredibly bound: all of us. It's like there's a common thread through our hearts. That went for all six, and certainly goes for the five of us now. I don't believe it's changed. I think, in the very early stages, it certainly made us closer than we were; but I really don't believe that you could make our family any closer than it always was. It's just one of those unique things.'

'As a unit, we would all be together at anytime and pull our weight to help one another. There would never be a situation in our family of seriously not talking. I speak to my sister every day; I probably speak to my brother every couple of weeks, but that's not for anything else other than his life and my life. My relationship with Mum and Dad is probably even stronger and closer than it was, but it was close before.'

'In the very, very early days, we were inseparable: all of us. I guess the sad part through trauma, especially the death of somebody who is truly missed in life, is that the world goes on. But you can make a choice; you can either go down the drain— and that would just have been so easy, and in some ways could still be so easy—or you can decide you've got to go on. So life returns to where it was before, if you make that choice. I guess that's where the family unit is now; it's back to where it was before.'

'I don't pray. And I don't question if there's really a God, on a daily basis; but I certainly did when I was sitting in synagogue. I thought, "What the hell am I here for?" I guess it's made me understand, in some ways, a lot less than I understood before; because now I've got so many questions that we'll never have answers to. But it hasn't really changed my faith. I mean, I'll still go to synagogue, but I guess I probably believe less than I did before. I've lost a little bit of that: though not about the Jewish faith thing, the family bond and the things that we love doing at home. But I would say that I've lost a little bit of the need to go to synagogue, even on the high holidays, at this point in time. If there was a call to go to synagogue tomorrow, I think I'd probably make a choice and say, "No"; because I'm not quite sure what place being in that synagogue has any more.'

'I'm not quite sure where Simon is now; he could be in a number of places. There are times that I believe his spirit is definitely around. I believe that he's somewhere around, without a doubt, and that we are connected in some way. But I really don't know how much of that is just my own belief, in that part of him now lives inside us all, and certainly inside me, or whether there is a spirit, or a soul, or something flying out there. I'm not sure; I guess that's something else that I've started questioning, you know—whether there is a spirit world or not, or a reincarnation. I just know that the person I knew, and the person that is no longer with me, is not suffering in this physical world. That I know.'

'The traditional Jewish view is actually very beautiful, in that the soul lives on. And I guess without being a traditionalist, or looking at it from a religious point of view, I think that's probably how I really do feel. But I'm not able to be definite about where the soul actually is. I mean, his soul lives on; he is gone from this physical world, but there is plenty of him and plenty about him that is still around. So I still feel him very much in the physical sense, because of a number of reasons. His room, his things, paintings on the wall, art, photos: all of those kind of things. He's in my heart.'

'We have a tradition where they bring little stools to the house. When you're in mourning you're supposed to humble yourself before everybody that visits. You're not supposed to sit or stand higher than the people that come to show respect, and therefore you sit on these stools that look like kinder-garten chairs. The immediate family sits on those stools during the shivah.'

'The Jewish faith has a thirty-day mourning period. Nobody actually tells you that you have to be any different, or tells the parents not to go to a wedding or a function and have a great time, to be sinister. It's actually saying that for twelve months, you're not going to feel like it. So maybe the religion actually caters to what a normal grieving process is for anyone. I mean, twelve months after the fact, maybe it will be easier for Mum and Dad in particular to go to a wedding and go to a function and relax. But now, they couldn't get up and be carefree.'

'I would imagine it is harder—it's something totally different—for a parent to lose a child. I mean, it's been very traumatic for me to lose my brother, but it is something completely different for a parent to lose a child. The religion respects the proximity of the relationship. I mean, child/parent: parent/child is the closest bond you're ever going to get in life; and it will take a period of adjusting to get used to this new life: a new existence without that person. I think it basically says, "It's all OK; everything that you feel is normal". It's allowing you to go through this process—which is a normal process to go through—not having any expectations put on you.'

'There is nobody that doesn't understand. Even non-Jewish people certainly understand Mum and Dad. I mean, they're grateful for them attending something that is important to them, and being there and sharing the occasion. But nobody questions their inability to get up and dance. To actually get up and dance takes a lot more than just functioning as you normally would.'

'I don't think that everybody understands death and the process that goes with it. What they don't acknowledge is the individual situation every time. Just because you can lose a grandparent and go to a funeral and be back at work tomorrow, doesn't mean that I'm going to survive the loss of my cat. You know, it depends on the person and on the importance of the relationship. Every situation is so totally different: you function differently.'

'Simon is in the orthodox cemetery. There was a time when, if you took your own life, they wouldn't bury you in the orthodox section, or if they did, they would put you right at the back. But this was a different case. Because he was ill and it happened through the illness, they didn't treat it like a normal self-inflicted death. There used to be a lot more trauma connected with that sort of dying than there is today.'

'The Jewish way is to buy your own grave, but some people are not prepared. It was a conversation that we'd had in the family at odd times and nobody really wanted to discuss it. I know that up until my brother's death, Mum and Dad certainly didn't have anything. Since, they've got themselves a plot next to my brother.'

'I've now gone through three phases of what the cemetery actually means to me. Very early on—like within the first couple of weeks—I was dreading it. It was such an issue to go to the cemetery, and I kept saying, "It's just a place; it's just a place; it's not where he is. That's not where he is; it's just a physical thing". It is traumatic; it is an absolute reminder every time of the truth. It is not in any way peaceful. The cemetery can be peaceful because it's quiet, but it's not peaceful in that particular place.'

'There isn't a monument on his grave yet. The marker there is just a piece of wood with the name, which is very typical. That's really what happens until a monument is erected. It's just a mound of soil; or you can order a metal cover, which protects it from the rain and stuff like that. So yes, it does have a cover over it, and there's just a wooden plaque with the name.'

'But then I learned another thing that the cemetery means to me. On one visit, when I came home I was quite emotional— almost traumatised—because I realised that it's the only place I know that I can identify as where he was, is, or is around. It's like the only place that I could identify in a physical sense with the last existence of him as a person. That made me understand why people do go to the cemetery. I could never understand why people go all the time; and I still couldn't go all the time. But the people who do go every week go because they're looking at that place and saying, "That's where that person is; that's where that person lies". And therefore, to visit and see and communicate or contact that person, they must be in that place.'

'To me, there was never a question of Simon not being buried in a Jewish cemetery. Simon did leave a note. I know for a fact that he didn't think he'd be able to be buried in a Jewish cemetery. I'm pretty sure it's because he took his life that he didn't think he'd be able to be buried as a Jew. And really, for a great part of his life, and even through his illness at various times, Judaism was really important to him—not that he was any more orthodox than anybody else was. But there were times when he really did believe that he had a calling almost. He had a real essence about him. So I think, if he had a choice, he would be very happy that he was buried as a Jew.'

'I don't feel especially close to Simon at the cemetery; I feel more distant probably. But you can always feel different things when you're at the cemetery. It's normally a chilly, freezing cold place; there is not a time that you ever go there in your T-shirt, because it's not warm there. But on the day of his funeral it was just absolutely beautiful; the sun was shining and the birds were flying, and the bugs were around. Every time we've gone to the cemetery to visit him it's always been a beautiful sunny day. You can stand there and feel the sun directly on your face, and you can say, "The sun's shining on me: it's Simon". It's a beautiful thing; but whether it's real or not, I don't know.'

'It's not a holy place, but is a religious place, in terms of the standard of what goes on there. But I don't feel closer to God, because I question him at the moment. To me, the cemetery is not sacred—as in holy like the synagogue—but I respect it. I would never do anything that would show any disrespect: as much as I'd love to go there, light up a cigarette and blast some music. At the synagogue you can have a wedding; there are some happy memories attached to a synagogue. There are no happy memories in the cemetery. There are lots of people we know who are buried there. It definitely has heritage value. If there wasn't a Jewish cemetery as such, and you were able to be buried anywhere, then I don't think it would have any heritage value.'

'I personally would never have just gone to the cemetery for the hell of going to the cemetery. I've always gone to the cemetery because it was—like I said before—the high holidays or anniversary or something like that. If it so worked out that Mum and Dad said that they were going to go to the cemetery and I could meet them, I would go and meet them at the cemetery. The monument is being organised at the moment; and next month we will have it consecrated by a rabbi and we'll all probably go to the cemetery.'

'I don't think the pain for that particular loss is ever going to be any easier. All that we really do is survive or learn how to cope. I probably survived in the first instance, and now I'm coping. I think life changes and you have to work around it. And you do to the best of your ability.'

'There's always going to be a memory: a reminder and an acknowledgment of his pain that nobody ever understood. I guess that's the hard thing, and the difference with mental illness. While cancer is devastating, harsh and physically destructive, because you can see it and feel it, you can identify with somebody who has it. Their body changes and you've got something you can relate to, whereas, with mental illness and somebody in Simon's situation, you can never quite grasp it. You can't really say, "Well at least they're no longer in the pain that they were dealing with". You know that must have been the case, because of what they did, but you've got no physical proof.'

'Jewish law actually states that it is more important to go to the cemetery on important days like birthdays, memorial days, prior to high holidays, and the anniversary of the death. It is not required to go daily, weekly or on a fortnightly basis and have a routine. Some people would actually condemn frequent visitation to the cemetery. After a funeral, the immediate family is not permitted to go to the cemetery for thirty days, or four weeks. So, as a family, we all went four weeks later. After the thirty days we have a special service.'

'I wouldn't be surprised if the thirty days was to be gentle to the mourners, because the religion and things that you're meant to follow seem to be pretty kind to the individual. So maybe it's because every time you visit the grave it's another sort of emotional upheaval that you go through. Maybe it's something to do with trying to remove yourself from that for thirty days to be totally engrossed in yourself, because that's really what it's all about. I mean, that's why they say the mourning periods are stipulated, because it is hard to get through life: it is. It's a process that destroys part of you. And you do change; you are vulnerable; you are weaker. And I think the religion says that it is OK: that it is normal.'

'As time goes on, I don't think that I'm ever going to be a frequent visitor; it is far too traumatic. I don't know whether I still believe that it's the only place I can find him; I just know it has to be there. I don't know that I'd have it any other way, unless there was ever a Jewish lawn cemetery or something like that, which is very peaceful and pretty. I can't identify with anything at the cemetery—although the monument has been incredibly important to us.'

'I've been maybe only half a dozen times. Whether I visit frequently or infrequently is entirely up to me. I don't find that it is a lack of respect not to go there. I guess I feel him and think about him every day; I think about him probably fifty times a day. I mean, there are times that I dance with him in my lounge room. Yeah; he's with me all the time.'

'I don't want to make it a routine in my life to go there, because he's everywhere; he's not just there. So I guess I don't have to identify with it as being the only place that

I can find him. I just couldn't. I'd be destroyed, because it is a really, really hard thing—a heart-wrenching experience—to go. I don't want it ever to change from that.'

'I don't want to ever be able to walk up to his gravesite and not cry, and not feel, and not hurt. I don't want to ever get used to it to the point where you go every Sunday and wipe it down and clean it; and that's what you do next Sunday as well. I don't want it to become a routine that I just get used to.'

'I think it is traditional when you visit a gravesite—in Jewish religion—to put a pebble on the grave, as a mark of respect, and to mark the fact that you've been. I don't spend a lot of time there. I know when my grandmother passed away I thought that I would. I always talked about taking a deck chair and sitting down for a whole afternoon and sitting by her side, so to speak. But I guess I've grown up a little bit since then and matured and maybe become a bit more spiritual. And I know that I can't do that now, because Simon's everywhere else, you know.'

'There are times when I wish I had a specific prayer that I could say. Maybe that will come, or maybe that will happen. I just have really nice, pleasant thoughts about him and shed a tear, and I guess I say, "I love you". But I say that every day. So for me, I guess it's a respect: a respect for the place as a final resting place. But I haven't yet gone through all the mental processes about what sort of role it really takes and what it really means. When I'm there I identify with him and his last moments of pain. It's not a future thing; it's definitely a past thing and a definite loss for me. It becomes real; it's there, and there's the proof.'

'When I visit, I don't think I'd spend any more than five minutes: tops. It's not that I can't stand being there; it's a matter of not being quite sure what to do when I stand there. You know, even if I was to say a traditional Jewish prayer, that would probably only take a minute: maximum. And there's nothing else to do; I mean, there's nowhere to sit.'

'There have been a lot of new burials since his funeral, because it's a new area of the cemetery. So there's a lot of death visible around him, which I guess is a fact of life for a cemetery; but because they're all relatively new there aren't many tombstones.'

'It's not very pleasant to stand there and look at the graves behind and read familiar names. There's a Naomi there, and the names of my parents and both brothers are on other graves. So it's really quite a hard thing to stand there, also knowing that the two spots next to him are for Mum and Dad. I picture myself very, very briefly—in a millionth of a second—visiting Simon and Mum and Dad together. Then that's it: I've got to go. I don't think I have to stand there for that long. I don't think that he would expect it, and I don't think there's anything to stay for.'

'When the tombstone's up, maybe one day I will go there and sit down and talk to him, and sit on his grave or lie down and bask in the sun or something, and do something really wild and whacky, which is what I'd love to do. But being in the cemetery, you've got to come down several pegs; you can't light up your cigarette and just chew on the grass, because you'd be condemned as a lunatic in about three seconds. And if the rabbi catches you you'd be kicked out anyway. But I guess, if I had my choice, that's what I'd like to do.'

'I think monumental masons need to be educated about servicing the mourner better: without a doubt. I mean, they've got a lot to learn about compassion and understanding and knowing people. I think it is crucial that they know and understand and learn how to service people properly.'

'Each situation I'm sure is different. You know when an elderly grandparent dies you have to pick a straight monument: maybe black or a grey marble. But in Jewish religion, you know that there's a Star of David and there are certain things that go on it; it goes to a form I guess. It's the same with Greeks or Italians.'

'But when you're talking about somebody like Simon, who was a unique individual, you couldn't just give him a black piece of marble with the Star of David and normal writing. You have to go a little bit different, because that's the kind of person that he was. So you need somebody who is prepared to listen and understand. You don't want somebody who says, "Yeah, yeah, yeah; that'll be right mate". And then it's nothing like what you're looking for and you've got to go through the same thing all over again. It's so traumatic. It's one of those things that are a necessity. It has to be done because of our religion, but nobody wants to do it.'

'Nobody wants to have to think about what needs to be written. Nobody wants to really have to go through the process of picking a colour or looking at 55 photos of other monuments, while they say, "Now; which of these do you want it to look like?" "I don't want it to look like any of them. Listen to me". I think that they could learn how to service a little bit better, and be a little bit more compassionate and understanding.'

'We went to several stonemasons. The main reason we did was because we've got such a special need. What we've got is a situation where we needed to be able to communicate and have some understanding. Simon was artistic, creative and young; and these were things that we wanted to reflect in the monument. And it was also for us; I mean, we've got to go there, you know.'

'If they haven't got the colour you want they tell you, "That's not the right colour for you". So you wipe them off and then you go and speak to the next person. The next person actually shits you, because there's just no dynamic personality between you, and they're telling you what you should have and you're saying, "But that's not what I want". So we go and talk to somebody else.'

'And then we finally found somebody who seemed to understand. He took the time and actually came to us with a load of samples and drew a sketch; and looking at it we thought, "Yeah;

that's what we want. Yeah; you've got the marble. Yeah; you get what we're talking about".'

'He was not a Jewish man, but he does a lot of work at the cemetery. It wasn't anything new to him. He just seemed to understand, because he belonged to the association and was recommended. I even said to him, "Thank you. It is so pleasant to talk to you. You've been very helpful and very compassionate and understanding". And he said, "Well, that's what I do; I've done this for so many years". But he let us down completely. He never got back to us. He was supposed to come back with a quote, but didn't.'

'Three weeks later, after ringing him three times and leaving three messages, I eventually got him on the phone. He said, "You were one of the people that I was going to contact". I said, "Thank you very much. What time are you working till tonight?" He said, "Seven-thirty; but by six o'clock you'll have it. I'll fax it to you". He never faxed: never rang. We never heard from him again.'

'In the meantime, Mum and Dad had been pestered by this Jewish man who does it for various people. And we couldn't get him off our backs, because one of his kids went to school with my brother. He said he really wanted to help Mum and Dad, and do it more as a good deed; he wasn't in it for the money. But Mum said, "Sorry. We're basically committed to this guy". He said, "Please, please let me help you. Once he sends the thing through, let me just give you another quote, and see if I can help you. I really want to help you". We were saying, "Jeez: this is just ridiculous. We're talking about something that we don't want to do and we're having to deal with it like a normal business transaction".'

'Then, as it turned out, because the other guy never got back to us and this other gentleman was really persistent, we ended up saying, "You've got the job". He said, "Here's a picture. It will be just what you want. Just give me the words and leave the rest up to me".'

'But that's not what we wanted. It wasn't the right colour or the size. We didn't want the Star of David; we wanted a treble clef instead. He was like the others. They don't want to understand special needs; they're used to just selling people a traditional, typical monument. He said his computer had about two hundred fonts, but not the one that we wanted. So there's been about fifty faxes sent back and forth trying to get it right this time.'

Stronger Person Now

Andrea was born in northern Queensland 43 years ago. She was the sixth of eight children: four boys and four girls. Her parents separated when she was twelve. 'I had a fairly traumatic upbringing. We moved down to Brisbane, but my father stayed up there. When I was eighteen I went to New Zealand and met my husband on the ship.'

Andrea has now been married for 23 years. She lives in Victoria with her husband and four children: aged fourteen to twenty. 'The youngest is still at school; the others have all got jobs. I was a nurse, but then my husband bought a manufacturing business and I worked there and reared the kids at the same time. My eldest daughter works with my husband now.'

'I don't get to Queensland to see my family very often. My Mum's a pastor of the Assemblies of God church, and my second-eldest brother is also a pastor, so I was brought up quite religious. I was raised in the Assemblies of God, and religion was rammed down our throats from when we were knee-high to a grasshopper. I was a Sunday-school teacher and that sort of thing; then my faith drifted. I stopped going to church when I was sixteen. That's when I went nursing and had shift work, which was just a poor excuse. But that's when I was able to not turn up, or whatever. But it was rammed down our throats.'

'When I turned twenty, I married a Catholic. That was seen

122

as a bad thing, because Mum used to be Catholic. It's like an ex-smoker or an ex-drinker or something. She did everything to stop our marriage. She didn't like my husband because he was Catholic.'

'Then I chose to bring the kids up Catholic, because if my husband's Mum and Dad struggled to bring their six kids up as Catholics—in private schools and everything—well then, I could do the same. My husband didn't take the kids to mass, so I took them, and I would sit there. It is different to what I was brought up with; but they learnt the Catholic side and I also told them the Protestant side. So they actually got two sides of the coin. And it's what they believe that counts, it's not a bunch of laws up there that you've got to do.'

'I went along to mass and all that sort of thing with the kids, and they went through Catholic schools, but I didn't actually accept the Catholic faith myself. Now they've got their own beliefs, but it's not Catholic and it's not Assemblies of God. I don't really believe in churches to give a person a safety blanket. I think it's what you believe in, not the name of the church that counts.'

Three years ago, Andrea suffered a severe mental breakdown following the death of her brother-in-law in a horrific car crash. Although much improved, she is still under treatment and has not returned to work.

'Bob was fifty years old. I have known him since I was ten, so that loss was pretty heavy. He was like a brother; I was very close to him. He had a sort of hobby farm really. He was a plumber by trade and they moved north from Brisbane. He couldn't get work for a while, then he milked cows and that sort of thing, and he ended up working on a cane field.'

'His father died of a heart attack at the age of forty. When Bob was forty he was very afraid of dying of a heart attack, but he lived till fifty. I was only ten when he was going with my eldest sister. He was sort of like a father figure I suppose. They've got four kids of their own.'

'His eldest son, who was seventeen, was driving the car and Bob was the front passenger. His other son was in the back. They were turning off the highway into the road that goes to their farm, and were somehow hit head-on by a car that was towing a boat. There was no one hurt in the other vehicle. But the eldest son lost half his face; the youngest son was scalped, and Bob was cut in half; so he died instantly. The two boys weren't expected to live, but they did. The older one has now only got a little scar on his head; they were able to put his face back. And they sewed the younger one's scalp back on, but he's got a little bit of brain damage. They both had every bone in their bodies broken, but they've come through it fine.'

'My sister is 47, and she was very, very close to Bob. The day of the accident, she was working in town and as she was coming home there was a news report to say there was a horrific accident on the highway. And she just got this cold feeling and thought it was her family. They'd been south to a car meeting or something. And she kept driving and they kept saying over the radio, "There's been a massive accident; avoid the area".'

'The road was all closed off, but she got home, because there are two ways of actually getting into their farm and she came home the north end. When she got home no one was there, so she got in the car and went out the south end and saw the accident. The helicopters and all that sort of stuff had arrived. They wouldn't tell her that Bob was dead; and they wouldn't tell her about her sons. It must have been terrible for her.'

'The boys were flown to the nearest hospital and they couldn't do anything for them, so they flew them straight down to Brisbane. The younger boy was in the children's hospital, and the older one was in the adult hospital; they were both in comas. The ambulance chap at the scene had been in the service for thirty years and said he had never seen an accident like it.'

'My sister eventually found out what had happened and insisted on going and seeing Bob. The doctors didn't want her to, but she pleaded with them that she needed to see him, so they ended up taking her with them. She said her goodbyes to him and then was flown down to Brisbane to the boys. With that, I got the phone call, so of course I flew up.'

'It was about a week and a half before they had the burial. Because the boys were so bad, they needed her there; she had to live in Brisbane. Their lives were so touch and go. They'd say, "No; they're going" and then, "Oh, they're back". She never left their sides; she just went from one hospital to the other the whole time. Then, once the boys were actually stabilised enough, we had the funeral. It was just a small burial. And then after the funeral she was back down in Brisbane again to the boys.'

'She needed to be with her boys, which would have been extremely hard for her as well. They had operation after operation. The boy who was driving had massive, massive injuries, and he had just one operation after another. And they'd think he wasn't going to pull through and then he would pull through. It was the same with the younger one.'

'She's a firm believer in prayer—so is my Mum—and she just stayed by their sides. Her daughters also stayed there and they were her strength; they held her up. Then gradually, her boys just started getting better. But they cannot remember the accident whatsoever. The older boy doesn't believe his Dad is dead; he still talks about him as if he's just gone off to work and hasn't come home yet. My sister found that very hard to understand.'

'The younger boy also had a hole through his skull, so he's got a plate in his head. He's not severely damaged; he's just a little slow. His brother has still got pins and plates and goodness-knows-what in him, but no brain damage whatsoever. They thought that he would be blind in his left eye, but even his sight came back.'

'They had a very big inquest into the accident. The driver of the other vehicle, an off-duty policeman, said that Bob's car went onto his side of the road. But because the boys can't remember they had to sort of try and work out how it actually happened. And they came to the conclusion that no one knew. There was no evidence of the boys going on the wrong side, or of the other driver's vehicle being on their side.'

'I believe it was meant to be. The boys were meant to live. It was Bob's time to go and he didn't suffer any pain at all, it was so quick. The ironic part about it is my sister always said that Bob wouldn't wear a seatbelt; he didn't believe in seatbelts. And the day of the accident he had a seatbelt on and that's what actually cut him in half.'

'The moment my Mum found out about the accident she rang me and I went up the next day. I met my Mum at Brisbane and then we went up to my sister's place, and then back to Brisbane. We just stayed in Brisbane, because that's where the hospitals were and Mum wasn't capable of driving at that stage, because she was just in complete shock.'

'Not long after the funeral, I went home. There was nothing else I could do and my sister needed her space; she needed to grieve with her girls. While the boys were critically ill, she actually lived at the hospital. They gave her a unit there just near the hospital. I stayed with my Mum, and my sister from New Zealand came over and she also stayed at the unit. But it came time for me to go. I'd sort of been there and she needed to grieve. I don't think she ever grieved properly.'

'Bob was a good man. He would help people; he would help people before himself. Many times he would give someone his last egg, because that person needed it, or he'd fix their fences when his fences were falling down. But he didn't have any insurance policy; he didn't believe in that. His house was falling down—and I mean falling down. He never showed his boys how to put a washer in a tap or how to fix the pump that comes from the dam into the house. When we stayed at the house, for the funeral, there was a massive hole in the floor. There were white ants through the house. So the family had to start from scratch.'

'My sister had to go into a lot of debt to actually fix the house. He was always going to do it, but he always did things for other people first. But he died and he left her with everything. And I think when I look at it now, that was meant to be, because my sister relied on him so much that she had to stand on her own two feet. In a similar situation, I had to stand on my own two feet, because you can't rely on a partner or anyone else for the rest of your life.'

'So she hit rock bottom and then had to get up and learn how to put a washer in the tap, how to fix the dam, how to get builders in to fix the hole in the floor, and plumbers and all the rest of it. She'll work for the rest of her life. She'll never sell the place, because it's Bob's. Bob left so much behind. There were a lot of good things, plus all the other things that he never got around to do. I know with Bob's death my husband learnt a lot: don't put off till tomorrow what you can do today. So we've all learnt a lesson out of one death.'

'My grandparents died many years ago. Also, many years ago, my husband's brother went on a cruise and disappeared off the ship. He was out in international waters on a foreign cruise ship and he went up to the top deck to watch the sunset with a mate who left him and went to bed. One of the crewmen also saw him there on a deckchair, but the next morning they stopped at some islands and he wasn't around. His mates just thought he'd gone ashore, so they went ashore and when they came back he wasn't there.'

'When the ship started to pull out, they went to the Captain and said, "Look: we're missing a passenger". But the ship kept going. They stopped at the next port and radioed back. Then they ended up searching the cabin, and his passport and everything was still in his room.'

'It was the biggest bungled job that you could ever come across. I was actually at my husband's Mum and Dad's house when the phone call came to say that he'd disappeared, presumed drowned. They never, ever found his body. The

Australian consulate wouldn't do anything because it was outside their waters; and the French consulate wouldn't do anything because it was outside their waters.'

'It was days before they got a plane up to look for him; and that was only because of pressure from the family and a media network. It was horrific for my husband: absolutely horrific. I was extremely pregnant at the time with our first. My husband's other brother and their lost brother's girlfriend ended up going over to the islands a couple of weeks later. They went to the islands and had a look around, but they found absolutely nothing. There's never been an answer.'

'His mates say that aliens got him. I've been on a ship, and if you're on the top deck you can't fall off into the water, because there's another deck that sticks out and there's another deck. So if he had fallen he would've been on the next deck. Then they tried to say that he'd committed suicide. The crew had changed ships. Another ship had come up and the whole ship's crew had changed around that area, so whether he had seen something he shouldn't have seen and something happened to him, no one knows. He just disappeared off the face of the earth.'

'Then after seven years, they said, "OK; he's dead". I think my husband's used to the fact that he's not going to come back. I think that was the closest thing that I've had to do with death really.'

'Just before Bob's accident, my Mum's sister died of leukaemia; I was very close to my aunty. And Mum's brother died of cancer at the beginning of this year. I also had a scare with my Mum. She had breast cancer and had a mastectomy only a month before Bob was killed. The mastectomy was very quickly done; I didn't go up for that. My sister in Queensland was with Mum for that; and then with the news of the accident, I went up. I think I was actually on the verge of a breakdown when the accident happened. It toppled me over.'

'Around the same time as Mum's illness, I had two operations on my breasts to remove lumps. I'm in a very, very high category for breast cancer. I was petrified of the first operation; it was very, very frightening. I thought my husband wouldn't love me any more, and all that sort of thing. The second one was after the breakdown, and I thought, "So, if I get it, I get it". I thought, "Oh, well; so be it. If it's there, it's there. If it's not, it's not". And that's how I look at it. If I'm going to get breast cancer, well I'm supposed to get breast cancer and then I'm going to learn from that.'

'I have a very, very close friend who's dying of breast cancer at the moment. She's younger than I am, and I find that hard: very hard, because she's been sick for six years. The doctors said, "Oh, no; you haven't got breast cancer". And now she's dying of it. She was the bubbliest person you could meet, and we are very close; we're like sisters. So I think that might be a pretty hard thing when the time comes.'

'I wasn't involved in Bob's funeral. My second-eldest brother did the service: he's a minister. One of his sons played the saxophone and the other son played the piano. They played *Amazing Grace*, and because that was Bob's favourite song, it was extremely emotional. And my Mum got up and read; so a lot of the family actually took part.'

'I remember my son saying that it was the most beautiful funeral, and the happiest, he's ever been to. Not that he's been to very many funerals. My brother did the talk on him—he and Bob were mates—and he brought up all the happy things that he and Bob had done. So there was a lot of laughter in the church. It wasn't all crying; it was a real lot of laughter.'

'About two years before that, my second-eldest brother and his wife and kids lived with them for about twelve months, so there was a very strong bond there. But he spoke about all the good bits—all the funny pieces of Bob's life came out—and people who hadn't seen him for years could remember those funny pieces. So it was sort of a sad occasion, but it made you feel really good, because he was such a good bloke and had done so much. It was a very nice funeral.'

'If someone suffers before they go, I think it's harder for someone else to cope with that, because they know that the person has suffered and there is a lot more grieving and sorrow to go through, because of that person's suffering. But Bob didn't suffer at all; it was just: Bang! Goodbye: gone!'

'And I think it was different because of the other two boys being so critical. The funeral was left for such a long time because of the boys; and then they couldn't even go to the funeral. That was sad: that his own two sons couldn't be at the funeral. But it works out that they don't remember anyway, so they've never gone through a grieving.'

'I've had a mental breakdown since then. I think it was Bob's death that actually popped it. I think it had been coming, but I just went and fell off the top as soon as I heard about the accident; but I stayed pretty strong when I was up there with Mum and my sister. I more or less collapsed when I came back. I didn't know that I was having a breakdown until I came back; but one day I just knew I was, so I went and sought help.'

'I think Bob's death didn't cause the breakdown, because I was already starting. I had migraine every day; I just lived with migraine. But it was my body saying, "Excuse me; slow down". But because I wasn't listening, I just kept going and going. I sort of look at it now that the soul said, "Well, OK; here, have a breakdown, then you'll listen". And that just happened to be when Bob was killed. That just toppled me over the edge. Then I had to start from right down the bottom and work my way up again. So yeah, I hit rock bottom.'

'My breakdown has been very, *very* difficult for my immediate family. My husband didn't understand what a breakdown was. He thought I should just snap out of it. Most people think, "Well, OK; so you're depressed. Now get better". But it's like a disease. Mental illness *is* a disease, and you can't snap out of it. It put horrific strain on my husband and me, and the kids. I couldn't do basic things like get in the car and go to the shop. I had agoraphobia. I couldn't cook meals. My second daughter cooked meals for twelve months. I can't remember a lot of that twelve months.'

'My husband would take me to the psychiatrist every week. To start with, it was twice a week. He actually wanted to admit me in hospital, and I said, "No". I was on a lot of medication. I could not sleep and I couldn't eat. I went down to 45 kilos. I had OCD, which is obsessive compulsive disorder. I was afraid of germs. I would wash my hands until they were bleeding. I would disinfect the ceiling, the walls, everything. And I would run. I could not stop. I couldn't go slowly. I had to go very fast, which was a strain on the family. I didn't stop running. There was something in me that just couldn't stop. I just had to keep going, and going, and going, until I was so exhausted I couldn't breathe.'

'I felt that it was my husband's fault, and I hated the business. I thought it was the fault of the business. I felt like a nobody at work. I had started off with the business and I had been told what to do the whole time. I started out the back, in the factory, like the factory workers. I had the kids and still went to work out in the factory. Eventually I got to the front office, but I didn't have a desk and I didn't have a chair. But I needed to be there for moral support. Whether there was work for me or not, I was needed. So I sort of stood around like a wallflower—which I felt. I put up with that for a long time, because I didn't know any different. That was the old me.'

'Then the migraines would come and I still had to go to work. I still had to stay at work and do deliveries in the car. They tested my brain to see if I had tumours; they did every-thing. I got to the stage where I hated work. A lot of pressure was on my husband at work, and I felt it was all my fault, so I took everything on. This was before Bob's death and I didn't know any different, so I just kept pushing, and pushing, and pushing myself. I had to be the perfect wife and perfect mother. Well I couldn't be; there's no such thing. Then there was Bob's death and I had the breakdown. So a lot of things were causing me a lot of stress at the time; the accident was just the icing on the cake, as they say.'

'In Queensland we didn't really have a lot of time to grieve, because the boys were so ill. But we knew that Bob was gone and there wasn't anything we could do about that. Everything was then focused on the boys. I think my sister didn't have time to grieve for Bob.'

'Everything was just focused on how the boys were going. Just about every organ in their body had something wrong with it. They're miracles. The doctors say they're miracles, and the ambulance drivers said they're miracles. They should not have survived. The older one's now married. But yeah, she didn't actually have time—we didn't have time to grieve. There was nothing we could actually do for Bob; he was gone and that's it.

'It's a bit strange really; the car that the accident was in is in their backyard. Now I couldn't have that myself, but the car that Bob was killed in is still sitting there. It's very hard to let go of the vehicle, but it doesn't mean a thing to the two boys. I don't know whether they'll ever go through a grieving time, or one day it will just hit them and all of a sudden their memory might come back. I don't think their memory was supposed to be there, because if they remembered the accident they wouldn't have coped with their own injuries. I think the universe was looking after the boys, so it worked out just right. "Bob's time was up—Bang!—Gone!—but you two can't remember it".'

'I had a lot of psychiatric help and counselling. Then I got into yoga, which has been absolutely fantastic; it helps you balance. You're thinking not only physical, it works on four levels: your physical, mental, emotional, and your spiritual levels. I'm now doing a course to become a teacher, and I'm doing esoteric studies as part of my course. The last five weeks of the esoteric studies course have been on death. And it just works out so simple, how it all is.'

'I do look at death differently. When your time is up, it is up. When your soul is ready to leave, it leaves: and that's it. So I think if anything does happen, at least I can understand what death's all about and the stages that you go through after death, and the stages you go through before death. I think if anything happened now, my grieving would be different, because I can see it differently now. So the yoga and the esoteric studies have helped me heaps: absolutely heaps.'

'I know I'm a stronger person now; I'm mentally stronger. I was weak before; I'm not now. I'm stronger in my personality, stronger in my thinking and in my understanding of things. I class my mental breakdown as a breakdown that was meant to happen. I'm not a person's person; I am my own person now. I just look at life differently. We're here for a job and that's what we're here to do, so get on with it. Enjoy life, but you're here for a purpose, so find that purpose and do it.'

'Bob's death brought the family closer together, but also put a little bit more tension between myself and my eldest sister. Her eldest daughter got married two years ago, only twelve months after her dad died. I went up for that. I was very close to her, so she insisted on us going and staying with her. I didn't really want to, and she pleaded with me to stay. I thought, "Oh, you've got enough on. You're going to be the mother of the bride".'

'But we stayed; and she was so stressed. She'd never really got over the grieving, and I could not handle all that. It sort of brought back everything, so I was busting my neck to leave. She found it very difficult, and I actually said something pretty nasty to her at the time. It was her daughter's wedding and we were all there helping, and she was doing the wedding cake and she was getting extremely frustrated and she was nasty to everybody. She was nasty to her daughter. Wedding presents were coming and she didn't care. It was really getting to me, because it wasn't her daughter's fault.'

'I had been through a very bad time with my Mum before

I got married, and I didn't want that to happen here. On the morning of the wedding, she asked me what was wrong. She said, "You don't seem very happy. What's wrong?" Well, the honesty came out instead of a white lie and I said, "It feels like we're here for a funeral not a wedding". And she got extremely upset and did grieve. She grieved. I'd never heard anybody wail so much; but it released her.'

'I went to pieces and I told my husband to go to her. She just wailed and wailed something terrible; but as it turned out it sort of snapped her out of this grumpiness and all the rest of it. My husband calmed her down and nobody else knew, so it didn't spoil the wedding. The girls were at the hairdresser's and when they came back she was a different person. She was happy and was nice to her daughter and the wedding turned out beautifully. But I never forgave myself for being nasty to her. That day she actually grieved.'

'The next day she came to me and said, "I hadn't cried". She said, "I've had little weeps, but I had not cried since the accident". She was not thanking me of course, and it did put a strain between us. I couldn't wait to leave; I couldn't stand it.'

'Oh, because she didn't have time to grieve when Bob died—because everything was put on to the boys, she hadn't actually had a good howl at all—she just kept going. Then her eldest daughter decided that she was going to get married within that twelve months, and that was on the anniversary of Bob's death. That was sort of very heavy for my sister, but I think in that way she actually did release all the emotions that she'd been hanging on to for such a long time. She was able to release it and then let go; and then she was able to get through the wedding.'

'Her eldest son gave the bride away. He was able to walk down the aisle and give his sister away. It was a beautiful wedding. But I sort of went through a little bit of regression, because it took me back to the accident time. I'd only just started getting strong on my feet from it, and then this toppled me back down again. By the time we got back from Queensland, I was a wreck again and I had to start off again.'

'I actually stopped taking my medication a month ago now. I still do see the psychiatrist, but not very often. I know he is there if I do need him. I can always ring him or whatever. But the yoga teacher training course that I'm now doing is a very heavy course and the esoteric study hits a lot of raw points. So I was told not to give up on the psychiatrist just yet, but to get through the course and just see how I'm going, because there's a lot of things that can be brought up. I've had a couple of not-so-good days in class, talking on death and things like that. Mental stability is like that; it sort of hits home a little bit to me, but I'm getting a lot stronger through it.'

'I don't attend church now, but I still find that I am religious in my own way. I'm not Assemblies of God, I'm not Catholic, and I'm not Church of England. I'm not a name as such; it's what I believe. My husband doesn't go to church and the kids don't go to church, but I do have faith and I believe in God, and I do read the Bible and all that sort of thing.'

'I suppose there is an obvious connection between Bob's death and my faith that I believe in now, because I had the breakdown and then had to start from scratch. I never said, "Why me?" and blamed God. I don't believe in that personally. But it was going to yoga and doing the teacher training course that has brought me closer to God, because you study a wide range of religious beliefs. It's not a denomination or anything like that. It looks at a bigger picture in understanding death, and understanding life and why are we here, and that's given me a lot of understanding and growth.'

'I personally don't believe one religion is correct, because Jesus didn't have a religion. He wasn't Catholic and he wasn't Protestant. It is only in the last two thousand years that religion has actually come with names. And a lot of religions are there to frighten people. I do have a lot of faith, but it's not under a name as such.'

'I believe in reincarnation: our soul is put here to learn something. I believe in karma: what goes around comes around. I think Bob was a very giving person and a very kind-hearted person. I don't think he's in heaven to stay in heaven, but he's gone up. He'll see what his plan on earth was supposed to be, because we're all here for a purpose.'

'And whether he's actually done his purpose I don't know, but it will be shown to him. "Now you should've really done that, but your personality got in the way and you chose not to, because you've got free will. So now you've got to go round and do it all again. You're going to go back and learn; and you can do something very nice to that person. So you're going to cop it when you go back, so you know what it feels like". So I think he's up there, but he's going to come back in another human body to learn something else.'

'The day before my niece's wedding, my husband took my sister out to the cemetery to sort of help her get through her depression. We thought it might have helped her, but it didn't. We haven't been back since the wedding. The older son got married earlier this year, but I didn't go to that.'

'I don't think I would have liked to have gone and visited Bob's grave. Why put yourself though another sadness when you don't need to? I know that if I went there all these memories from the accident would all come back—so it's best I think. Maybe it's because we're in Melbourne and they're in Queensland. I don't know what the situation would be like if I was up there, but I don't think I would go. I'd hate to go back to where I was when I had the breakdown—not that I'm going to go right back to the beginning, because you don't. But I don't want to go anywhere near that spot.'

'I think if someone said, "Oh, look; do you want to come with me while I go and visit Bob's grave?" I'd say, "Oh, OK". But I really don't think I would just make a special trip to go and see the grave, because it's only a grave. I haven't dwelt on that a lot, because I can get on merry-go-rounds and I can't get off them. So I try not to dwell too much on one thing. I also think a goodbye is goodbye, and you should move on. I don't know whether my sister goes to the grave, but I don't think the boys do.'

'Bob was supposed to have a monument on his grave, but I haven't seen it. I think a plaque saying something about the person is beautiful, but it's not necessary for me to go and see that. I think it would probably be a little different if it was my husband or one of my kids.'

'My husband's aunty died about sixteen years ago. She'd lived with his Mum and Dad for eighteen years and I went to the funeral, but I've never been back. I've never had an urge to go to the gravesite. So maybe that's just me, whereas the next person might have to go each Sunday or whatever; but I don't get the urge to go.'

Death of a Spouse

Respecting the Memory

Born in Sydney, 62 years ago, Bruce describes himself initially as 'nominally Catholic, but lapsed and verging on atheistic'. He now lives alone as his two sons, aged 35 and 33, have 'gone their own way'.

Having retired from a military career, Bruce is currently undertaking tertiary studies in business. He left school with the Intermediate Certificate, completed the Army's First Class Certificate of Education and a technical certificate in the early 1960s. More recently, he qualified in financial planning and attained industry accreditation.

Bruce's wife Erin was born in northern Victoria to an Irish family that 'had been there since the convict days'.

'They were on the land and were squatters who drove sheep 180 years or more ago. She strongly identified with her Irish ancestry, her Roman Catholicism and her rural background. She was a happy-go-lucky vivacious person, but very serious about her responsibilities as a mother. She raised the children and I went out to work. From the advancement of her first pregnancy, she didn't work for wages again'.

Bruce and Erin had what he described as 'the old-fashioned idea that the husband was the breadwinner and the wife was the home-maker'.

Erin died four and a half years ago, at the age of 53. The couple had been married for 34 years. Bruce recalls: 'She was very much into raising the children and virtually took total responsibility for the family unit as such. Being a soldier means prolonged periods of times away from the family. And the wives of professional soldiers do all the things, which, in other ordinary nuclear families, the husband does or they both do together. Wives of soldiers are much more experienced in just about everything. If there's a nail that needs to be driven they get the hammer and they drive the nail. So she was the lynchpin of the family.'

'We had a very happy relationship. The only point of strain was me getting out of the army. I did go back in again, because I thought it would make her happier; but it made me dreadfully unhappy. She was the family if you like, and I funded it.'

'The only people that had died in my family were my grand-parents, three uncles and an aunt. No one closer than that had died until my wife died. She was the first person very close to me that died.'

'She got breast cancer. They did what's called a lumpectomy, as opposed to a mastectomy, where they remove the lump but leave as much of the breast as they can. Then they gave her massive radiation treatment. They thought they had it, but it came back in both the liver and the bone. In the liver it was inoperable. From the time she got the breast cancer to the time she died was eight years. And she fought it every inch of the way, but succumbed to leukaemia in three and a half weeks. So she actually died of a combination of breast cancer and acute leukaemia.'

'Having her last as long as she did with the breast, liver and bone cancer, it was quite dramatic how quickly she went downhill and died with leukaemia.'

'I got a phone call the day she died saying, "Get in and get the family together and get here very quickly". As it happened, it took quite some hours after that. I was with her, as was our eldest son, when all of a sudden she started slipping away. I had to run and get a priest, because I knew that's what she wanted. It was important that I'd done the right thing: that I had kept the faith with her. I was not keeping the faith with the church, but I'd kept it with her.'

'I had a chance to observe myself at the funeral—if one can be objective in a subjective situation—mainly because the funeral director was a personal friend of both Erin and myself; we went back a long way. I was more concerned about my two children, to see how they held up. But there was no reason for me to have that concern. A more dramatic impact was obvious on Erin's elderly mother. It's a dreadful thing for a parent to lose a child.'

'Because her family are such devout Catholics, there was a requiem mass and everything else. The requiem mass was important in the sense that it was familiar—though not from any spiritual sense—but it was familiar, and I think that was comforting. Because I'm used to the military way of reducing things to routine, I consider an acceptable routine is the right final thing to do: and you do the right thing. I wasn't touched spiritually, but I was touched.'

'I think I drew more solace from the number of people who came to the funeral; it was quite an enormous turnout. Many came because of the military association with myself, but a huge amount were people whom Erin had somehow touched in her lifetime, even back to people she went to school with.'

'She organised her father's funeral during the early stage of her own cancer. So I had the opportunity to see exactly what she wanted, and I did liaise with her mother and her sister as well. I knew that the religious aspect was important to them. This is again fulfilling a duty in terms of the ceremony itself. My grieving was internal and I tended to privatise it.'

'I think Erin is dead. And as harsh as it sounds, I think that a human being is no different after death than any other living animal. I think dead is dead. If people live after death, they only do so in the minds of the people they leave behind. I don't believe that there's some place somewhere where they all go; and I have no concept of the pearly gates, or anything of that nature, nor any fear.'

'I recall a tremendous sense of loss at first when she died. Although I was surprised and even felt somewhat guilty about the rapidity at which I seemed to get over it. But I had eight years to prepare for it.'

'Her mind had gone that day. We were talking to her earlier in the day, and then—you know. I don't feel I had a good opportunity to say goodbye, particularly from one who's not unfamiliar with death. I never broached the subject and she was such a fighter. She kept fighting and I hoped that she would get better. She wasn't acknowledging the inevitability of her death, and I wouldn't want to discuss it with her, because it might sound like I would be contradicting her hope. It would have been the wrong thing to do. It was not only important to maintain that hope, but it was even more important not to be the person who destroyed it.'

'As I was some years older than she was, I had originally looked forward to travelling around with her and enjoying old age together. I mean, that was the way one thought, since women outlive men. To bury a younger wife came as a surprise. But as I had the opportunity to prepare for it, I think it wasn't as jarring as it would have been to a friend of mine whose fifty-year-old wife had a cerebral aneurysm and virtually dropped dead last year. He had no chance to prepare.'

'At first I found myself saying, "I must mention that to Erin". And of course there's no Erin there to mention it to. The house was large and empty. I could hear the echoing of my own foot-steps around the place, because there's nobody there in the house, and that initially exacerbates the sense of loss. But that was diminished by the fact that she spent so much of the time in hospital. Particularly in that last year and a half, she was in hospital almost constantly. So again, I had a period of time to adjust before the actual death itself. I'm not a psychologist, but

I suspect that lead to a more rapid adjustment and acceptance than it would have otherwise.'

'I am by nature a pragmatist and, in private moments, engage in what's called 'self-talk'. That is, to get yourself to do things, you might say mentally to yourself, "Get off your backside and do this", or whatever. I simply told myself, "Since I come from a family of notorious longevity, then in all probability I have a long time yet to go. It's about time I got off my backside and got on with the rest of my life". And I did so.'

'There were occasions in the early stages when I felt a bit guilty about this attitude, but again I think pragmatism steps in. You begin to think to yourself, "Well, you're not helping anybody by grieving excessively. You don't help them; you certainly don't help yourself, and you're certainly not much fun or pleasure to be around for your family or for your acquaintances".'

'I have now put my loss completely behind me. By that, I mean that I'm totally accepting of the fact that she's dead. She's gone: I'm not. Therefore I have to get on with my life. I'm sad that she's gone of course, but I'm not going to allow that to affect the rest of my life. It makes no sense, and she wouldn't want it anyway. In fact, I now have a lady friend whose company I enjoy, but because there's quite an age difference— a quarter of a century's difference—it's not going to lead to marriage or that sort of thing. If I were a younger man it probably would, but I'm not.'

'Again, you have to confront reality in life and deal with things on the basis of reality, but I've certainly resolved my grief. There are times when I develop some nostalgia—something will trigger that off—but I regard that as perfectly normal and healthy. But the effect that it had has passed. They say that grief is usually resolved—well I've resolved it.'

'Erin's death brought the boys and I closer together, in that, as I said earlier, it was she who raised them. My sons and I weren't terribly close then; it's surprising how close we are now. I think, because she was the closest person to them, that her going out of the picture changed things.'

'I think they first came to see me out of a sense of obligation or duty. We were never enemies, but because of the nature of the life that we'd led, weren't close. Then we discovered each other and got friendly. It was not just a matter of the survivors clinging together. The three of us are not the type to show our emotions, particularly in that way. We would by nature try to conceal our emotions. There's also something of a loner about me, and I think the boys are that way as well; so this removes the clinging bit.'

'Even though I had full medical insurance cover, the cost of supporting my wife for eight years was quite horrendous. But since leaving the army, I've earned very well in this business. Financially, my situation has improved dramatically. It used to bother my wife the amount of money it cost to support her; it never bothered me at all. So the fact that I am now financially so much extraordinarily better off is just a side effect. I've now got no dependants, so I don't work as hard, which is why I've been able to find the time to become a geriatric undergraduate. I've got time; I've got money. I'm in a different situation, I suspect, than most people.'

'My religious perspective did not shift at all in response to Erin's death. I think one would be more likely to feel that way if it had been suddenly dramatic, but it wasn't. Again, I had this adjustment period prior to the dying, rather than having to do it from scratch. I've seen an awful lot of death; I'm not unused to death.'

'My Catholicism probably started to die when I was still a teenager, but this was certainly accelerated by violent military service. It's very hard to see the hand of God in the midst of such lifetime experiences. I never voiced that to my wife but she was certainly aware of it. I think it's more a journey of intellect. I just find it impossible to conceive of an old man with a beard sitting in a cloud looking down on earth. Of course, I realise that's not the concept of the theologically educated; but I'm afraid I am an evolutionist. For me, it's been a journey away from faith, and I don't think Erin's death played a part in that at all. I'd already arrived at that destination well before. However, it could make you think again that if there's a God— and she was so religious—then the old adage that only the good die young tends to have some element of truth in it.'

'The cemetery is emblematic of the respect with which we held the people who are there. It marks us as a civilised society in that we show respect by honouring that memory. But it's the memory you're honouring by the method of disposal of the remains, and by maintaining a place where you can go and can mentally think back, reminisce, engage in nostalgia and think: what if she hadn't died?—and all that.'

'As I drive through the cemetery and see other people there, I believe it is significant to society. I think cemeteries play an enormous role. If, in my lifetime, they are going to dig up my wife's remains and put someone else in because they wanted to recycle the ground, then I would be looking around for a weapon—metaphorically speaking—and going out hunting. I would be very, very annoyed.'

'I see the cemetery as being sacred to the memory of the people who are there, rather than sacred in the Catholic sense. I would never knowingly engage in a sacrilegious act. Now that's not a matter of trying to be euphemistic, or having two bob each way, nor do I believe a bolt of lightning would come down from the clouds and strike me dead, or anything of that nature. I believe it's a respect for people, it's a respect for culture, it's a respect for tradition, and it's a respect for customs, which hold a society together.'

'Even though there are so many disparate parts of that society who have different customs, I would suspect that respect for the dead, and those things which are emblematic of that respect— which obviously includes cemeteries—is common to all. And I think it distinguishes the human animal from others. I mean, really; what is the difference between us and any other animal, but the capacity to reason? And if we are a reasoning people and we understand things, cemeteries do bring solace to an awful lot of people and become a focus in their lives. A cemetery should be treated with the same respect that the people who are there should be treated with if they were still alive.'

'I think the lawn section where she is, is visually relaxing. I find tombstones quite harsh. In fact, some of them try to outdo you—"I'll have a bigger one than you have"—and that sort of stuff. This is obscene to me. However, I would defend everybody's right to have it: totally. But for me, that's not the way. I'll probably finish up in the same hole in the ground myself anyway. I think it's peaceful. I feel possibly a trifle guilty because I'm relaxed there. I find it quite a relaxing place, except when there's a funeral being carried out, because I feel for the people whose grief I understand. But when there's no funeral going on there, I find it quite a peaceful place.'

'Somebody once said that when emotion comes in the door, logic flies out the window. I think the reverse may also be true. When logic comes in the door, emotion flies out the window. It's also an indication of one's own mortality. I mean, I'm looking at the place where I'll be buried. And I say buried because she was. Maybe I'll get cremated and they'll bury the ashes there. I don't know.'

'I don't consider reuniting the remains to be very significant, but I know that for my kid's sake it probably is. I think it is convenient and it's neat. My brother has Mum's ashes in his attic. When Dad dies, we'll have him cremated and I'll sprinkle their ashes together where they lived. They liked that place. But what they do afterwards with me, from my point of view, is not relevant.'

'I don't want a large funeral. I intend to sit down and write a note to my sons, my executor—who is my brother—and our funeral director friend, or whoever his heirs and successors are—stipulating that I would simply like a quiet funeral with two or three members of the family present. I haven't decided on cremation or burial. A week later, there should be a notice in the paper, under the regimental badge, saying that I was privately interred, or cremated or whatever—and that's it.'

'I've been to enough funerals myself where we've buried the bloke and then gone to the pub and gotten pissed afterwards. For myself, it's not what I need to know, but I certainly recognise a large number of people have a great need to know what's going to happen to their remains. For them it's significant, but it's not for myself. I'm back to my original point, and that is when I'm dead, I'm dead! I'm not going to know what the hell what is going on, so why should I care when I'm alive.'

'We found that one of our blokes was buried in a country cemetery in an unmarked grave. We immediately combined with the commando association, because he'd been a regular army instructor in the commando unit, as well as being in one of ours. He was also ex-Vietnam and an Anglican. We got a bronze plaque and a retired Anglican army padre—a chaplain who was also a Vietnam Veteran—who'd actually buried him, and we had a memorial service there. Then we went into the local RSL and had our few beers and what-have-you. It's a respect for the man. Now if I'm driving past, I'll pop around there and just cast an eye on his grave and let the blokes know the next time we get together. We have a bit of a "sticky" at Snowy's grave, and I look after it. I think that little lawn section in the cemetery is well tended and that's good.'

'Having travelled through Europe—and particularly Ireland, because my ancestry is Irish—I found it fascinating to go to churches in England and Ireland where they have the names of the priests going back a thousand years recorded on a board. And you could go out into the churchyard and there was their grave—very often difficult to read, because they'd weathered over. The stone wasn't of the quality it is today. I think that people such as these are part of our history. It's people who made history. So, if we are going to show any recognition of our history, then we should surely show recognition to the people who created and maintained that history. That, I suspect, means that you maintain the cemeteries, which also allows people carrying out research, for example, to go and do so in those cemeteries.'

'I am appalled that in a country as large as Australia we think we can recycle gravesites. I can understand it in countries where land is at a premium, such as Japan and in parts of Europe. But we don't have that problem. The problem may come of having to put a cemetery somewhere where it may be difficult for people to get to, if you run out of space in suburbia, which we will do. Land is finite, but I think the loss of heritage is terrible.'

'I go out to the cemetery with my friend, who goes regularly to look after her father's grave; it's one of those marble Italian ones. And I find myself in the midst of a dichotomy there. The style and money spent on those Italian graves do not appeal to me one bit. I think the money would be better spent on the children in helping them put a deposit on a house or something.'

'Now that's the pragmatism coming out again. They do not appeal to me personally, but the first person that wanted to change them would find me as a warring enemy, because if we're going to respect the fact that we are a multicultural society, part of culture is the way in which we differ. We must show respect for other people who have different traditions. If that is important to them, they are important, and each group is important to society, then their traditions and their icons need to be honoured as well. So if anybody starts buggerising around with graves, I tend to get quite irritable.'

'Emotionally, I probably wouldn't be quite as defensive of the graves of people I didn't know as I would be toward my wife's grave. But philosophically, I am—as an exercise in logic and as an act of what I believe to be decent civilised behaviour. And I know that may sound strange from a person who earned his living shooting people and reducing things to basics.'

'If, for example, they were going to destroy the Italian, the Greek, or whatever section of the cemetery, and they wanted people to go and demonstrate against it and sign bloody petitions, I'd be there in a flash. I'm reminded of a Lutheran minister during the Second World War, who said: "When they came for the Jews, I wasn't a Jew, so I didn't worry. When they came for the Catholics, I wasn't a Catholic, so I didn't worry. And when they came for the Gypsies, I wasn't a Gypsy, so I didn't worry. But by the time they came for the Lutheran's, there was no one else to defend us". Where we draw the line in the sand, as human beings, is for other human beings, because that's the only group we actually belong to.'

'These louts that get into cemeteries and break graves and what-have-you: I know what I'd do to them. I'd start off by handing them a shovel and pointing to a plot of earth. You've touched a raw nerve here.'

'I now visit Erin's grave about once a month. But initially, I wouldn't drive past the area without going there. I'd go down that way very often. I sort of felt that somehow it would be disrespectful: selfish: in bad taste, not to go in there. I'd have been going there at least twice a week—sometimes three times a week—for the first six to eight weeks, and then it rapidly tailed off. I'd go back and I'd start thinking, "I'm not doing myself or anybody any good here". But I still missed her.'

'Initially, I found that instead of giving solace, going there tended to make me remember the immediacy of the funeral, including the pain in her mother's eyes and that sort of thing. It brought it all back. And initially, there was nothing to do around the gravesite. That was part of it. I hope I'm not rationalising here, but as one begins to get on with their life, the tendency to revisit their old one—which is what I think they're doing when one goes to the cemetery—diminishes. Part of what one is doing is revisiting their past.'

'I then found that I wasn't feeling guilty about not visiting the grave. And, as other interests in life began to intervene,

I found myself more and more involved as a trustee of a local RSL and on the committee of my regimental association. Then I started going out with my lady friend and she introduced me to wine. I read up on it to blazes and enjoyed it. I enjoyed it before I knew anything about it, but that's another story. These things began to occupy time. I elected not to work harder, because I couldn't see any sense in working hard for the Federal Treasurer.'

'Initial visits did evoke memories, but I didn't feel that I was in contact with her, or with God or whatever. Initially, some memories were quite painful, but because of the inherent discipline that my previous occupation engenders, I didn't show it. To do so would be a sign of weakness. But there was an occasional time when there was a bit of a catch of the throat, metaphorically speaking.'

'I found then that I would be saying to myself, "Oh, God! I haven't been to the cemetery. I'd better go over". I would go as a matter of deliberate intent, because I'd say, "I haven't been". So I'd go and get in the car, and I'd drive over there and tidy up around the grave, which served a few purposes. First of all, it stopped me feeling guilty, because if I hadn't been there for a while I might feel a bit guilty about it, so I went. Now, who the hell I would feel guilty to is another matter, because who the hell would know? The dead don't. And the kids hardly ever go there. It's like a reflex. I think that is interesting. Well, why the bloody hell should I feel guilty?'

'I've only been over there a few times with my friend when she's been going to her father's grave. On that basis I thought, "Oh well, while I'm here I'll go to Erin's". Now that's an interesting thing to do. I observe that she is far more attentive to her father's grave than I am to my wife's. I believe that makes me feel guilty too. Also, of course, I wouldn't want a friend to regard me as being a terrible person who doesn't go. So maybe there's a bit of hypocrisy creeping in here at the same time. So yeah; I don't have a need to go there, but yet if I've forgotten for any period of time, I feel guilty and I assuage that guilt by going. It's interesting, isn't it?'

'I visit Erin's grave about once every four weeks or so now. That's because I simply clean up the bronze plaque. In the boot of my car I've got a tiny pair of grass shears, a little hand broom, a bottle of baby oil, and a rag in a plastic bag. I just keep it clean and tidy. Now it might be a moot point to ask whether or not that's part of respect for Erin, and part of it is the habit and the instinct almost of looking after and keeping things neat, clean and tidy. It seems disrespectful not to. I'd say I'd be there about twelve times a year, but I used to go there every week. At first after she died, every time I drove past I used to feel that I had to go, otherwise I was somehow letting the side down.'

'I don't feel any communion with Erin at all. I'll often think about her, but that's a matter of reminiscing; it's a matter of casting the mind back. But I have no sense of being in contact with her, or God or what-have-you. I believe that you should honour and respect the memory, but if somebody asked me to be logical, I would say, "Well it probably accomplishes nothing".'

'I take flowers on Mother's Day and her birthday. Maybe I shouldn't be telling you this—I'm probably an annoyance— but I also bring a little grass seed along and a bit of soil. If I notice bare patches in the cemetery lawn, I'll sprinkle seed on the bare patch, and a little bit of soil over it. This probably annoys the hell out of the cemetery people. There aren't any weeds there yet, but if I did find a flat-weed or what-have-you, I would most certainly root it out.'

'I think it's a combination of a mark of respect to Erin, but also part of the old soldier's habits. I think someone skilled in psychology would be able to determine exactly what it is, but I would say it would be half and half. Let's put it this way, if one let the whole thing go—and imagine the cemetery authorities also let it go—I would find that quite disgraceful on my part not to go to the effort to maintain it properly.'

'I spend around five minutes at the grave—as long as it takes just to tidy up around. I'm not given to prayer or anything like that. I just trim the grass around the concrete base of the bronze plaque. My next-door neighbour told me that the way to keep the bronze plaque up is with a bit of baby oil rubbed into a rag. I've also got an old toothbrush, which I use to get into the lettering and what-have-you, just to make it look neat, clean and tidy.'

'I think the memory fades, and the sense of identification with the individual fades. Now I don't mean that it vanishes at all, but the sharpness of the immediacy of death fades. If you're not religious, it tends to become a combination of a sense of obligation, a sense of duty, and a habit, and the need to maintain the plaque and the gravesite at a standard which satisfies me. Now this sounds rather selfish I know, but it's as if I'm deriving a sense of satisfaction by fulfilling a duty to maintain an emblem of what was once my wife.'

'I think my sons are probably not likely to visit anywhere near as often as I do. I'd never ask and they never volunteer, but I was pleased that the older one was able to say he had found the plaque nice and clean and shiny. So he had been there not long after I'd been: only a matter of days. So maybe there's a sense of indicating to my children—who are well and truly adults—that I'm remembering their mother and treating her memory with respect.'

'What has happened progressively is that a sense of logic began to take over from the emotions. And logic says that underneath the ground is a coffin in which is what's left of the body; and that's all. Therefore, although the scenery has become progressively more and more peaceful where she is buried, and because I am by nature a pragmatist and a realist, then there's not the emotionalism that there was initially.'

'There's not a sense of visiting her, but there is a sense of duty done and respecting a memory: of ensuring that anybody else who goes there will see that the memory is respected and not neglected. It gives a sense of peace that I am doing that, but I don't have to do it as often to feel the same peace. That's what's happening. It's like weaning a drug addict. The time between hits becomes greater. The space has become greater as realism, logic and objectivity all begin to play a much larger part.'

Better to Keep Busy

Elisabeth was born in England nearly 67 years ago. Her mother died when she was a baby. 'My Aunty brought me up and played the mother role. I was about a year old when I was taken to live with them. I had one older brother and three sisters. My brother and sisters were still with my father in the family home, but my eldest sister was actually married. My brother was about seven years older than I was. My aunt had one girl who was also older than me.'

'I'm on the pension and I do some voluntary work. I always worked in the past. I worked in an office and then I worked as a weaver. Here in Australia, I did clerical work at a hospital for a while and then paymaster work, you know. I worked part-time while the children were growing up. I'm a Christian. I'm a member of the Salvation Army, and I've got three boys who are all married and gone. Now there's only me and the dog.'

'Richard and I were married for 45 years, and we came to Australia 32 years ago. He died nearly four years ago. He was really lovely and kind: a good father, Christian, Salvo—you know—hard worker. He worked at jobs he didn't really like when we first came here, to just keep a roof above over our heads and food on the table. He was very caring and conscientious.'

'He was 73 when he died. He retired when he was 63. So he'd been retired ten years. He had a slight heart attack then, so he had to give up work. He was the chief cashier where he worked. Previous to that he did all sorts. He was a miner for twenty years. He'd done a lot of work.'

'Richard was musical; he played a tenor horn and trombone. The boys were all musical and the grandchildren are fairly musical. In fact my grandson, who gets married in a couple of months, is doing music at uni. He's going to be a music teacher. So it's a very musical family. I could sing, but that was it. I played the tambourine when I was younger.'

'Richard had motor-neurone disease; it started a good two years before he died. It started in his feet and worked its way up. But it wasn't until the September previous, that we actually found out what it was. Because they thought first of all he'd had a stroke or a heart attack, or it was muscular, but we weren't sure. So we were going backwards and forward for tests—about once a week for tests—and in between for getting the results. So he was affected for about two years altogether, but it was very brief that he was really bad. He was totally helpless by that time, but I nursed him at home.'

'He died at home. We were actually just getting ready to put him into a nursing home, for me to have a break, but it never occurred. He died before that happened. It was a shock when it happened, but it wasn't a shock like he'd gone out and got killed in a car crash, if you know what I mean.'

'The children all came, of course, as soon as they knew what happened. Because two of them are Salvation Army ministers, their work's always taken them off. They've lived all over the place—like Tasmania, South Australia and Western Australia—so they'd been out of the state for years. But we always went to see them. That's where all our money went: travelling to see the children.'

'We were always laughing, outgoing and positive, we were. I probably cry more now. I was more positive than Richard was. He was a bit more negative, but I think that probably stems from the fact that they were very, very poor when he was younger—and things like that, you know. He came through the war, of course, as I did. He wasn't a military person, because of the job he did. He was a miner. And they weren't allowed to go into the military, so he never went into the military, because they needed the coal.'

'I'd virtually lost him previous to his death, if you know what I mean. He was just a shell of the person he was. Usually he wanted to get up straightaway, but he didn't that particular morning. And then a lady came to talk to me about his diet. And when she'd gone, I went to see if he was all right. He was just lying there and he wasn't breathing. I thought he was breathing, because he had oxygen tubes in, you know. He slept with oxygen tubes in his nose and that, so I didn't know. I didn't get to say goodbye.'

'I rang the ambulance, because I thought that he'd better go into hospital. And they said, "You don't know how to do CPR?" They explained, and I said, "Yes, I did". And they said, "Well, try that until we've come". Of course, he always sat up to sleep, so I laid him down. I tried that and I yelled at him and I screamed at him, but it didn't work. And when the ambulance people came, they said it wasn't worthwhile using those electric things, you know, because of the condition that he was in. He said it would probably break his ribs, because he had no flesh on his bones. So they thought the best thing was just to leave it go—which we did.'

'The ambulance men wouldn't go until I had somebody here. I had to ring up somebody to come and stay with me. And the band was going away overseas that morning—the Salvation Army band—so everybody had gone to the airport. It took me ages to find somebody who was still home. They'd either gone to see to them off, or they were going. But I found a friend—an old retired brigadier and his wife—and they came and stayed with me, so the ambulance men could go before my family started to arrive. All the children came eventually.'

'I stayed with him in the bedroom, but the dog went and stayed under the bed—because she was really his dog—and she got on the bed close to him, and she never moved till the people came to take him away. She just stayed there. She really missed him, you know.'

'That year, in the January, I lost my brother; the February, I lost a sister; and in the April, I lost Richard—all in the same year. It was a bad year. My brother and sister were in England, but we stayed fairly close.'

'We used to travel about, and we went over there about every four years. I was over last year, actually, but I didn't get over to either of those funerals. When you go and book a seat it's just a terrible price. I couldn't really afford to do it. You can't do a deal with, you know, 21 days in advance, or things like that if it's just up and go. Consequently, nobody came for Richard's funeral from England. There were five brothers and two sisters in Richard's family.'

'We didn't actually talk about his funeral and things before he died. No we didn't. Because you know, we were too busy living—because we still went out. Even the day before he died, we'd been out in his wheelchair and that, because he couldn't just stand sitting there and looking at the four walls. We'd have to go somewhere, even if it was only to the shopping centre. But we'd always been used to going out and doing things—picnics and stuff like that—you know. So we just kept that up right till the end. We never did talk about a funeral.'

Richard was cremated after a service at the local Salvation Army church. Elisabeth planned the service with the funeral director. 'My sons were here too, so we chose the songs that he liked, and I liked. We had it all written down like a lot of people do now. Yeah; some people have it all planned. Our eldest son read the Scriptures.'

'The hall was packed. It was a very packed hall. And the veterans' band played. I thought that was really nice that so many people were there—and that was helpful. We have a nephew in Adelaide, and he came over for the funeral.'

Elisabeth does not have any more or less contact with her own children and their families now that she is on her own. 'They are so busy with their own families involved in what they are. I mean, they come. Like, one son came yesterday, because he had a day off and his wife's away. I am so busy as well; they've got to book to see me—you know what I mean? I find I have to keep myself busy. That's my salvation if you like, you know: better to keep busy.'

'I'm quite a positive person. I've continued to do what we always did, you know, when Richard was alive. I've continued to do those things, and I have my voluntary work: the Girl Guides at the Army and things like that. I took some of them to England last year to a big jamboree type thing. Yeah; I'm still involved in that. There was only four of us went, because money wise it was very expensive and some of the girls just couldn't afford it. There was about a thousand in camp. It was great. And then I took them all round England to show them all the things and all the places that I like. I'm in charge of the regional division, so that keeps me occupied. But then I've always been involved for the past 45 years; it's not something I've just taken up.'

Elisabeth says she has always had a strong faith and, that if anything, Richard's death has brought her closer to God. She believes that Richard is now in heaven. 'Well, his soul's in heaven. I mean, I know his body's not, but his soul's gone to heaven. Because that's our belief, that as soon as you die your soul goes back to God. But he's here too; his spirit is still here. I really don't know. Nobody knows what heaven is like; it's only what you read and what people tell you. You just know it's a better place. I mean, you get a long white robe. It's no good them giving me a harp, because I'm not very musical; so they'll have to give me a triangle when I go.'

Richard was cremated and his ashes interred in a rose garden at a suburban memorial park. 'I chose that. The roses are beautiful there. I've got photographs of them somewhere when they've been in bloom. The cemetery is beautiful. It's really nice, you know. It's not a morbid, dreary-looking place, like some cemeteries are. There are beautiful flowers. But then, I'm a rose-freak, so I think it's beautiful.'

'To me, the cemetery is no more sacred than any other place. Everywhere is sacred really, because God is everywhere. I mean, some people consider churches are more sacred than anywhere else, but they're just fellowship centres to me. I worship God everywhere. I do my ironing saying my prayers, you know.'

'This cemetery doesn't have any history to me. All my family is buried in England. When you go to England there's really old, well-known people buried there. Like we went to Keats— where Keats is buried—and other places, you know, where people of note are.'

Elisabeth reckons that she would visit Richard's memorial every couple of months or so. 'On his birthday, anniversary or Father's Day, I take flowers in. I'm not one for going every week, like on the same day: just when I can, and when I feel I need to. I went for Easter last year as well. With Easter coming up again I'll probably go then. It was his birthday in January, so I went then. It's also our anniversary in January, so that was a combination one; but I don't make it a ritual. Just after his ashes were put in the garden, I might have gone about once each week for perhaps the first month, but no more than that, because it's just a symbol.'

'I take flowers every time I visit; I usually buy them on the way. Sometimes I'll take roses, if there's any decent ones in the garden, but I'll put them in with whatever I buy: carnations usually, because they seem to last a bit longer. But it's only a ritual; it's got no significance that I can think of.'

'The rose garden area is very well looked after. I just sort of take up any leaves that might have dropped on the plaque. I seem to brush them off; that's all. I would pray, because it's something to do. I talk to Richard as well, but not about anything in particular, because I can talk to him anytime. It's the same with my prayers; they're no different.'

'I drive to the cemetery and don't stay there long—probably about five minutes to ten minutes would be it. I don't hang around long. If it were raining, I wouldn't go. I don't think I've been when it's been raining. I just sort of get the water, put the flowers in, and—you know—stay for a couple of minutes. My dog always comes, and she knows where the plaque is. I know of one or two others that are there; but no, I don't visit those.'

'The cemetery is a peaceful place; I don't ever feel frightened. There is a sense of sadness when you see a plaque with somebody that's young. Sometimes I'll read some of the plaques as I'm walking around, or coming back, or throwing the rubbish in the bin; and I feel sad when I see a little person that's died.'

'I feel sad about Richard when I'm at the cemetery. But I've got his photo and everything around me; that brings back memories. And I've still got things I haven't let go of yet. I don't hold them to remember him, but I keep them in memory of him. I mean, if I didn't have a photograph it wouldn't make any difference, you know. I still have him in memory, and I've got all these photo albums anyway, besides the ones that are around, you know. I took a lot of photos, I did. I still do.'

Elisabeth says that she does not really know why she visits the cemetery. 'I mostly go for a special reason, you know. But then I just think, "Oh, I'll go and get some flowers and take them". Or if I'm going away, I'll go before I go away. I don't feel that I have to go; it's just, I go on special occasions. It seems to have settled down to anniversaries, birthdays, and before I'm going away, you know. It's just that I can't buy him presents— because we always exchanged gifts on these occasions.'

Safely With God

Rosa was born on a farm in south-east Italy, seventy years ago. She received no formal education. At the age of 29, she came to Australia. She married Angelo two years later. Before the birth of her second child, Rosa worked at various production jobs, including making jumpers, dolls and bicycle components. She also worked in a private hospital, but has not been employed since having her children.

Angelo was born in Sicily 72 years ago. He immigrated to Australia at the age of 34, and after 28 years as a telecommunications worker, had been retired for ten years. He died in Melbourne almost three years ago, after 36 years of marriage.

Angelo and Rosa's two daughters are both married with children of their own. After their elder daughter Maria married, Maria and her husband (and eventually their daughter) continued to live with Angelo and Rosa for some years. The young family had not long moved out into their own home when Maria suffered a debilitating stroke at the age of 34.

Angelo had been unwell with kidney failure and dementia for some months before suffering a fatal stroke only a year after Maria's incident. According to Rosa, 'He had a few things wrong with him, and although I sort of knew it was coming, it hit very hard'.

Rosa 'knew a bit' about Angelo's cerebrovascular disease, as 'lots of strokes were picked up by a head scan'. And her daughter had tried to explain that 'he didn't have long to live'. Nevertheless, she found that: 'when it did finally happen it was still very, very hard' and she 'was greatly shocked'. She had still been endeavouring to cope with her daughter's incident, which she believes also took its toll on Angelo. Rosa suggests that rather than endeavouring to prepare herself for Angelo's inevitable death she 'went into denial'.

Angelo died in hospital, with Rosa and their family present. 'I also spent some time at the hospital with him even though he was unconscious. We had as long as we wanted to be with him once he passed away. But after that, the next time I saw him again was at the funeral, because he had an open coffin.'

Rosa was 'very pleased' with the funeral service and considered it 'very, very nice'. She believes that the ritual of the requiem mass and the whole funeral service helped her to cope with her grief. 'As Catholics, we had a rosary the day before the funeral—that is the blessing of the soul of the dead. The priest who does the rosary usually does the funeral as well at the same church. We have a rosary first; the next day we have the funeral. It's like saying goodbye. The funeral itself is very, very emotional. The funeral is actually good. But on the day, I just felt very sick: really, really sick.'

According to Rosa's daughter, 'She is quite a different person now. She is more withdrawn and doesn't see the good side, but always sees the negative side of things. She doesn't really enjoy life now. It's really hard for her. She'll have good days when everything's fine. But then little things constantly remind her of him, and it comes to her. She sort of keeps to herself now.'

Rosa says that she often feels 'very lonely, very upset and depressed', but finds that on 'some days' she is 'all right'. She is 'still getting there', but hasn't yet reached the stage where she 'could sit back and remember the good times and start enjoying life'.

It took Rosa 'over a year' to get herself 'back together'. Now she is 'gradually doing more and more, like working the garden, which was always Angelo's garden'. While he was alive she wouldn't go near the vegetable garden. This was Angelo's domain: his main interest and source of much pride. It was always neatly and efficiently planted, meticulously maintained and highly productive.

At first, she 'wouldn't go out there, because it was his area, and he had just recently passed away'. But now Rosa feels driven to work in the garden, partly because she wishes to maintain what was most important in his life and to carry on his work, and also 'to feel close to him'. She also acknowledges that it gives her 'something to do instead of sitting down dwelling on things. You know, the more you do the quicker the day goes and the less you think.' Rosa recognises that as she is 'getting older, it is getting too hard to do'. She regrets that, before long, she will 'have to stop doing Angelo's garden'.

Rosa's second daughter and family (comprising her husband and two sons) now share the family home with her. They moved in to keep Rosa company 'about two weeks after Angelo died'. She considers they have been a 'great support' to her.

Rosa believes that 'Angelo is now safely with God' and waiting to be reunited with her. Since his death she feels 'a little bit more dependent on God now that Angelo has gone'. Rosa's bedroom dresser (which must be negotiated on entering or leaving the room) now serves as a shrine to Angelo, complete with photographs, remembrance card and vigil lamp. With the aid of this memorabilia, Rosa focuses her thoughts on him each day.

Following a requiem mass, Angelo was buried in a pre-purchased, double-depth concrete vault. Some years earlier, Angelo and Rosa had purchased the grave and erected a large granite monument of their choice. The monument already included inscriptions, with just the date of death and a photograph to be added following the interment of each of the couple. According to Rosa, 'the cemetery is a place where the people die and go and relax. It is a sacred, holy place like the church is.'

Rosa visits Angelo's grave 'once a week: every Sunday morning' and feels that 'once a week is enough'. She considers that her faith influences the frequency of her visits, as 'the Catholic thing to do is go once a week'. She sees her regular visits as 'a religious obligation and a duty to Angelo and to God'. Rosa insists that the frequency of her visits, and personal need to be there, have not changed since the first week after his funeral. However, she does feel that her 'emotions have got better'. She found that 'at first, visiting was more difficult: it was very, very emotional. That has got a bit better now; I definitely feel better.'

A friend (whose husband's grave is in the same area) drives Rosa to the cemetery. When she visits, Rosa will 'pray, wash the monument and put some fresh flowers every week'. Depending on the weather, she says she spends about fifteen to thirty minutes at Angelo's grave. 'Even when I was really ill, I had someone place fresh flowers on his grave, because I couldn't go there; I was too ill'.

Some Sunday mornings Rosa feels very upset and doesn't want to go. 'But once I get there, I feel happy: quite happy. Being there, I feel close to God and Angelo. Just bringing the fresh flowers and things gives me a good feeling'.

Magnetic Personality

Michael was born in Holland 51 years ago. He was the first of seven children. When he was six, Michael's family immigrated to Australia where his youngest two siblings were subsequently born. Michael identifies himself as 'most definitely Australian'. He says, 'I went back about fifteen years ago to see where I belonged, and I definitely belong in Australia.'

Michael has been dairy farming since he left school. Originally in a partnership with his parents, he has now managed his own property for almost twenty years. His family was Roman Catholic, but Michael supposes that he now has no religion. 'But I'm not against religion either; I just don't participate in any religions. I leave the census form blank on this one.'

'I've been married twice. The first was about twenty years ago, but that ended in divorce. We had no children. Then I married Anna twelve years ago. Anna grew up in a sheep area of New South Wales. I think she went to a local primary school and then to a private secondary college in Melbourne. There are no children by that marriage either, but Anna already had six of her own. Her eldest is now 29 and the youngest is eighteen. Only the girls lived with us; the three boys were all older and they stayed with their father.'

Anna died just over two months ago at the age of 49. 'She had a very magnetic personality; people were drawn to her fairly quickly. She loved flying and just loved life and the family.

She loved her kids. She was Anna. She was fun to be with. She kept our place together. Not a night went past that we weren't together, till she got sick.'

'Anna had a seizure one morning and that was the start of it. She was diagnosed with a brain tumour and was ill for fifteen months. She had radiation treatment for six weeks, and the tumour reduced about sixty or seventy per cent in mass. They expected her to be right for another seven or eight years, but within six months she had another seizure. They found another tumour, which they treated with chemotherapy, but that didn't work. Two months later she had another MRI scan. They found another tumour and treated it with another sort of drug, and that didn't work. She had a bad fall during an interstate holiday, and then she had another scan. It was really diseased. She only lived about eight weeks after that.'

'We were very lucky. She only spent ten days in hospital after the first seizure; they only did a biopsy. And then we had six weeks of radiation treatment, and then she went back to milking cows for the whole year. Well, there seemed nothing wrong with her. She did everything again. She had a terrific year right up until she had that fall. She had an excellent life till then, but it went downhill very quickly after that. The last five and a half weeks she spent in the local hospital, about fifteen minutes from home. And the rest of the time she was at home. For two weeks she was in bed.'

'About six months earlier, I was pretty sure she was going. Once she got the second lot of tumours we knew she wouldn't last too much longer. We just hoped against hope that she would.'

'The week before she died, I'm sure she didn't know who people were. Or if she did, it was only for a split second, because she was on 600 milligrams of morphine plus boosters. I suppose that in the last fortnight she wouldn't have had too many boosters: just every now and again. I feel this worked out because we could boost her ourselves. And a few of us worked out that if she got upset or aggro, we could boost her and bring that right. I suppose it was only the Sunday before she died that she really got bad. She couldn't swallow any more and saliva was running out of her mouth, and she didn't know anybody. She just lay there; she didn't move any more."

'I think I went home and did the milking, and when I got back she was really bad. Her mouth was open, her tongue was half hanging out and she started vomiting blood. That's when I called the main people who had helped look after her, because I thought she's not going to last much longer. Her kids then went home about ten o'clock. She was really bad. She just kept vomiting blood every half hour, and she was sort of whimpering like a baby. It took a while to come to terms with boosting her morphine, but we did it. Then she went to sleep just after midnight: about 12.30. So she died peacefully, but she had hell for four hours before. I'll never regret doing what we did.'

'There were only four of us there at the time she died—plus the nursing staff. And we could've stayed there all night if we wanted to. I had heaps of opportunity to say goodbye and sorry for the stupid things I've done. Though at the end, you couldn't hold a conversation with her. I split my head open very badly about a fortnight before she died, when I came off my motorbike, but I don't think she ever knew I got hurt.'

With both of his parents still alive and most older relatives in Holland, Anna's death was Michael's first significant bereavement. 'I still haven't lost a relation: just one old bloke. He was pretty close and that affected me a little bit, but nothing like a close relation would I think.'

'Her illness prepared a lot of us. For the last seven or eight weeks, she had someone by her side 24 hours a day, and that was a group of about six or seven people. We used to sleep there; we had a roster made out and it was good. That's a stupid thing to say, but it was. It was good.'

Despite the recency of bereavement and self-acknowledgment that he is still going through 'quite a bit of turmoil',

Michael believes that he has changed a lot. 'I don't think I've got a temper any more. I had a very bad temper. The little things everybody carries on about just aren't very important any more. I'm probably more emotional; I cry and laugh more. I just appreciate things more. Laughter and tears tend to come a lot easier. I appreciate life more.'

'I wouldn't be able to comment on her kids, because I don't see them much any more, but I'm sure Anna's death has had a big impact on her eldest son. He used to ring her up every couple of days. He's still quite emotional about it, actually. I get on with him the best. He hasn't got the influence of the father, I'd say. He's a different bloke altogether.'

'Anna's death hasn't stirred a renewed interest in God, or made me hate him for everything. I can understand why people do turn away from their faith after something like that happens. Or, I suppose to some people, it's a good crutch to hold on to. But to me, it's made no difference whatsoever.'

'I was ready to give the business up about thirteen years ago, then she came along. She loved it and made it good. She made me want to save it. It was a good working relationship and we worked well together, all the time. I always said that if Anna left, I'd leave the farm. And it was on the market just before she died. Only Anna kept it going. So it's now time for me to do something different, or do nothing—whatever I feel like doing.'

Anna was buried in a lawn cemetery, just out from a nearby country town. 'We had the funeral at home. Before she died, Anna said there were three things she wanted: there was to be no cremation, no church, and she wanted to be buried here—not where her family and ex-husband lived. I was going to get the celebrant that married us to do the service, but when she died it didn't seem right. Anyway, there was this little Anglican minister who used to pop in once or twice a day and who used to say, "G'day. How are things going, kid?" He never pushed religion or anything. And the minute she died, I said, "I want him; he'll do it".'

'I organised the funeral with an especially close, mutual friend of ours. Apparently there were 300 people there. It was probably one of the most moving and best funerals I've ever been to. It was at home in exactly the same place we were married. The flag was at half-mast, and the cows were in the front paddock. People came from everywhere. I didn't know the music was coming; our best friend picked that. I didn't cry before then. We had a viewing the night before and that didn't worry me; it was really good. But when the music came on, I just went to pieces.'

'The viewing was good, because only a couple of days before, we saw her being sick and all that. She didn't look very nice then. She'd lost heaps and heaps of weight, and she looked like a skeleton. It was just good to see her virtually looking well; because she did. They did a really good job; they had even done her nails. She looked like a big china doll, and she was buried in her wedding dress.'

'I told the minister heaps about her and said, "Look; keep the religion as low as possible". Her father was a bit put out when we said there would be no church and all that sort of thing, but that's what she wanted. Her father is very, very religious, and his wife is a lay preacher. But Anna was the same as me; she had no religion.'

'I was very proud of the funeral. We had the service at home, and then we drove to town, to the cemetery. There we had a graveside service, and that's where the minister did his bit. Our best friend also said something, and then she had a five-aeroplane fly-by. That was just magic, because she was very active in the aero club. She made that club. At the service at home, the aero club gave a eulogy. And they've even got a perpetual trophy in her honour now. But the funeral was very moving. It was spectacular; it really was. If I ever planned one for myself, I think I'd want one just about the same. It was great—especially the fly-by. It was beautiful and very moving.'

To Michael, the funeral was everyone's opportunity to say a final goodbye to Anna. 'After the viewing, you couldn't just leave; you'd have to have something else. So it was the final goodbye: the end of a chapter.'

'The cemetery is just a cemetery. It's where Anna's body is. I used to go down there nearly every day, for a couple of weeks after the funeral, and there was sort of nothing there; it was just a pile of dirt. I don't know what it will mean to me in the future. I don't know how often I'll go. I suppose it's been ten days since I've been there—no; it's probably only a week. It doesn't seem to change much. It's only a bit of bare dirt at the moment. I suppose I'll go there every now and again, but I don't know.'

'I believe that Anna is not really at the cemetery. She's not in the ground just under a bit of dirt over there; I think she's probably everywhere. Whatever I do reminds me of her. I think she's looking out over us. Don't ask me why, but I think there's something out there. I don't know what it is, but I think there'd be something once you've gone. I suppose the reason is probably that you'd hope for yourself that there is something after you die. I don't know.'

'The cemetery tells you a lot about the town, because you can usually see in a mining town that the people died a lot younger—mainly accidents—than in an agricultural town. You can learn a lot about a place by its cemetery, and they are interesting places.'

'I don't feel close to Anna at the cemetery, probably because we did everything together. It doesn't matter where I go—in the house, or on the farm, or wherever—she's been there. She's done something here; she's helped me with something there. So I feel her more at home than I do at the cemetery. Sometimes I feel a little bit of sadness at the cemetery, and other times I have a laugh and chuckle; it depends on what I think about at the time. If you think about a good time, you sort of laugh and chuckle, but if you're thinking about sad things then you will be sad.'

'I guess the cemetery is a sad place, not because Anna's buried there, but because of some of the other people you see come there. Like, there's a little old lady who just sits there; she's done this nice little garden and she just sits there for hours on end. She brings a cup of tea and dinner. That's sad: not that it's a particularly sad place.'

'That bit of ground doesn't do much for me at all. It doesn't make me feel sad; it doesn't make me feel happy. It's just a bit of dirt, but I know Anna's buried down there somewhere. I think putting a permanent marker there is important. Well, that's where her body is, and it was important to her. She used to look up old family graves in other cemeteries. And once we couldn't find a grave, so she wrote to the cemetery trust and got a map, and she found it. It was just a bare bit of dirt, and she was very upset, because there was nothing there. So it's important I think; it's very important. When I die, I think I'd like somebody to say, "Look; he's buried there".'

'In the beginning, people expect you to go there. If I were really truthful, I'd probably have to say that most of the times I went were because people expected me to. To be honest, I felt a bit guilty if I hadn't been when people thought I should have. Now I go when I want to go—when I feel like it—and not when other people think I should be going. I probably also had a need to be there in the beginning; I wanted to be there.'

'I mainly visit on my own, but sometimes with someone else. It's a funny thing I know, but I was there probably only a couple of days after the funeral, and there were these two bottles of wine that she just wouldn't let me open; I don't know why. They were nothing special—just two bottles of plonk—but she just wouldn't let me open them, for no reason at all. So I went down and opened those bottles of wine and poured them all over her grave. I had a mouthful of each and threw the bottles in the rubbish bin. Why I did that I don't know. But I couldn't drink them after that. One bottle wasn't bad actually; it was a waste.'

'If I go to town to get pizza by myself, I'll eat it near the cemetery. That's when I sort of think of her. When I've talked about her to other people then I probably tend to go there a bit, if I've got nothing else to do. I've only ever driven in there a few times just to go and see her.'

'When I visit the grave, I just stand there for a couple of minutes. The time varies, but I suppose five minutes would be the longest. I wonder what she's like down there in the coffin. I wonder what stage she's at. I know the coffin is good wood; it's supposed to last 25 years, but I wonder what she would be like in there. It's pretty clinical I suppose, but that's the thing I mostly think about. I suppose now and again I say a few things, but I don't know whether she hears me. I took flowers out of our own garden for a while, but not the last few times.'

'I suppose I'll probably go at Christmas and on important days. And I'm sure I'll go on her birthday, and maybe the day we were married—a few things like that. I've now got past the stage of going because I thought people expected me to go there. I'll go there when I want to go there.'

It Does Get Easier

Elsa was one of five girls and three boys born to 'a typical large European family' in Libya, 66 years ago. She is a devout Roman Catholic. At the age of 26, she came to Australia, landing first in Perth and then sailing across to Melbourne. Four years later, she married Italian-born Giovanni. The couple subsequently raised two sons and a daughter. Elsa and her adult children all speak Italian and English, and identify their family as Italian.

Elsa had no paid employment while raising her family. 'Before I married I worked, but after I married my husband did not want to look after the children'. She considers that was a 'very European' thing to do. 'No; you do not work'. Neither did she work before immigrating. 'No, no, no! In my country, it's not good that the girl goes to work. It's very hard: not like here.'

Giovanni came to Australia as a young teenager, shortly after the Second World War, to join his father who had immigrated about ten years earlier. 'He left his family very, very young in Italy. There were two girls and one boy that he left over there. After he left, the war broke out and they were separated. He could not go back. He was one of the first Italians across here from his region back in Italy. He came to Australia and started bringing them all across from that village, or area, that they were all in. One sister stayed in Italy.'

175

'Giovanni started as a farmer when he came to Australia. Then I think he had a few odd jobs: cleaning jobs. And then he worked at the brewery for 23 years. He did a lot of shiftwork. He never missed the nightshift for 23 years, you know. And he would never be sick. He was working every day, every night, every afternoon. And after it all, this happened.'

Five years ago, following three years of retirement, Giovanni succumbed to lung cancer at the age of 63. His illness had been diagnosed only three months earlier.

'He had couple of problems, including diabetes, but when it came, it came pretty sudden. When he went in hospital last— three weeks before he passed away—the doctor she was telling me, "You better go home, you together with your children". She did not tell me straight away, "Your husband is going to die". But I'm not stupid, you know. He was very sick, but I came home. One day she said, "You know, he's very sick". It was Friday, and he passed away in the night. The family was all there. In his last few hours, he closed his eyes and did not open the eyes, you know.'

Prior to Giovanni's death, Elsa's most recent bereavement had been the death of her mother, thirteen years earlier. Her mother was buried in another suburban cemetery. She also has a deceased brother buried in the same cemetery as Giovanni.

After a requiem mass, Giovanni was buried in a lawn grave at the local cemetery. The funeral meant a lot to Elsa personally. 'Oh, yeah. All the time I remember the funeral. He had a good funeral. Good people came. The church was full. Yeah; it was full. There were his mates from work, and my relatives and my friends. He had a good funeral.'

After the funeral, family and friends called at home. Elsa felt that the funeral helped her in working through her grief. 'It was an important part of all that. Of course, I'm very sorry for him to go. I said goodbye, but in my heart it's very broken, you know. The doctor she gave me some sedatives to calm me, but

I was fine; I don't need them. Of course there was some preparation during the sickness'.

Elsa considers that she is 'a different person now' as a result of her bereavement experience. 'Sometimes I cry more now, but not always. Anyway, I remember I had a good life with him. I'm all right one day, and—you know. I still get angry, but not for a long time—just for a minute—enough for everything to pass, you know. I remember how he used to just yell for about five minutes, you know. But you just forget these things.'

These days, Elsa lives with her daughter and one son. Her older son is married. 'We get on with each other; we stick together.'

Of her faith, Elsa feels: 'It's pretty much the same: pretty strong and remained constant.' She believes that Giovanni is now in Heaven. 'I pray every night for him, and when I go to church. But what can you do? Nothing. He's not coming back.'

The cemetery is quite important to Elsa. 'It is sacred. It's nice. But when you go, it's very sad, you know.'

Within the cemetery, Elsa feels a sense of God's presence at all times. And sometimes, she also feels a sense of Giovanni's presence there. 'At the cemetery, I feel close to God: close to my husband of course. I feel very sad of course. I remember it's a love and I am alone. I don't play cards. I don't play anything, you know. When I go, I remember when we were together. But now I really feel sad when I go to the cemetery. Now I go to see my brother in the grave, and that is very, very sad too. Sometimes I think I go crazy. Sometimes I forget about everything. But what can you do? Nothing.'

These days, Elsa would like to visit the cemetery each week. However, she actually gets there only 'about three times a month: just when it comes up'. 'My daughter usually takes me, or my son does sometimes. Always I go with my son or daughter, not by myself: no. At the other cemetery: yes, because I have my mother in another cemetery. Sometimes I go there by myself, because it's easy, you know. The tram stops there, but not at this one.'

Elsa makes a particular point of visiting on several special occasions, including Giovanni's birthday, Fathers Day, their wedding anniversary, and All Souls Day. 'Fathers Day is big at the cemetery: Big! I go up early in the morning, because it's very hard to go inside with your car.'

She considers that her faith strongly influences how frequently she visits. 'Of course, that's what you feel. That's why you go into the cemetery, because if not that feeling, well what for do you go?'

When she does visit, Elsa always places flowers. 'Sometimes I talk to him; sometimes I pray. I definitely maintain around the plaque, you know. When I'm there, I stay about a quarter or half an hour—yeah: definitely half-an-hour. It depends on the day; it's different. We clean the plaque; we take our time. If it's a nice day we take a little bit longer. Then we visit my brother in the Italian area on the other side. That's another fifteen— maybe twenty minutes.'

Elsa says that would like to visit her husband's grave more often than she is able to get to the cemetery. 'Sometime I have the feeling to go, but my son is at work; everybody is at work. I wait for Sunday to come, or Saturday to go over there, because who'll take me? I don't drive, you know. If I had a chance I would go every day: but no.'

'For the first six months after he passed away, I would go every Sunday. And after that—you know—not so much. I don't need to go so much.' Elsa also feels that visiting her husband's grave has become less of an emotional strain. 'Oh, just a little bit, yeah. It's now a little bit easier. You know the feeling you get; it does get easier with time.'

Very Lovable Woman

George was born into a Maltese Catholic family 66 years ago. He met Olive when they were both seventeen years old, but he came to Australia by himself at the age of 22. Olive joined him six months later; they married the day she arrived. The first of their two daughters was born the following year and the second, two years later.

'In Malta, I was working first as a bus conductor when I was sixteen. Then I worked as a building contractor: just a labourer. That's when I decided to come here, because the job was hard and money wasn't much. When I came to Australia I worked in a small paint factory—just very small; there wasn't many people—maybe about twenty. Then I got another job making plaster, and then in the boot trade for seventeen years making shoes. Then after that, I got a job with the airline, and that's when I retired. I retired seven years ago, because I had a serious car accident and I couldn't work any more.'

'Olive was 62. She passed away over four years ago, one year after she retired. She wasn't ill when she left; she was still good. She worked in the same place for 33 years. She had ovarian cancer and was ill for six months before she passed away. As soon as they told us she had ovarian cancer and it's spreading very quickly, we knew. Ah, well; I accepted it, but the kids didn't want to accept that she was going to pass away.'

'Olive was a very strong and happy-go-lucky woman. She was very active. She worked for 33 years without being sick, except when she had the kids. She never had a day off from work or anything. She was just really strong and she never saw a doctor until she was ill.'

'Olive and me went to Malta nearly five years ago. And while we were there, my mother passed away. My mother was a bit crook and I wanted to go in the summer. But Olive said, "No; you better go early, because you might not see your mother". And sure enough, when I was there, my mother passed away. I was lucky enough to see her, and I was with her when she died, you know.'

'Then that's when Olive started to get sick. When I was in Malta, I realised; because we went to the doctor there, and the doctor said to me, 'How long you staying here?" I said, "Not long". He said, "Well as soon as you get home go and see a doctor, because your wife is very sick". A week later we just left Malta, because I knew Olive wasn't well. Olive went six months after that.'

'Olive passed away in hospital. The whole family was with her: my daughters and my son-in-law. We didn't want the kids to come, so we left the kids; but the children loved her.'

'With Olive, we didn't talk about her dying—to keep giving her hope; because she sort of knew she was going to die. But she never brought it up: not to me and not to her daughters. She never talked about that. She fought strongly all the way. She never showed anything: not to me, not to her daughters— not to anyone. She was very ill—especially the last six weeks— because she had a blockage and she couldn't eat anything. For six weeks, she never ate anything: just liquid, and that's all.'

'The six weeks she was in hospital we never left her side. I would go home and have a bit of sleep, then one of my daughters will be there. When she went home to look after the family, the other one goes in. So we were all taking turns. So for six weeks she was in hospital there's always someone there. After she'd passed away we spent maybe an hour and a half with her, because it was very early in the morning. One o'clock in the morning she passed away; so we stayed there till about three, then we came home.'

'I was still getting over the loss of my mother when Olive died. Because, although I hadn't seen my mother for a long time—I was very young when I left my mother—we were still very close. I used to phone her very often, you know.'

'They were very different experiences: totally different. I was very, very sad in my Olive's death, but it was to be expected with my mother. She was 88; although she wasn't bedridden or anything, you know. But I wasn't with her that often, you know. Like my sisters for example, they took it very hard, because she lived with them. But me, I was too far away. It was easier to accept my mother's death because of her age. My mother was 88, so it was expected, you know. She wasn't going to last that long.'

George and Olive's eldest daughter was widowed about twelve years ago. Her estranged husband collapsed and died at the age of 33, within two hours of his own father's death. But George feels that, in some ways, this resolved serious family concerns, rather than imposed any significant grief on his immediate family. 'My daughter practically had no say about what happened. Mostly his mother and his brothers were involved; they buried their father and the son together. They had one funeral for both.'

'Olive had a lot of friends at her funeral. There were a lot of people who came. Even from the hospital, half a dozen nurses came to her funeral. Because, even though when she was in hospital she knew she was sick, she always used to joke with the nurses—even with the professor that operated on her. Sometimes she used to say to him, "Today you're going to do a bit of butchering". So she had a very, very big show, because people from her work were there. The church was packed, because she was a very lovable woman. I think the funeral is how people come together, you know, saying goodbye. Yeah; I think it's more saying goodbye.'

'The funeral director was very, very good. We got exactly what we wanted. The kids and me were involved in planning the funeral. But I tell you, we made the right decision, because we didn't know much when we were going to bury her. At first, we thought we were going to bury her in another part of the cemetery where there is already plaques. Then a friend of ours, who recently lost his wife too, sort of said, "Why don't you go to the cemetery and have another look, and tell them to show you where my wife is?" So that's what we did. And then we changed, and we're very glad. My daughters came with me— the two of them—because I didn't want to do anything without them, you know. Just whatever was good for them was good enough for me.'

'My daughters and their families, they come to my place every Sunday for lunch. That started when Olive was alive, you know. We'd been doing that for maybe the past fifteen years without missing. They always come to my place. So when Olive passed away, I didn't want to break that tradition. I just kept getting the kids up at my place. I suppose I look forward to the Sunday when they come.'

'It is more important to me now than ever that they come, but I don't sort of feel happier than I was—no way known. I do get very sad. I don't show it very often in front of the kids, because I don't want to get them upset by it. You see one of my daughters—the eldest one—doesn't go to the grave very often. Because even though four years have passed now, she still doesn't accept the death of her mother. But the other one, she goes every Sunday. I go every day—every day without missing one day—except when I went to Malta for a visit. I go every day, and it just helps me to sleep. I talk to her about the kids.'

'Actually, since Olive passed away, I went back to Malta twice. Once, I took my daughter—the widow—and two of her sons with me. And I went again later. So I went twice since

Olive passed on. I only stayed six weeks. I have all my relatives still there: my two brothers and two sisters. I have no one here.'

George considers that Olive's death has drawn the remaining family closer together. 'But it's hard to explain. The grand-children are all grown up now—the youngest one is fifteen, and the other one is close to seventeen. When the other five go out, they all go out together. They don't go their separate ways—so the family is much closer. And the sisters, they see each other very much more than before these days, and they ring up each other twice a week or so.'

'I go to church every Sunday—that's the Catholic Church. I believe Olive is now in heaven, because she never, ever had a cross word with anyone. She never hated anyone. And I think that's the worst sin, if you hate anyone. And she was very Catholic: confession and communion every Sunday. She was very religious, and you never heard her say a bad word. I really believe she's in heaven. I don't know what heaven is like where she is. We were always taught that when we die we all get together again—like your immediate family—you meet God, and that's all.'

Olive was buried in a lawn headstone section of a nearby cemetery. 'It's a good area. We couldn't choose a better place. I'm happy to go there too.'

'The cemetery is a quiet place. Every day I go, ever since she passed away. Except, like I said, when I went to Malta; otherwise every day I go. If I'm doing something at home and sometimes I forget, even if it is half past four, I just leave everything and I go before the gates close. When I go there I just always stay for about two minutes, but just say hello to her and talk to her about the kids; but I do it every day.'

'I look forward to it actually. I look forward to going to the cemetery. I talk to Olive about how things are going, and when someone is sick from the family, I just ask her to pray for them. I also pray. I say a few Hail Marys. I don't take flowers every day, but as soon as they start to wilt, I just replace them. I usually buy them. I get some from home too, but not very often. Once a week, I wipe down the monument. I get a small bucket to carry the water, but I usually have a damp cloth.'

George acknowledges that he feels a sense of Olive's presence at the gravesite, but no sense of God's presence in the cemetery. 'I come to the cemetery every day, purely because—well Olive and me have been together for close to 48 years, so I just want to be with her for a few minutes—no other reasons.'

'I don't feel sad every day when I go there; I just feel unhappy till I go there. I'm happy to be with her for those few minutes. Occasionally, I get a bit emotional. But it's been nearly five years now. On a long visit—for example, some special occasion—maybe I stay ten minutes. Earlier on—maybe the first six or eight months—I used to stay much longer, like half an hour or so. I stand at the grave praying and talking—mostly about how the kids are growing up and how they're progressing, because she loved those kids so much, you know.'

No Future Without Him

June was born in Melbourne 75 years ago. 'My dad was an Irishman, and we were very strict Catholics. My parents drank too much and were cruel to us kids.' At the age of fourteen, June fell in love with Edward. She married him three years later. 'He'd just turned 23 a week before the wedding.' June insists that from when she was fourteen years old, until Edward's death fourteen months ago at the age of 79, 'Not a day went by that we didn't see each other'. She now lives alone.

'I have a daughter who's 56, and a son who's 46. And I have another: a fostered daughter. She's forty now, and I've had her since she was two years old. So she's really our daughter now, isn't she? She lives up the top of the hill from here. My other daughter lives across town, and my son lives in north Queensland. I've just come back from a couple of months up there, and he keeps ringing me. He wants me to go up there and leave here. He really worries. He doesn't like the lonely part of me any more than I do. I miss him.'

June was employed 'only for a short while' before having her first child. 'I worked in a factory: a stinking shoe factory. It was much against my brain, but that's all there was for kids in my day. Then I stayed at home, and was always there when they came home. I was there when they went, and I was there when they came home.'

According to June, Edward was as dependent on her as she was on him. 'We shared everything. Raising the children was our role. Everything was ours: everything. We did everything together: the housework and everything. We even washed half the car each—would you believe? We were never apart: no, never! He worked at the government aircraft factory. That's why he didn't go to war; they wouldn't release him. He was a supervisor at the aircraft factory for 42 years there. They tried to send him interstate, but he wouldn't go. He said, "If I can't take my wife, I don't go". They made quite a fuss about it there for a while at the aircraft factory, but he just refused to go, and said, "I'll leave the job first". There was nothing going to separate us.'

'I was a pillar of the church until I started to do a bit of thinking and looked around. The Vietnam War actually started me off. The Vietnam War was on, and I found my church— my beloved church—was supporting it, and supporting them going over there and burning women and children. I thought, "Something's wrong here somewhere". I started to do a bit of thinking, and gave the church away. I suppose I would've been about forty at that stage. So I didn't have any religion for many, many years. But I've wandered back partially to my Catholic faith.'

Edward retired from work fifteen years before his death. 'I got him out of work. He had a year's sick pay, and he wasn't the type to tell lies to the doctor; so I did it for him. I went up and told the doctor that he was very tired and couldn't sleep. But he was sleeping very soundly. I was very nervous, and the doctor said, "Oh, we'll retire him". Then, as I was going out the door, the doctor told me I hadn't fooled him at all. He said, "I just think you want him at home; don't you?" And I said, "We all do".'

'Then I ran straight across the road to the public telephone and phoned Edward. I said, "You've retired!" And he said, "Oh, wonderful". I though he'd never have to go to work again, and we could be together every single minute of the day. It was a great day when I went out to that telephone and said, "Guess what? You're coming home!"'

'Edward had a heart bypass operation two years before he died. It seems to be all they get out of a bypass—about two years. He had chest pains and went to the hospital. And the cardiologist said he'd do a balloon that would fix him and he should be all right, and he did that. Then I rang Edward up and said, "How do you feel?" And he said, "I feel good". I said, "I'll come over and see you". And he said, "Don't come. It's too late". I said, "Yes, I will. I'm coming over, because I love you". And they were the last words I ever spoke to him, because when I got there he had died.'

'When we got to the hospital the nurse came and said, "He's very, very sick". I said, "What's happened to him?" She said, "He's got chest pains and he's up in the theatre. He's very, very sick". We sat there for about three-quarters of an hour. They had him on the heart-lung machine, and they tried to get a surgeon to see if they could do a bypass, but apparently they couldn't. Then our cardiologist came around the corner and just said, "We've lost him"—just like that—"We've lost him".'

'The cardiologist was distraught: absolutely distraught, because he didn't know why. And I still don't know what happened. They were to have an autopsy, but apparently the coroner decided against an autopsy. I suppose—he being an old bloke of 79, and with a heart history. So we still don't know what happened: I don't know. He was to come home in two days, but he was dead when I got over there.'

'I couldn't believe it: just couldn't believe it; no. I had all the faith in the world. The cardiologist and I knew that these fellows could do so much with these sorts of things. And we'd been going to the cardiologist for so many years that he was our friend as well as our cardiologist. I had too much faith in him, I think. I thought he could do anything. I thought when Edward went over there and had this treatment that he'd be all right for a few more years.'

'The cruel part about it is that he had a stress test about a month before, and that showed him to be remarkably well. The cardiologist said, "Ah, you're remarkable: absolutely remarkable". So we were elated: absolutely elated, the two of us. We thought we'd have a few more years. And he was dead within a month. It proves you should never trust a stress test.'

June chose not to view Edward's body. 'The girls did that; but me? No way! I wouldn't go anywhere near him: no way. I never wanted to see him for the rest of my life as a corpse. I wanted to see him how I saw him in his bed: smiling and happy the night before. That's who I remember, not a corpse.'

'It worries me that I don't know if he knew he was dying. I went over to see the cardiologist, but I didn't ask him. I wanted to know if he knew, because if he knew he was going to leave me—then how terrible for him!'

'Edward was one in a million, believe you me: one in a million. He'd help people. He took food to people. He had his own meals on wheels. If anybody was sick, he'd cook a meal. He got a few widows around here, and he'd look after them and take them meals. And he looked after an old man one time—shaved him and so on.'

'Edward never suffered. That's the only way I can bear it now. That's the only way I can stand it. I think, to have him come home an invalid would have been a bigger hell than what I went through. If only you knew the man. He'd have crawled on his hands and knees rather than be an invalid. He never sat down.'

'But two days before he died, I walked in and he just stood up and put his arms around me and said, "I'm feeling sad. You know, we really haven't got all that much time left together, have we?" I nearly fainted! It was uncharacteristic of him: completely, absolutely uncharacteristic. Oh, it made me feel cold. Of course, I don't believe in premonitions; I think all that's a lot of nonsense.'

'I'd never seen the man down in my life. He was on an even

keel: never depressed or anything. He had a wonderful attitude: wonderful, very strong-minded and strong-willed: very. That's why it surprised me when he said it. A couple of things like that happened a few days before. But I never think of them. Just before he went to hospital, we were laying in bed and I felt him just touch my leg, and I woke up. He said to me, "Sorry I woke you up". He said, "I was just laying here and feeling so full of love for you: just so full of love. I felt that if I touched you, you'd feel just how much I love you, in your sleep". He said, "I'm sorry I woke you up". I was 73 and he was 79.'

Prior to losing Edward, June had lost both of her parents. 'But we also had a tragedy with the daughter—or the foster-daughter. She had a wonderful partner—just a beautiful partner—who was like a wonderful son to us. But he got killed on a motorbike about nine years ago. That was pretty terrible. He was a lovely fellow.'

'Mother died fifteen years ago now, at the age of 91. My father died thirty years ago. They both died of boredom. When my mother was 91, the doctor said she could make a hundred, easily. She said, "I'm not into that". And so she stopped eating and drinking; and that's a fact. It's a fact. Mum eventually become dehydrated when she stopped eating and drinking, and they wouldn't do anything about it. I asked the doctor, and he said, "No; it's her choice". When she became badly dehydrated they put her on a drip, so I assume that her kidneys would have failed and she died.'

'I don't know what happened to my father. He was in hospital with prostate trouble. The doctor said he could live many years with it. But, seeing he was 85, he just sort of laid down and said, "I've got cancer", just shut his eyes, went into a coma and eventually died. So I don't know. When people ask me what they died of, I say boredom. One of these days, I'll get their death certificates and see what it's got on them.'

'Edward was buried. I said to the kids, "If you cremate your father, I'll never forgive you". He was buried. I couldn't handle that cremation bit. My mother said to me when she was dying—or some time before—"If you cremate me, I'll come back and haunt you". I didn't want to burn him up: no way!'

June did not attend the funeral. 'I wasn't well. I wasn't going to sit there in front of a box and know that he was in it. My daughter planned the funeral—my two daughters—I had nothing whatsoever to do with it. They're planning a gravestone now, and I want nothing to do with that. I don't even want to know what's on the headstone. I don't want to know anything about it: nothing. I signed the cheques, and that's all.'

June says that on the day of the funeral she just sat in her 'brown chair'.

'A friend stayed with me. They all went away, and I just pretended it wasn't happening—you know—just pretended it wasn't on. Then they all came back to the house after the funeral, and they were around for days. My son and his wife came down from Queensland, and he stayed. Oh, the family was great for a week or so; they were here all the time. They slept overnight. They stayed with me. Oh yes, they were very supportive: very, very supportive.'

'They didn't talk to me about the funeral. I didn't want to know anything about it, but they made a tape of it and I could listen to the tape. It was not a religious service; it was a celebrant, you know. I'll listen to the tape. There are different ones—our friends—who stood up and spoke. It's beautiful, you know. And I could listen to that. I got some comfort out of listening to that, for some reason or other.'

'I can even read the book. They had a book, and all the people that were present wrote their names in it. And they got some really beautiful cards. It was beautiful; everybody was beautiful. I could just listen to the tape of the service, without even crying. But it doesn't at all make me wish that I had gone to the funeral. No way: never! No: I couldn't. It'd be the last memory—you know—a box with his body in it: no way!'

'I think of him all the time: every day, non-stop—but not

when I'm with other people. As soon as I get out of bed, I cry. I cry in the middle of the night. I cry when I'm going to bed. I just can't stop it. I say to myself, "I won't". And every time I open that door and walk in I say, "No". But I walk in, sit in that chair and sometimes cry for half an hour before I can even do anything. It will wear off eventually I suppose, but I don't know. I've never been through it before, so I don't know. I just have to wait and see what happens. I was on medication. I'm coming off it gradually now, because I don't want to depend on medication. I've got to do it on my own, someway or other—sink or swim.'

'I never turned the television on for a year, and I cancelled all the papers. I was a great reader; I used to read five or six books a week, but I never read a book or turned the television on for a year—never. I read nothing; I watched nothing. But now, I put it on for the news and the 7.30 Report, and then I go to bed. I've read a couple of books. I started to show a little bit more of an interest in the world that way. But I'm off reading again. I can't be bothered reading.'

'We got the newspaper every day, and that was a whole lot of our life. We used to sit over the paper every morning at breakfast and do the crossword puzzles. That was a whole lot of our day, was breakfast with the newspaper. They kept delivering it, and I must have just hurled it over to the next-door neighbour's. I never, ever touched it: never opened it.'

'We've always been a fairly close family, you know. We've never had any problems in the family, though I'm a bit disappointed in the younger daughter up the hill. When Edward was alive, she used to come here three nights, and sometimes four nights a week. He was a great cook. He cooked everything we ate. She'd come down for meals with her little girl—a beautiful little girl I love dearly.'

'Since he's gone, I see her now and again, but not much. I miss the little girl; I miss her terribly. I adore that little girl, and she adores me. She comes out and we will sit and cuddle together. She pats me and kisses me and says, "I love you Nanny". You know, I miss that like hell.'

'I had all that up in Queensland too, with the three girls up there: just beautiful—absolutely beautiful—those girls. I went up there for two months. My son, his wife and the girls were just so beautiful. Now the son's on the phone every night and wants me to come back. He gets very emotional, and he said to me, "Oh, if you won't come back, it means that you don't love your grandchildren". But that's blackmail. That's stupid.'

'He gets very busy. He's a barrister, and he can't just walk out at any time. He can only come between briefs, if he's got time off. He said he's coming down shortly and wants me to go back with him. But the heat—it's so hot. I don't like to leave the house; I hate it. I can't see any way out of it though.'

'Sometimes, I feel a bit let down by the family, like when I was very bad. I was like a zombie when I went out, you know. People would say, "Come out." And I'd go with them and try to shop. I'd push a trolley and pick groceries up, and that. It was incredible. I just couldn't do it, you know. I just had no concentration: no interest. Now when I look back, I think the kids could have rallied a bit more and helped me out a bit more in that way; but they were pretty good. I just came back from my daughter's. I had a weekend up there with her, and I think that sometimes they could've helped me a bit more, you know. But that's the way it goes.'

'Since he died, I'm down the gurgler a bit. He had good superannuation, but the wife just gets seventy per cent. But I'm quite all right; I'm quite comfortable. My son said, "You shouldn't worry about money, Mum". He's very successful, and he's got a successful surgeon wife. And he said, "I could keep you out of my petty cash".'

June was 'absolutely dependent' upon Edward to drive her anywhere. 'I had a chauffeur. We only had the one car, so I couldn't have learnt to drive while he was working. And when he knocked off work, he was just a chauffeur. It didn't matter where

I went to—the dentist, the doctor, the hairdresser: everywhere—
he was there. These days, I get a half-fare taxi. But there's not
many places I want to go to now.'

'I met a particular priest who came to see me, and I was
surprised that all the things I found wrong with the church, so
did he. I was quite delighted, you know. He came a couple of
times. I really enjoyed talking to him. I thought back over the
years—the stupid, ridiculous things that they taught us and
brainwashed us into believing—it's criminal. And he agreed
with me. He's a beautiful man. He said, "Typical Catholics".
Really: I couldn't believe it.'

'So I did go back to church. They have a healing mass every
month, and I go to that. I find that a little bit helpful. I felt the
priest really understands. When I went up to the altar and
received communion, he leant forward and kissed me on the
cheek. I though, "Oh, I'm just with somebody who understands". I thought he was beautiful. He is beautiful.'

'He should come more often, but he's the only priest in
charge of the whole parish. If it had been any other priest that
came here and started all this preaching, I wouldn't have given
him a minute. They're no good to me. I can't handle a lecture.'

'But the church has changed so greatly in those years that I've
been away—well ours has. The change has been tremendous.
They've done away with all that garbage. And it was a hell of a
lot of garbage. He said, "It's a lot of —".'

'Well, I won't say what he said it is—all that garbage and
rubbish. "We're trying our best to change it all".'

'Yeah; they told us we'd go to hell for eating a meat pie on a
Friday; and then they changed it. And I spent months wonder-
ing what happened to the poor things that went to hell
previously for eating meat pies on a Friday. Now we could eat
them. I must have been very simple and stupid, I think. There
must have been something wrong with us to believe them.'

'Underneath it all, even through those years, I've always been
a bit of a believer, you know. But my own religion was between

God and me; the church had nothing to do with it. It's a private thing. If there is a God—and I'm not one hundred per cent convinced there is—then it's just between him and me. I do like this healing mass though; it's good for troubled people like myself.'

'I wouldn't have a clue where Edward is now—wouldn't have a clue. Sometimes, I've got him up in heaven with God. At other times, I've got him out there with the lid screwed down, and that's it. I don't know. Who knows anyhow? Who does know for sure? I know no more than anybody does. If I could feel sure there is a heaven and God, and that he's up there and I'm going to meet him one day, it'd be wonderful. But I don't know.'

'I'm not trying to rebuild my life in any way. A couple of days recently, I went to bed and just stayed there all day, for two days: just didn't get out. I don't see any future. There's no future without him: no future at all. I can't build a new life without him: I can't. He was there for nearly sixty years, when you think I was fourteen, and I was 73 when he died. From fourteen to 73, he was there all the time. Even at fourteen, I saw him practically every day. And I didn't have much of a life at home. He provided more of the things I never had.'

'The children haven't provided any real support or assistance since he died. No, nothing interests me: nothing. I don't think anybody can really support me, in any way. I just miss him. I miss him like hell, and I just won't do anything without him. It'd be very easy to take to suicide, even now.'

'I go out sometimes. I go in a taxi to the shopping centre and just wander around. I have to wear my dark glasses, because I walk around just crying all the time. I go out on occasions and I visit people. Sure, I visit people. I've always done that, even after a few weeks, you know. I went in a zombie-like state and walked a little bit; it was dreadful.'

'I couldn't do anything for myself: breakfast or any meals out in the kitchen. I shake bad, you know. I couldn't hold anything.

I just dissolved into tears for about an hour and a half, and I was thinking, "Why aren't you here to help me clear up?" I still don't touch the house. I've got a housekeeper, a lady who comes in once a fortnight and does it. I couldn't be bothered doing it. I'd like to keep it clean, but I just haven't got the interest.'

'My daughter is a social worker, and she asked me about a counsellor coming, and I said, "No". I said, "I don't see how anybody saying words can help. I know what I should do, and I'm fully aware I've got to be brave, and go forward and go out and make friends. I know it all, but nobody's going to tell me how to do it. Nobody tells me. I know exactly what I should do. I couldn't see the point in somebody coming and saying what I already knew. But I said, "Well let him come just the once". And he came.'

'He's a beautiful person; he's a beautiful man. I looked forward to him coming; I really did. But as soon as he walked out the door, I'd dissolve into tears, and all his work—you know. I think he gave up in the end. I think the counsellor gave up on me. I think he thinks I'm one of his failures. I suppose I saw him about half a dozen times, at least. He called a few times while I was out and left a note on the door. I was sorry I missed him a couple of times. I did find it helpful—a bit—because I got a chance to talk to him about Edward. I wanted to impress on him what a wonderful fellow he was: what a fantastic man he was, you know. I don't know why.'

'I've got a friend who used to drive me up the wall. I've got to drop her. She's very good and very kind, but—oh. She's got a photo of my husband on her kitchen table. "Why haven't you got a photo of him?" she asked me. She said I couldn't have loved him. I said, "No; I couldn't stand the man". She's ridiculous, you know. She carries on like this, and is overpowering people. I was up there one day, and she had this photo on the table; she put it right in front of me. Then I had to visit the doctor, and my blood pressure was right up when I got there.'

'When I went back to see him a week later, it was down to normal again. The doctor told me, years and years ago, to keep away from her. She's very kind, but as he said, "She's a morbid person. She's not suitable for you". I'd hate to ever tell her that, but he said that she'd understand. She's a very morbid woman: very morbid. But other than that, she's got a heart of gold. But I had to stop going to see her: just gradually weaned off her, you know.'

'She would put this photo right in front of me. I don't know her reasons, but it's weird. Isn't it? I think it's rather wicked also, because she knows I won't have a photo around. I can't understand why she does it. A couple of times I've had a peep at it. A couple of times I've thought of our young days, and I go right through to the present—a little peep and I put them away again. I'm gradually working myself up to it, I think. When I'm ready, I'll have one; but not until then.'

'I know exactly what I should do to brighten up. You do this and do that; now she's telling me how to do it. There's no way of telling a person how to do it; is there? That's what I think of counselling. I don't know how many people really get help with counselling. I suppose young people are different. We're all different. It must help a lot of people, perhaps, to get over it and start a new life. I think a lot depends on the relationship too. When you've had that sort of ace relationship—two old dears.'

'We used to sit in the back room there at night with his arm around me. He was mad on music. After me, his greatest love was music. We used to sit in the back room there with our music, holed up together like a pair of teenagers. I won't go into that room now. I've never put his music on—ooh, no way I'd put the music on. I won't even go in the room. I stop in this room. We never used to come in this room: never. I couldn't stand it. I'd start crying and carrying on; I just break down. I can't see any point in doing a thing that's going to make me breakdown. One day, perhaps –. I don't know.'

'Bringing back these memories has not really been difficult, because actually, when no one's here, I'm thinking about it anyhow. It doesn't make that much difference; I think about it most of the time, and my mind goes over, and over, and over.'

'I'm sorry I've been crying. I'm running out of tissues. I can't afford the tissues. I'll have to give it away sooner or later. I usually have a small towel: my special "crying-towel", as I call it. I have a good old cry and say, "Come on, have a coffee". And I go and get a cup of coffee and sit down, and I'm all right for a while. I haven't got any interest in the television. That's just the trouble; there's nothing on that thing through the day.'

'My friend that I used to go and visit—who has the photo— she lost her husband shortly after I lost mine—she says to me, "Put your television on. There are some wonderful things on in the day". But it's unadulterated crap. And she sits and watches it all. It's unbelievable that people can watch it. Oh, it's all trash. It's the age of trash, you know—trash on television: trash on radio. Plenty of things are trash these days—like McDonald's.'

'I recently read an excellent article about what to do with mum, when dad goes; or dad, when mum goes. One woman said they weren't getting her into a nursing home, or to rent a retirement village with old wrinkly bodies like hers swimming in swimming pools, and some old dodderers dropping dead in the grounds. She wasn't going where there were only two people that had their marbles: all the others were loonies. She said it was like One Flew Over The Cuckoo's Nest. I also read somewhere that old age is not for cowards.'

'I'm interested in euthanasia. I've been tempted a couple of times to do something about it, but I don't think I ever will. I think I'll just think about it. I used to think I wouldn't do it once, on account of the family. But I'm beginning to think lately that the family might be relieved eventually. They might cry and mourn for a while, then think, "Oh well; thank God we haven't got to worry about Mum any more".'

'You feel like a strain, you know. You can see the family saying, "Oh well; perhaps we can have Mum next Sunday. Oh, there's something on: perhaps the following Sunday". You can see it. I'll tell you something: when you lose your mates you're on your own—you've lost everything—you're on your own. That's life; isn't it?'

'That's where we went wrong: the only time he let me down. I always told him I had to go first. I told you he was stubborn. I should've gone first. I was in hospital once, and I rang him up and said, "What are you doing?" He said, "Nothing; just sitting here". I said, "Why?" He said, "I've got no interest in doing anything when you're not here. I've got no interest at all". And he was such a busy person; he was always doing something.'

'Every night when I go to bed, I pray, "Please don't let me wake up in the morning". And the next morning, I say, "Oh God, I'm still here. Now I have to live through another day". I am very interested in assisted suicide. I think I'd like that. But I guess I'm probably a coward at heart.'

'I think he probably would have felt the same way if I'd gone first. But I think he would've coped better; I think he would've. He'd have been very sad: very sad. I remember when I went to a picture show one afternoon with his sister. I came home and he said, "Gosh, I missed you while you were gone". He said, "You know, the house is just not the same. It's awful without you: it's terrible".'

'So one of us had to be left behind and I was the unfortunate one. On Saturday nights, I think to myself, "If I was only with him". And then I console myself by thinking that if he had lived another couple of years, he may have developed cancer or something. That would have been worse; wouldn't it? That'd have been worse: watching him rotting away.'

'When I go shopping, I see all the others walking arm in arm. And I see the young couples together, and that makes me feel terrible. Then, I think to myself: "Well, you had your day; you had all that". You know, when we were out in public, he wouldn't walk holding my hand: no way. He wouldn't ever hold my hand or show affection in front of anyone: oh, no. Even before we were married, we'd be walking home from the films with his arm around me; if he'd hear someone come, he'd pull his arm away. He was a very self-effacing person, you know: very tranquil, and no show at all in front of people: no kissing. He never kissed me in front of anyone in his life. Where nobody would see us he was very, very affectionate: very.'

'I embarrassed him once in front of his sister. I said, "You watch this". I went over and threw my arms around his neck, and I said, "You're just absolutely marvellous, and I just love you so much". You know, he just didn't do anything, but he said, "Oh that's nice". But after she went, he shut the door, and he came back and said, "Come on now; where were you up to?"'

'My daughter said to me, "Mum, you must realise that you and Dad had a most unique relationship: absolutely unique". And I said, "Well, all these things just make it harder, don't they?" Can't I be forgiven for taking so long?'

'The cemetery really means nothing to me. You've got to be buried somewhere—apart from cremation. You have to be buried somewhere, and I didn't care. It just had to happen. Didn't it? What happens to the body is not a particular concern. But I wouldn't have had him cremated; I wouldn't have done that.

I've never visited my parents' graves. I've never been back to the cemeteries to see my parents. I went to their funerals. I could handle that, because I had him supporting me every inch of the way. That was different. You grieve for parents, but after their funerals, I never went back to the graves. My parents weren't buried together; they're in different cemeteries. There wasn't enough room where Dad was buried. He was buried in a family grave, and there wasn't enough room for Mum. We thought it advisable, because they had continual warfare between the two of them. Everybody said, "The best thing to do is to separate them". We felt sure they'd find a way to keep it up, if they were together.'

June has never been to the cemetery where Edward was buried fourteen months ago. 'I feel that if I went to that cemetery, I'd feel that it just happened yesterday. I would feel that I'd lost him all over again, and I'd start from the beginning now. It makes it definite, you know. But perhaps I'm playing a game where I think he's away somewhere, and perhaps he'll come back. I don't want to look at that ground and know he's there: it's too final. It's absolutely too final. I keep away from there.'

Life Is So Precious

Marie is a 34-year-old technical assistant. She grew up in South Australia with a younger sister, but her parents separated when the girls were very young. Ten years ago, as a top amateur sportswoman living in New South Wales, she met Jon. He was six years her senior, and a professional in the same sport. The following year she moved to Victoria to live with him.

Marie recalls: 'Jon was a very confident, very knowledgeable person, even though he didn't have very much education. He didn't work at all, but that didn't worry me, because he ended up with money through his high-profit gambling and other activities. We never lacked for money. We used to fight a lot. But then we used to always make up really quick. We used to fight and make up all the time.'

'We had a good life together. We weren't in each other's pockets. We were just there for each other when we needed each other, and our relationship ran very well. Anyway, we fought like brother and sister a bit, but still loved each other as much, or probably more, after each tiff. We lived with each other for six years; and in the last fifteen or sixteen months of his life, we bought a house together. That sort of helped things a bit.'

'It is almost three years now since Jon died of AIDS. We think he contracted it in his previous relationship, before he met me. People were always questioning, "Oh, did he take drugs?" or "He wasn't gay, was he?" They just don't understand that heterosexuals are at risk as well. That used to get up my nose a lot, with some people.'

'His illness certainly helped me to prepare for his death. He told me what he had seven months before he passed away. He knew about fifteen months before he died, but kept it to himself for quite some time.'

Marie had planned to start a family, and had been trying to conceive 'for two or three years'. Initially, after Jon's illness was diagnosed, he avoided sexual activity. Going out at night to bring home money provided a convenient excuse, and allowed him to better support Marie, financially. When they did resume sexual activity, he insisted on using a condom 'to prevent pregnancy', suggesting that 'it would not be wise, in light of family history'. Also, 'as there was something wrong' with him, they should 'wait until the doctors know what it is'.

'When he did tell me that he was dying with AIDS, I was shocked. I was unable to speak for about an hour. I just sat there, rocking backwards and forwards. But when I got over that, I started talking very positively. I suggested we travel the world, and enjoy the time we had left together. Then he said, "And I've been worrying about telling you all this time". And we laughed.'

'We both just assumed that I had it as well; and I felt that we were sharing the ultimate experience together. But four days later, I found out I didn't have it at all. And it felt like we'd lost something, if you know what I mean. I was sort of disappointed that we weren't sharing it together, if that makes any sense. But you can't be disappointed that you haven't got AIDS! During those few days, I had mapped out the rest of my life. But this was now uncertain, and I was facing life without Jon. It upset all our plans.'

'I didn't expect him to die so soon, though. But then, it was his time. And he was lucky that he went then, because a lot of people with his illness suffer for a lot longer than he did. He virtually suffered only from when he told me, because he went right downhill after that. Well, it seemed like that to me. I think he was trying so much to keep it a secret that he pretended nothing was wrong. And that helped, because it's a mind control thing as well with that sickness.'

'Before that, we knew he was sick, and were trying to work out what it was. That is, previous to him knowing. But then, after he found out, he kept telling me that the doctors didn't know. Because I had been to the doctors with him before he found out, I just thought that the doctors were still telling him the same thing. I don't know if it's a bit of conscious blindness or not. I don't know if I thought that I really didn't want to know about it anyway. But then, I did want to know. Because during the month before he told me, I was on his back a bit about it. I assumed he had cancer.'

'We talked a lot of times about what would happen after his death. He used to talk about his wake a lot. And he said that he wanted a big party with lots of grog, and lots of dope there. He wanted everyone to enjoy themselves. Then he said, "Oh, hang on. I'm not going to be there, and it's going to be a real good party". Then he suggested we have it before he dies.'

'Another time, he broke my heart when I was giving him a bath. I had to help him in and out of the bath. He was lying in the bath, and was just in tears. He was crying and crying. When I asked what the matter was, he said, "I'm scared that when I die, I'm going to miss you too much. I know I'm not going to be with you. It doesn't matter if I don't know, but I'm scared I'll miss you." That really broke my heart. Ooh: I can still see him there crying in the bath.'

'Previously, my mother's parents had died, and a close girlfriend died in a car accident when she was eighteen. My grandfather was pretty close to the family. He had Huntington's chorea, which is hereditary. That was pretty awful looking, that sort of disease. It was a very different thing altogether: very different. I didn't have to care for my grandfather. Anyway, he was in a home, and I got over my grandfather's death a lot easier than I did Jon's. Sure, it was very sad, but it was just something that happened. That's just the course in life; when you get old, you die. He wasn't that old; he was only 65, I suppose. But back in those days, when I was a lot younger, I thought that people died at 65. So memories of his death didn't help me whatsoever.'

'We talked about whether he would be buried or cremated, just before he signed his will. He didn't really worry too much, but he asked me what I thought. And I said I'd rather get cremated myself. And he said, "Oh yeah; I'll just get cremated." He really didn't care. He's not into cemetery visitation that much, because he never visited his parents at all. He never visited anyone in the cemetery. He just wanted to leave the funeral arrangements up to me, and said so in his will. He wasn't really fussed, but he did put in the will that he wanted to be cremated.'

'I arranged the funeral. I specifically asked for a funeral director I knew, and he came after they took Jon away. He'd died in his sleep in the morning, and they waited very late that night to get him, and that was good. We had him there the whole day, which was good.'

'I didn't feel guilty after he'd died. I really believe that people grieve a long time, or grieve excessively, because of guilt. That's what I believe. But I did everything I could for him that I thought was appropriate. There were times when I told him that his demands were far too much, but I think that with time off from work, I had plenty of time to spend with him. We talked about things all right—just us, and the life he had.'

'I took extended leave from work, to care for Jon full-time, in the last few months of his life. After his death, I went and stayed with my mother for a month, before coming back home. I just wanted to leave work and go away for a while, to just cruise around and live everywhere. I didn't want to just hang around home.'

'I feel I was pushed back into work too soon by my boss, who insisted that I set a date. So I set a date, and returned to work six weeks after the funeral. But for the next three months, I hated work and didn't want to stay. I wanted to sell the house, to drink, and do all sorts of dreadful things. But then, I took two weeks holiday, and came back bright as a button. I just needed a taste of it, and then to go away for a couple of week's holiday. Then I was back, and I was fine.'

'I never admitted to too many people that, in the morning, when I was trying to wake Jon up, half of me was saying, "Wake up", and the other half was saying, "Don't wake up". A sense of relief went right through me, including my mind and body, when I knew it was over. I had lost a lot of weight without having to go on any diet, so it was a sense of relief at first: just a sense. I'm not saying that I was relieved, but there was a sense of relief there.'

'I was very well in control for a week. And then after that, I lost a bit of control. That's when I did go into shock, I think. For the next three months, I was a bit out of control. Then they put me on those tablets, and I started to regain control.'

'I think I'm beginning to part with him now. For six months, I felt that I had to tell any man I met that my fiancé had died. Then my Mum told me that I didn't have to tell everyone about my past partner. I thought I had to, because he had AIDS. I certainly didn't experience any social withdrawal after his death; I was actually the opposite. I just wanted to talk to everybody. It really depended on who I met, whether I told them that Jon had died of AIDS or not, but I definitely told them that he had died recently.'

'He had acquired a bit of money, and we took out a mortgage to buy a house. But a month after moving into the house, he found out he had AIDS. After that, he wasn't well enough to do all the things that he had been doing and earning the money. But we had a bit of backing there, and so it was a lot easier to get through the few months that I had off from work. We actually survived on the pension, plus our savings.'

'Jon's parents left their house to him and his sister, and she lived in it. He left part of his share to me. And I then needed money to pay a lot of bills, including medical and funeral costs, and to maintain the mortgage repayments. Jon's sister wouldn't buy my share of the house, and she refused to sell her part, or pay any rent. So we ended up fighting through solicitors.'

'Eight months after Jon died, I became pregnant. But I don't still see the father. I now had something new to live for. It gave my life a new focus. I stopped drinking, and everything else I shouldn't have been doing. But then, I think I needed to do those things as well, to get them out of my system.'

'I lost so much weight just before he died, and didn't put any weight on until I was pregnant. The weight loss was due to stress and worry. I was eating the same as him, and was giving him eight small meals a day. Jon was eating more, but the weight wasn't going on him, or me. Other physical changes include the acute stress, which comes in patches, and the chronic stress, which is always there.'

'I feel I'm tougher than I ever have been, and I lose my patience more with people. I'm definitely against suicide, and that sort of thing. I don't have as much sympathy for people as I used to. I'm less tolerant with people who might be complaining about something of a more minor nature, like a headache. They don't know what a headache's all about. Jon had shingles on his head, and excruciating nerve pain going through his eyes all the time. Shingles is very painful, especially around the eyes and the head. I have toughened up a lot. I now say what I think more, and people have to accept me. If they don't like it, it doesn't worry me.'

'Some people, like nurses and even some friends, said, "Oh, you were so lucky not to get it too". But I feel I am very strong and healthy. If my body can reject or beat HIV—and with what I've been through—I feel I can now cope with anything.'

'I have no sympathy for people who kill themselves, unless they themselves are dying in some horrible way. Suicide pacts are senseless. It is stupid for both people to die. Thinking you can't live without your partner is a load of crap, and just shows cowardice. Life is so precious. There are too many people out there fighting with all they've got to stay alive.'

'I was talking to a counsellor during Jon's sickness, and went there once after he died. But I couldn't be bothered going back again. It's not that I didn't get anything out of it, it's just that I couldn't be bothered going there.'

Marie has experienced several significant 'turning points' in her life since Jon's death. She has progressed in her sport to become the national women's champion, and has twice represented Australia overseas. She also returned to part-time studies, to expand her professional knowledge and work role. In the meanwhile, she has moved closer to work, but has retained the house she shared with Jon. And more recently, she purchased a second home as an investment. She is also a very dedicated, single mother to her precocious two-year-old daughter.

Marie's spiritual life has reawakened since Jon's death, but she does not attribute this to his death. 'We try to go to church every Sunday, but that's due to my daughter, since she's been christened. I really don't believe in having kids christened and then not doing anything about it afterwards. What's the use of getting them christened? Christening isn't just one act. It's for the whole of their life. I want to give her an opportunity to learn about God, so she can make a choice later in life.'

'I did attend an Anglican Church when I was younger, but not while I was with Jon. He had no interest in that at all. I can't say that I didn't have any faith in God; I just put my faith in myself more. I mean, I didn't think about it. Jon did pray to God daily that I wouldn't have HIV. And when he told people about him having it, he would always say, 'Thank God, Marie didn't get it'. He talked about God just before he died. He'd been thinking about God. And then the night before he died, he went a bit strange in the head, and was telling me to go out and pray to the Lord on the lawn outside. He'd gone a bit crazy, you know.'

'I did have a funny dream on the first anniversary of him telling me that he had AIDS. It was about him in heaven. And it meant a lot to me, having that dream. It was like heaven, but there was nothing about God in there. It did give me the faith that he is waiting somewhere for me in years to come. His spirit is waiting for me. I don't necessarily know where, but I still remember the dream. He said we couldn't be together now, but we will soon—and don't be in too much of a hurry to join him. That was when I was drinking a lot.'

'We didn't discuss what to do with his ashes. It just didn't enter my head. I didn't think about it until afterwards. I just had the crematorium post his ashes up to Mum. But since then, I've had a lot of thoughts. They're still in my mother's top cupboard in the hallway. And she's asked me a couple of times what I'm going to do with them. I've thought about having a rose bush or something at the cemetery, but I can't justify the cost at the moment, because I've got others things to think about. But I wouldn't mind having a big pot with a bonsai tree, and his ashes buried in the big pot. Then I could move him around. I like that idea. I did think about putting them with his mother and father at their cemetery, but I haven't even bothered to ring up to see if there's any room. Keeping the ashes doesn't seem to worry Mum very much at all. When she comes across them, every now and again, she asks me if I've decided what to do with them.'

'Before I'd gone through the death of Jon, I always thought that placing cremated remains was very important. I didn't understand why some people wanted to scatter ashes. Now I understand how people can forget about them, and even leave them at the crematorium. It is just a lot easier not to think about it. You really don't know what to do sometimes; and what you get doesn't always justify the cost.'

'If I were dying, and someone else was going to clean things up and throw things out, I think I'd have his ashes scattered; but nowhere in particular. I have no idea, because I'm not a real outdoors person. Locating the ashes in a particular place is not all that important any more. I used to think it would be, but not for Jon. If it were for my mother, then it would be a different story. But because Jon didn't worry about it, it doesn't worry me as much. I feel it's important to do what the person wanted done with their remains.'

'A cemetery didn't have any particular significance with Jon. But with different people you're related to, things can vary. I think it is a bit of a selfish thing for me, as well. If I put Jon in a cemetery, then his sister could share him. And I don't want to share him with his sister, because I hate her: I really hate her. She was still giving me hell fifteen months later. But with Mum, I'd want to share her with everybody else. So I'd put her in a cemetery. To me, putting cremated remains in a cemetery is when you want to share.'

'My grandparents were buried in a very small cemetery in South Australia. Mum used to take us to visit them about once a month. I still remember going to that cemetery. I used to be scared to tread on the graves. I used to jump over them all the time. There were the Catholic, Methodist, and Anglican sections; because back in those days, you didn't mix the faiths.'

'If I'm visiting the cemetery, and someone else is bawling their eyes out and screaming, I think it's offensive; because they're intruding on my grieving. To me, that's not true bereavement; it's just an act. I really hate that. It seems to me that women who cry the loudest think they're the ones who grieve the most. But neither do I think that they should have to hide their grieving. I mean, if you want to cry: cry!'

209

Death of a Secret Lover

More Than Just a Friend

Marisa is 45 years old and has never been married. She lives with her parents and the younger of her two sisters. 'My Dad is retired as a blind invalid pensioner. My Mum worked when we were younger, but not since my youngest sister started school; so she hasn't worked for nearly thirty years. My sister and I have always lived at home. Twenty-two years ago I started at the business where I still work as an administration officer. I have been in the same role ever since.'

Marisa regarded herself as an atheist prior to Greg's death, but is now perhaps agnostic. 'I don't really have any religion, but I think I believe that there is something out there: more now than I've ever believed, I think. Before, I was clear that there was no God. Now, I believe that when someone dies, you don't just disappear: someone does look after you. So I'm really not sure what I believe, but I believe there is something up there.'

Marisa's family was unaware of the depth of her relationship with Greg. 'They thought he was just a friend, but he was my partner, boyfriend, my lover—whatever.'

Greg was 44 years of age when he died of a massive heart attack, almost three years ago. He managed a provincial sports venue. We had been going out off-and-on for nineteen years. He was basically a nice person. He was my very first boyfriend. We went out for a good year and had a normal relationship. Then we broke up for a while. Whenever he got sick, he rang me up and we continued our relationship right where it left off, up until the time he died.'

'The week before he died, I went for a week's holiday and stayed at his place. I noticed a difference in him from what I had seen the month before. His appearance had changed dramatically, going from a very clean and impeccable dresser, to a slob.'

'Greg had a very mixed up family. He was adopted; his sister was adopted too. But he didn't know that until he was in his late twenties. So he was very mixed up: very confused. He had a son, who he had distanced himself from. But I think that that was just basically the way he'd been brought up too. He treated him virtually the same. They were very mixed up. His son lived with his ex-wife and her new female partner. The son was 21 when Greg died.'

'Greg was on his second marriage, and all was not well with that marriage. She was away, staying at their friend's penthouse in Western Australia. Greg suspected that she was having an affair with his friend over there. And she has recently moved, and they've bought a house together over there; so –.'

Greg suffered a fatal heart attack in his car, while in his garage. 'The week before, he'd been feeling sick and had black-outs, and so he went to the doctor. He found out he had sleep apnoea, high cholesterol and diabetes, and was having tests for that. But actually dying of a massive heart attack was very unexpected. Some of his friends hadn't seen him for a while, but the week before his death his appearance and everything seemed to have changed. I mean, he was getting things in order: writing a letter to his son, and different things. Sometimes, people say that they think people know when they're going. He was just sorting himself out.'

'They thought he might've committed suicide, because his car engine was running when he died. Well, his car had run out of petrol the next morning when they found him, but the coroner ruled that out and said it was a massive heart attack.

'Apparently he had a meeting with a lady from the local radio station at midday. I'd spoken to him the night before—about eleven-fifteen—when he was doing some work on the computer. Apparently he woke up—or he mightn't have gone to bed—and they figure he had pains in the chest and tried to get into the car to go to the hospital, about two-fifteen in the morning. But he had a massive heart attack in the car. So, from two-fifteen until after midday, when someone came to find out where he was, he'd been in the car.'

'I found out a day or so after Greg had died, and was able to see him that night at the funeral parlour. It was my sister's birthday, and I felt I couldn't stay at home singing happy birthday and pretending to be happy. I had to get away and be by myself, so I went out. Coincidentally, a staff counsellor started at my work the very next day. Well, on his first day he really copped the whole lot; he really did. He listened, and he came back week after week to see how I was.'

Greg's death was Marisa's first close bereavement. 'No one else close to me has died. I mean, I've lost uncles and aunties since then; but his death was the most significant thing that I've had to deal with in my whole life.'

'Greg was a very popular person, and had lots and lots of death notices in the paper. I felt, because I'd known him for so long, that I should put one in too. Part of me was saying, "Do it". And part of me was saying, "No; don't do it". The counsellor suggested that I do it, because of my relationship with Greg. I only put in a very small notice, and there was no signature; so no one but me knew who it was from. I always called him 'Sunshine', so I just put his name, his date, and just "my Sunshine is gone"—and that was it.'

'And the next morning, the newspaper rang up and said the family thanked me for the notice, and would like to thank me personally. I thought, "No; this is not a good idea". Then they said, "Well, we won't get the family, we'll get a friend of the family to talk to you". And I thought, "Ooh, OK".'

'So I spoke to the gentleman that they asked me to speak to, and he asked if I was going to the funeral; so I arranged to meet him at the funeral. When I got there with a friend, I recognised him. He was looking around: I suspect looking for me. He'd given me a description of what he looked like. I went inside for the service, came out, and then went over to introduce myself. Then Greg's wife came over and introduced herself. We went to the crematorium. And in the line up to greet Greg's wife, we exchanged hugs and kisses like long lost friends, and we arranged to have lunch at a later date. And we did have lunch and have kept in contact with each other since; so it's a very strange situation.'

'Greg was cremated. And it was—it sounds very strange, but it was—the best funeral that I've ever been to. They had singing. They had funny stories. They had lots of people. The seating at the funeral director's chapel was reserved seating only, because there was just so many people there. He had people from overseas and interstate. And there were columns and columns of advertisement notices in the paper, from people all over the place.'

'Yes, it was a really big funeral, and really good. To me, it wasn't a sad day. It wasn't: "we're all sad because Greg's gone". It was like a celebration. It was a celebration of his life and what he'd meant to a lot of people. It was different.'

'At the funeral director's service, everyone was laughing; no one was really crying. Then we went to the crematorium. And at this place, they don't lower the coffins; they turn around in the wall. So it's like he's not actually going anywhere; it's just disappearing for a while. And still there were no tears there. I mean, there were hardly any tears from anyone. And that sounds kind of sick really; doesn't it?'

'I was very lucky; because I was allowed to go to the funeral parlour before anyone had actually found out he had died. He lived way out in the country, but he'd been taken to the Melbourne Coroner's office; then they took him to the funeral directors. The day I found out, I rang up the funeral directors, and I was allowed to go over there to see him.'

'People had told me that to see someone when they have died helps you accept death a lot better; so I saw him, and it was just like he was asleep. And I think that really helped me, because I didn't really feel that he had died—that he'd been in a lot of pain or anything—because he looked really peaceful. He just looked like he was asleep. I was very happy with the opportunity to see him at the funeral home. I feel that gave me a good opportunity to say goodbye to him. But I was crying leading up to the funeral. I think, at the funeral you realise that they're not coming back. I mean, they're going to be cremated, and you're not ever going to see that person again.'

'After Greg died, I was very, very angry. Very angry at him: very angry at friends. I was really quite a nasty person for at least twelve months. I had to go to the doctor and was put on medication for depression for about six months. I have mellowed now, and I feel that I'm a bit more compassionate to a lot of people than I was originally before Greg died. I cried an awful lot for that first twelve or eighteen months, as good friends know. I cried many tears, but you get back on track. I mean, you never forget them, but life just tends to go in a different direction.'

'After he died, I kind of went mad on shopping: mad on spending money. I mean, I spent an awful lot of money in that first six months; but it was just wasted things. That was part of my relief I think; I just went shopping.'

'I didn't think straight away that there was anything there: that he went to heaven, or he went to hell, or wherever. I went to a few spiritualists and mediums after he died. I just felt that there was something out there: that he is there. I don't think that when you die, you just disappear totally: no. I just got some faith. I don't really know what sort of faith; but it's there.'

'I am not so sure that there is no spirit world any more, but I don't believe Greg is now in heaven. I reckon he's in hell somewhere; I do. Greg was a really nice person, but he lied an awful lot to different people. I reckon he's somewhere off having a really good time. He's probably in hell, but having a wonderful time.'

'I believe there is something, but I'm not sure whether it is God or the devil, or whether he is on a plane waiting to go into another life, or whatever. I do believe he is somewhere, but I'm not quite sure where. I expect I'll see him again some day. But I've always wondered: if he died as a 44-year-old person, and I live say for another 46 years, then I'll be ninety.'

'I did go to a medium, about five months after Greg died. I'd been to the cemetery that morning and put flowers on his memorial. I went with a friend from work. And the medium said to me that Greg thanked me for the red flowers that I'd put there this morning. And I mean, she didn't know that I'd been to the cemetery. So I figure it had to come from somewhere. I just thought it had to be Greg thanking me for going to the cemetery, and that helped me a lot.'

'Greg's parents were quite elderly. About ten months after Greg died, his father died. His mother died exactly a year after Greg. A man rang me up at work and told me, "Greg's father has died". And he told me that he'd known about me for years and years. Then we arranged to go out and have dinner. He still rings me up once a month, just to talk about Greg and to see how I'm getting on; so he's also remained friends.'

'I told the counsellor at work about my family situation, about my situation with Greg, his being married at the time, and my relationship with Carolyn at work. He made it a lot easier to see why I was upset, and he just checked if I was all right. He's been really good through the whole process. At Greg's anniversary, he came in to see if I was all right: how I felt the year after. He checks in occasionally, just to see that I'm going along all right. Nothing is a secret; everything just came out in the open. There doesn't have to be a secret with him any more. And I kept Greg and my relationship a secret for all those years.'

'It's still a secret with my immediate family, but others know the details these days. I don't want to tell my family about it. Both my sisters and my parents don't know. I figure there are some things that you just leave; they don't need to know. As far as they're concerned, I just lost a friend. But he was a bit more than just a friend. And I miss him more than words can tell.'

'Greg was cremated and has a memorial tree at the cemetery. I believe it is a special place; they are really guarding the people that have been trusted to them. I mean they look after them: maintain the grounds, and it's locked up at five o'clock. It's like they're the custodians. I think it's very safe once the gates are locked. I think he's in a very safe spot there, and no one can really get in and touch him.'

'At the cemetery, I feel safe. I feel it's sad, and I feel safe. Sometimes, I've even gone in the evening: during summer particularly. They leave the gates open until seven p.m. So I go after work sometimes; there's nobody else around. It's a bit eerie, because they've got a musical garden there too, and the music wafts around the ground. There's not another living soul around.'

'For the first eighteen months, I used to go once a month. But it's gone to about once every three months now. I often wonder why I go to the cemetery. I think I like going to see him, but I get really sad walking away, because he's there. I mean, he's never going to leave there. And this cemetery is a very tranquil spot. It's very pleasant where he is. But as I said, I get very sad. I think I stopped going because of that reason. I like to visit, but I get very sad when I walk away. But I go there often enough.'

'For the first year and a half, I would go monthly. But it changes; it's just something that happens progressively. At first, soon after he died, I cried when I went there and I cried when I went away. Now, I visit his plaque, put the flowers there and I just cry walking back to the car. And I think it's because I feel guilty about leaving him there. I think it has become easier to visit these days. It's not as painful now as it was. But I get angry at him too: more than anything, because he's actually died. He had so much to live for. The pain of going to visit is all right, but it's still that going away and leaving him there –.'

'When I go, I feel that I'm doing so for my own benefit, rather than for his benefit, but I'm also not quite sure what that personal benefit is. I feel good going there, but I feel very sad walking away. I don't look forward to going. I think it is perhaps a sense of duty that I feel to go there now. I feel it's a duty to me because—it's a silly thought—if you don't go, you feel that you're forgetting the person. By not visiting them, it's like you've forgotten them and you're not going to see them any more.'

'I always drive to the cemetery by myself; but on his first anniversary, two friends came with me. I usually try to make it around the anniversary of his death. I know his ashes are there, but he's not. But it just kind of helped me when he first died. I also visit on his birthday, but not Christmas, because Greg wasn't really big on Christmas. I don't think that you have to go to the cemetery to remember the person. I mean, I used to think when he first died, and I used to go every month, that it's like going to visit him. But then I thought, "Well, that's silly, because he's not there". I mean, you remember what you remember yourself. You don't have to go and visit a cemetery.'

'I don't really know what I get out of visiting there myself. I go and place some flowers, talk to him, and just walk away. They have the plaques on a concrete base, raised out of the ground; so I just push the tan bark around a bit more, but that's basically it. I'm happy with the way they maintain it.'

'In the first year or two, you feel that it benefits yourself to go to the cemetery. But as time goes by, you realise that you don't have to go to the cemetery as often, because the person is inside you. I mean, the memories are there. You don't have to go to the cemetery to visit the person. But even so, I still like to occasionally. But it's not as urgent as it was before.'

Death of a Parent

God's Will

Adriana was born in Melbourne 27 years ago. She has not married, but lives with her father and only sibling: her eighteen-year-old brother. Ten years ago, on leaving school, Adriana commenced her career in the bank where she still works.

'Mum was born in Greece 48 years ago. When she was four, she came to Australia with her parents, two brothers and her sister. They first migrated to northern Queensland where my grandfather worked in the sugar-cane fields. But it got a bit too hot for them, so after a few years, they moved south to Melbourne. Mum went to school here, so she was virtually more Australian than Greek. She didn't speak much Greek.'

'She went back to Greece when she was eighteen or nineteen, and met Dad there. He was born in Greece four years before Mum. They decided to come back to Australia and get married. That was a year or so later. Mum never had a professional job; she mainly worked in sales. When I was five, we all went to Greece for about three months. And four years after that, my brother was born.'

'I used to go to a Greek Orthodox college. All students there are Greek Orthodox, and they focus on our religion quite a bit, as it's run by the Archdiocese in Melbourne. So during our schooling, we always had a religious influence on us. Then once leaving school, it sort of died down, because I didn't have that fed to me. I didn't go out myself to find out more about it, or to be involved. I wasn't attending church on a regular basis at that time. Well, of course I went at Christmas and Easter, and in between, I'd say every two or three months; but not on a regular basis. However, that didn't stop me from being religious. It didn't stop me from praying and what-have-you; it's just that I wasn't directly involved with it.'

'Six years ago, we discovered that Mum had cancer. They virtually gave her about three years of life. But with a lot of chemotherapy and very good support from our doctors, she managed to go on for six years.'

'This year was very difficult. I think it was about this time last year that she was actually free from cancer. They had cured it, and they had great hope for her. So we actually went away to Queensland, where her brother lives, and spent Christmas there. When she got back, she had gastro. That deteriorated her immune system; and by April, she had lost quite a bit of weight.'

'She was in and out of hospital about twelve times in a matter of three months. So every few weeks, she'd be in hospital, out again, at home for about a week, then back in. She was very nauseous, so she couldn't keep food down; and that was the main reason she was in hospital. We didn't know that the cancer had actually hit her lungs, but that's the reason why she couldn't eat.'

'Mum passed away four months ago. She was actually at home that day, and she requested she go to the hospital. I remember her saying, "I have to go into hospital, because they have to do something to me. I can't live like this any more". So, I don't know whether she actually felt that this was her last day, or whether she still had hope. I really don't know what she meant by that. I happened to take the day off from work, so Dad and I took her in to hospital at about twelve o'clock. Our oncologist spoke to Dad and myself while she was having X-rays taken. He said, "You know, it's a only matter of days left". And even at that stage, I didn't want to believe it.'

'My brother was still at school, and Dad asked me to go and pick him up, so we could all be together. After I'd picked him up, I went by my grandmother's (my mother's mother's) place, and I told her that Mum didn't have long to go; and of course she wanted to come. At that time, Mum's sister was with my grandmother. They had originally planned to spend that day over at our house, but as we had told them that we were going into hospital, they stayed at my grandmother's house and were going to make their way to the hospital late in the afternoon. So we all went to the hospital together: my grandmother, aunty, and my brother and me. But by the time I got back with the others, Mum had already passed away. So it was a matter of hours more than days.'

'They allowed us to stay there with her as much as we wanted to. That was very healing in my view. And as we left late that night, it was just Dad, my brother, and myself with Mum. I think that even though they were around, that didn't bother me. I still paid my final respects to Mum in a way that I wanted to. And I still spoke to her in a manner that I would've if others weren't around me, so I don't think that made a difference.'

'Mum's dad passed away when I was about twelve. I only remember bits and pieces of it. The young kids—or the grandchildren—weren't directly involved in what was really happening. We knew that we had lost our grandfather and that we were grieving, but because we were so young, we didn't go through the whole thing that I am going through now. We were the young kids, you know. And we sort of just did our own thing and didn't play much of a part in the whole grievance process.'

'My Grandfather's was the first funeral I'd ever gone to. I'm sure that it helped me a lot and did prepare me for Mum's in some way that I didn't expect. I sort of looked back and remembered some of the stuff that we did do for my grandfather—the traditional Greek customs that we've got—and that sort of prepared me for now. I knew what to expect and what to do, so it did help me a bit.'

'As Mum was ill for such a long time, I don't think her death actually changed my emotions or made me feel any different. I think that happened when we originally found out that she had this disease. I think then, my whole outlook on life in general actually changed, and my emotions changed as well. So I'm still the same person, and I still have the same emotions I had before she passed away. Maybe, if she didn't have an illness and it just came as a shock, then I'd probably feel different, but I think her illness changed me more than her death did.'

'Mum's illness brought us a lot closer. We respected each other a lot more. When we found out she was ill, I was only 21. And back then, a normal 21-year-old only thinks about herself and having a good time. So I think, once we found out about the illness, it really hit me first of all. And it definitely did bring us a lot closer; we did a lot of things together.'

'Now that I look back, I think she tried to prepare us for her death. Any time she spoke of it, I couldn't actually confront it. I couldn't sit there and listen. I'd just break out, so I had to leave.'

'There were certain things that she would tell us she wanted, without us realising that she was actually talking about her death. For example, the photo that she wanted on her tomb-stone, and the dress that she wanted to wear at her funeral. She was sort of telling us in a way not to upset us, but to give us the idea that that's what she wanted. So that was really good, but we only realised that after she had passed away, and everything sort of started coming back to us.'

'But we never actually sat down to discuss what she wanted from us, and what she expected from us, because we never thought that it would get to that stage. We always had faith and hope that she would always be with us.'

'But I always knew, at the back of my mind, that she would no longer be with us one day. It's very rare that someone who has cancer actually makes it through. So it was always there.

Being close to our religion and having that faith, you never stop believing that there might be someone that can help. So yes, there was always that hope that she would be with us forever.'

'Mum's illness bought us a lot closer to our religion, especially for herself. She always enjoyed going to church and finding out about our religion. But I think she had a need to know what to expect. She also had to prepare herself for her death, and she prayed for God to help her. So it did bring us all a lot closer to our religion.'

'Our religion helped us prepare for the time when she actually passed away, in that we knew she would be finally resting, and we hoped that she would be in good hands, which we're now sure that she would be. By understanding a lot more of our religion, we then knew why she left. So it helped to answer a lot of questions that we did have. I mean, throughout the time that she was ill, we always questioned, "Why did it happen to you?" But you know that if it's God's will, then it will happen, and there's no way out of it. And it was God's will for Mum to have this illness. And of course, that might have been a way of getting us a lot closer to our religion. So that's how we looked at it.'

'I think my relationship with God has virtually stayed the same since Mum passed away. Before that, when Mum was ill, we had that bond, and we found religion and we often did pray. So it really hasn't changed that much, except for the fact that I go to church regularly now, and she's there with them. I tend to know that I'm talking to Mum through God, so there's actually more than just a reason to pray now, if I know that Mum's there listening to me. I don't pray any more now than I would have when she was ill, it's just that my prayers have changed. Whereas, before it was a lot of pleading, you know: "Please help us", now it's more like a conversational type of prayer.'

'I believe that Mum is now in heaven: the reason being that she had great faith. She loved her religion. She loved God. She loved Jesus. So I do believe that she has gone to a better place. Also, I've had a close bond with our priest. He would often come to the hospital and talk to Mum and say a few prayers together. And just before she passed away, he gave her final Holy Communion. Once she had her Holy Communion, it was only a matter of five or ten-minutes later that she passed away. And I believe that God waited for that moment before he took her. So I believe she left for a better place.'

'Mum's death has actually brought my father and brother and I together a lot. We're spending a lot more time together now, and we understand each other a lot more, because we're not afraid to show our emotions and how we feel. So we're able to sit down and discuss things now. Previously, just like any other normal family, it was very difficult to sit down all together and discuss things. So I think it has brought us that little bit closer, mainly because that's how Mum always wanted it to be. So we're probably doing what Mum wanted us to do.'

'Once Mum fell ill, it was just like a blessing that everything came to me again. I started meeting people without really going out looking for them. It was just out of coincidence that I was meeting kids: young kids from different Greek Orthodox youth groups. And to me, that was a sign: "You've got to come back to us". So that sort of helped me during that time. But it wasn't something that I actually ventured out to do; it sort of just came to me. So yeah, I find that a blessing actually.'

'I was very much involved in planning Mum's funeral. The funeral was something that had to be done, but it was also our final respect to her. It was the last time that we could actually show how much we loved her. To me, it was the last thing I could actually do for Mum, so of course you try and do every-thing to perfection. But it wasn't only a grieving day; it was also a day of relief that she's now at rest: she's now sleeping and going through no more pain. So the day had sort of two meanings, and there were two different types of emotion.'

'Dad, my brother and me were all involved in planning the funeral: just the three of us. In a way, working through the funeral was therapeutic. I'd been to a few Orthodox funerals—not direct relatives or anyone close to us—just friends of the family. I was very happy with Mum's funeral arrangements. I think I actually asked Mum through my prayers—after she had passed away—to help us in the way that she would want her funeral. So I just left it at that, and everything we did was something that Mum would have liked. I think that helped us a lot too.'

'The day before the funeral—the Sunday night—there were prayers for her up at the church, so she was there. The coffin was open at that time, and at her funeral. She didn't stay there at the church overnight; she was taken back to the funeral parlour.'

'The service was at our local Orthodox Church. There were actually two priests at Mum's funeral. The service included mainly hymns; and they asked for the soul to be saved, and for Mum to have repented during that time.'

'In our religion, for forty days the actual soul is still with us, then after the forty days it makes its way to heaven, or wherever. So it's a way of helping the soul find its home. And a lot of love is also chanted through the hymns, so we're also showing how much we loved her. I speak some Greek, and Dad speaks a lot of Greek, but most of the service is in ancient Greek. So, unless you have a clear understanding of the ancient Greek language, it's very hard to understand. I really wasn't familiar with what was going on.'

'After the church service, we went over to the new Orthodox section at the cemetery, and then there was another service at the graveside. I really don't remember much of that. I know that again there were certain hymns and prayers said, though I really couldn't say what they actually were. I think it's basically: that the soil put on top is not made heavy. So what they say is, "Let the soil be light for you, and may you not have any more burden on you". I think they say something to that effect, and that's about it really.'

'The cemetery is an important place. Well it's Mum's home. Actually, it's not her home; it's her body's home. Her spirit or soul is not there; it's just her body that is there. And, as Mum was a beautiful lady, I would also like her surroundings to be the same. So I think it's important that when we do attend the cemetery, it's not seen as a dull place. It should be something that is beautiful, even though it is such a sad, sad place. It still can be beautiful for others to visit, and for those whose bodies are in that area there.'

'It doesn't have any heritage value, although I do have a grandfather buried there. I believe the cemetery is a sacred place, but I'm not sure how to explain it. I think, on a personal basis, that it's not as holy as the church. It has that holiness in it, but it's not as holy as the church, you know. It's very hard to explain.'

'It's very difficult to explain how I feel. The fact that it's still hard to believe she has gone makes it difficult when we're going, and to believe that she is there. So at times—and I have felt this on quite a few weekends—we go there just because it's something that we do. It's just become a custom to us. I still haven't truly grasped the fact that she has left us; so I don't feel any closer to her there than I do at home.'

'The cemetery is a peaceful place. It's very peaceful. It is a place of sadness: quite a bit of grieving, of course. Whether it's a safe place, I don't know. I find it very difficult to go there on my own. I remember when Mum and I used to go to my grand-father's grave. But now, I find it difficult to go to a cemetery on my own. But I still find it to be a beautiful place.'

'I would be a bit happier, in a sense, if it was a little bit cleaner around us. I understand that certain Orthodox cultures have feast days on weekends, and they take their food and eat it with the person that has passed away. And then, of course, they don't clean up behind them. That's very disturbing to me, because it's like they're dirtying my Mum's house. That is very disturbing. I don't think it should be necessary—but it is, in this case—that maybe they should have someone that might clean up the place after they leave, because it is terrible. It is very disappointing.'

'I think it depends on which part of Greece you come from. I know that the northerners—which are mainly the Macedonians—tend to have this kind of feast at the cemetery. The rest would just take a little plate of biscuits, or maybe the boiled wheat on their Memorial Day. That would be about it. There's none of this carrying the Esky, and the tables, and having a whole feast there. I think, from what I've heard, they believe that they eat with the person, and the person's there eating with them. And they also leave food for those people, and the food attracts pests.'

'I've gone on Sundays and there are picnic baskets, and Eskys, and tables. When you're going there to pay your respects to someone, others are having a feast. I've even gone after they've left, and there are empty beer cans hanging around and bins are overfilled, and it just looks so terrible.'

'For someone's resting place to look like that is really heart-breaking. So that really annoys me. It should be a beautiful place: a place that you enjoy visiting. For example, the rose gardens are just beautiful; they're so clean and it's pleasant for someone to walk through. Whereas, with our area, down the road there's banana peels. It just looks really messy, and it's just not right. For me, there's no respect for those that are lying there: it's just terrible.'

'I still want to be buried there when I die. I would like to go in the Orthodox area because of my religion, and of course because Mum's there—I don't know if it would be in the same area or somewhere else. So of course the Orthodoxy does play an enormous role. I'd feel comfortable in the fact that I'm amongst others of the same religion. It's the place to be. It's just like when the Greeks migrated, they all landed in Richmond and Brunswick. It was the place to be.'

'Of course, once we go it doesn't really matter where our body is; it's our soul that plays the important role. But you still want to be amongst those who have had the same beliefs as yourself.'

'The fact that I work makes it difficult to visit Mum's grave as much as I'd like to. We attend every weekend, unless something major is happening: for example, a christening. Dad actually attends on a Tuesday and Thursday, so he comes every second day, and on weekends. Dad comes more often than we do. On the weekends, we visit both Saturday and Sunday.'

'Straight after Mum's funeral I went on a daily basis, because I had about two and a half weeks off from work. But since I've been back it's just on weekends, because I'm obviously unable to take time off work to visit. My brother only comes on weekends with Dad and me.'

'I think my faith has some influence on how frequently I visit. But I don't think it's only faith. I think it's also how much you love the person. I think that they go hand in hand: the faith and the love that we have for the person that we've lost. The church hasn't got any ground rules on when you should visit, or how often you should visit. It is up to each individual. However, I personally feel that the more you visit the cemetery, the more it helps you. And in visiting them, I also pray for them. So that sort of helps us to communicate in a spiritual way.'

'We try to go to church as a family every week. But then, of course, there are some days that we are unable to. Church starts at about eight, and finishes at about 11.30; so it's about three hours or so. If Dad might not be able to make it, I'll just go off on my own. And straight after church, we go to the cemetery. Even if we don't go to church, we'll still go to the cemetery.'

'On a typical Saturday, the three of us come by car, between two and three o'clock. We would stay for about an hour, or an hour and a half. It depends on how we're feeling at the time. Mum always believed in fresh flowers, so we bring her fresh flowers. Dad buys them on Friday, because he goes to the market then. The first thing we do when we approach her grave is our cross. We do the sign of our cross, and kiss her icon: her photo. And then Dad lights the little oil burner. There's a monument on Mum's grave with an oil burner sitting just in the front there. My brother usually lights the incense thing as well. And then, we just sit around and have a bit of a conversation between the three of us.'

'Dad always cleans the monument. He waters it down and then wipes it with a cloth. He enjoys doing that, so I just leave him at it. My brother doesn't do much. He just stands there, but he helps with the flowers. Dad talks to Mum; I don't—not out loud, as yet. But Dad tells her what we've done and what we're doing.'

'I pray pretty much the same at the gravesite as I do away from the cemetery. Whatever I feel at the time, I just let out and tell her through my thoughts. For most of the time I'm just watching Dad, and of course reliving some of the memories that we have. He usually goes for a quick walk around and just visits the other monuments, and that would be how it is. It's pretty much the same on a Sunday, except that we usually cut flowers from home and put them with the other flowers we bought.'

'I've always felt easy about visiting Mum's grave; I haven't had a problem with that. But leaving is difficult. I feel very comfortable being there; it's just a matter of when I'm actually leaving, you know. It's really heartbreaking to leave someone behind under those circumstances. It's a little bit easier to leave now, but I still have that thought. I wish I could stay that little bit longer.'

'Only the Macedonian Orthodox eat in the cemetery, not the Greek Orthodox. The only time that we actually take a few biscuits along—or boiled wheat—is on the Memorial Day itself; that's on the fortieth day anniversary. The first one is actually nine days after the death: and then at six months, nine months, and then the year. That's when the priest actually says a few words and blesses the grave. And they're the only times that we actually take wheat and some dry biscuits to the cemetery.'

'So the first blessing of the grave is on the ninth day after the passing, and then on the fortieth day after the passing. However, if the fortieth day falls on a weekday, it's always done on the weekend before the actual fortieth day. It's the same at the three months, the six months, or whatever the case may be. Then we have the year anniversary. And then it's up to each individual. They don't have to wait for the third year, they can do it at any time—whenever they feel they need a memorial service—and this can continue until the third, sixth or the ninth anniversary.'

'Blessing the grave is usually done on a Saturday. The priest will come to the cemetery where we'd be waiting for him at the grave. He prays for her soul, and we have a bowl of boiled wheat with raisins, sugar and almonds mixed in; and that symbolises the body of the deceased. The priest blesses the wheat, and then once it's all over, we just have a bit of the wheat and a biscuit or whatever anybody else brings along. We spend a bit of time there with the deceased, and then they usually all come over to the house and have a coffee.'

'All of the wheat has to be consumed, because it has been blessed by the priest. It shouldn't be thrown away. We usually take it home and then give it out to families who couldn't attend on that day. That's normally done on a Saturday, but the blessings used to take place on a Sunday as well. I remember that, with my grandfather, it used to be done on the Sunday after the church service. But I think now there are so many— I mean the Greek population has grown so much—that the priest doesn't have time to go on a Sunday, so he prefers to do it on the Saturday.'

Leader of the Family

Tony is a 40-year-old Roman Catholic father of three. He was born in Melbourne, of Italian parents. His only sibling is his younger sister. Tony's wife is also of Italian parentage, and they identify their own family as Italian. After completing his secondary schooling, Tony did a business course majoring in real estate. He has been operating as a licensed real estate agent for twenty years now.

'Dad left Italy in 1952. They did it pretty hard during the war and all that. Typical migrants: seeking a better life. He left the family at seventeen—obviously wasn't married—and came to Australia looking for a new start. He had various jobs, usually manual. He was a non-skilled labourer, I suppose. He worked as an assistant chef for a number of years, and enjoyed that; but the hours were atrocious, so he eventually left.'

'Dad worked for a company where they make communications equipment. He was a storeman, and loved it. And that's where he stayed until he died. So he did it pretty hard. He was just: work, work, work. When I was a kid, he was working seven days a week: two shifts. Of course, that changed in later years. But he was a typical migrant: came here with nothing, and carved out a future for his family and certainly put us on the right track.'

'Dad was always a little bit overweight. He had a bit of a cholesterol problem, and was always trying to keep that under control. He died of a massive heart attack, just on three years ago. He was 61 years old. It was very quick: very sudden. Just like turning off the light switch: flat on his back. His doctor said it was probably going to happen one day; there's just no way of knowing when. There were no previous warnings or anything like that. It just happened. It was very instant.'

'Dad and I were always close, but not as close as we would have liked to be. We never argued, even as a child. We never went through a teenage crisis, or anything like that. I was probably as close as one could be to a father who, when I was a child, was always working. We never really had family holidays, and things like that. But when we were together as a family it was fine. We didn't go away on camps or go fishing, because they just weren't the sort of things we did.'

'The European way of life is different to the Australian way. It's not that there wasn't love there, it's just that we didn't show that closeness. But now, for example, before my boys go to bed, I go in and hug them and tell them I love them: every night, without fail. That never happened, but that's OK. It didn't happen to anyone. It's just the way it was. But I don't feel that he didn't love me. He was a great father.'

'A funny thing happened just before Dad died. I would have gone weeks without seeing him, because of work and every-thing else. But two nights before he died, we went out shopping, And I don't know why, but for some reason, instead of coming home I said, "Let's pop in and see Mum and Dad". And so we did. That was the Friday night. And at the same time, my sister also decided to drop in, just by coincidence. I don't know why she decided to drop in.'

'So we spent that Friday night as a family. It wasn't planned. I remember distinctly that we had a family video— the home movie that we took—and we all sat around watching that. It was just amazing. I don't know why, but we all sat around in the room watching that video. And I remember dis-tinctly that I had just bought a huge warm coat. And it was pretty cold, and Dad said to me, "Oh, that's good that you've got that woollen coat. You need it, especially in your job. You need that woollen coat, and it's good that you're wearing it". And they were his last words to me as he said goodbye. So it really was an amazing night. It was a night that we all got together as a family, had a few laughs, a few jokes, and everything was great. It is a really fond memory to have, because that was the last time that I saw my father alive. That was just a terrific way of remembering him.'

'Dad died in the holiday house, near the beach. He loved going down there, fishing and all that. So, in a way, it was fitting that he died there, because to him that was peace.'

'When I was sixteen or seventeen, my aunty lost her child through cot death; he was eighteen months old. That was the first death in the family, and it was quite emotional, because we were all very attached to the baby in the family. It was a real shock. We used to visit the cemetery quite a lot soon after that, but then it dropped off a little bit. Then my grandmother—my father's mother—died. She came out after many, many years and lived the rest of her life here in Australia. You know, she'd got to an age where no one could look after her in Italy, so she came out and stayed with us—for probably ten years—and died a natural death at about 78. And then, after that, my grandfather died. But certainly, the death of my father was the most emotional. It was nothing like the other experiences.'

'I didn't actually see Dad when he died, but I saw him at the funeral parlour. It was terrific to see him then, dressed up and ready for his next adventure. We put his fishing rod in with him, and it was good to see him. To view the body was good.'

'The funeral service included a full requiem mass, which had to be done because—you know—it's just got to be done. But having said that, it still showed or brought home the fact that Dad had a lot of friends. The Italian way is that people come and visit you at the home, prior to the actual funeral, and give their condolences personally. The number of people that filtered in through those three days was unbelievable. That is just the Italian way, I suppose. It's just amazing to see how many people are actually prepared to do that. But then, they also come to the funeral. The numbers and just the support, it's just incredible. People you wouldn't expect just turn up. And it makes you feel that you do mean something to other people, and that's good. You know, a lot of those people came for Dad; but some even came just because they knew me—to show respect to me—and I thought that was just fantastic.'

'I think the funeral is very helpful. It helps you come to terms with it, because it's like final. It sort of ends the whole process from the time of death to the burial, and then you can sort of get back to your normal way of life. Obviously, weeks, months, or a year goes by, while you get back to normal; but at least it's a starting point. After Dad's funeral, we all went back to Mum's place—just the very close family—my family, aunties and uncles. We had a family dinner, and it was terrific just to sort of finish it that way. We finished it as a family, and then we've got on with our lives. It was a good experience.'

'We had our children at the funeral, so they saw the coffin being put into the mausoleum, and can now relate to their Nonno being there. It's not that he's in the ground; it's a different concept. They can still remember that Nonno was put in there. It wasn't as terrifying as seeing a coffin dropping into the ground, and then the dirt being thrown on top. That just seems cold. It just has a different feeling about it. The mausoleum seems cleaner and nicer.'

'I can honestly say there's probably not a day that goes past that I don't have a glancing thought of my father. Now, when he was alive, I don't think I ever really thought that much: not at all. I mean he was my father, and it was great, but I probably took him for granted. He was Dad and he was there, and that's it. But now, what it did to me was it really just focused—or brought it home—that I was now really the leader of the family. Being an Italian family, there's always a little bit more responsibility on the male, you know. I've got a sister; I haven't got any brothers, so I'm it.'

'For an Italian son who has just lost his Dad, there's a significant load of responsibilities. It doesn't mean that I'm going to take over the world, and all that. But what it meant—and I'd never thought of it before—was taking over that role. That thought only came to me once my father died. I realised that I was alone, in the sense that I am now the family, as far as the rest of the family is concerned.'

'There's only my mother, my sister, myself, and now my family; and that's it. And if there's a family decision to be made, or some consultation to do, it is now basically up to me. It is going to involve me a lot more than it did before—not that my father was overpowering. He was very easy to get along with, and certainly didn't impose his beliefs or feelings on anyone else. He never did that on me either, as his son.'

'It's interesting, that sort of concept, I suppose: not so much the physical actions of being head of the family, just the concept of being responsible. It's very strange, because I never thought of it before. It really did hit me; it really did. I often think about it. It's just strange how it sort of just happened.'

'There was initial grief, of course, and probably for a good six months after that, but I think I resolved it pretty quickly, just because of my own make up. I'm a very practical person: that's me. I'm pretty clear-cut, and I don't express emotion; I'm a bit reserved in that way. So I think I've resolved it in a short space of time, but the hurt never goes away; it's still there.'

'I suppose it made me focus on life a bit differently. You learn to appreciate what you've got in your family more than you did before. And also, you learn to appreciate others. I had a very close friend who lost his father about ten years ago, and I couldn't understand what he was going through. I couldn't work out why he was so affected by it. But I was younger then, and hadn't gone through the experience myself. Now, I totally relate to what he went through. I also appreciate the fact that he was younger at the time, and what he must have been going through was just unbelievable.'

'Ten years later, I had to go and get him aside and apologise to him for not caring as much, and not having understood. His father died of prostate cancer, and I didn't even go and visit his father in the hospital. To this day, I really feel a bit guilty about that. But I now think logically that I wasn't mature. But now I'd be totally different. So it has changed me. I think going through the experience definitely changes you.'

'The one most affected is Mum. She feels cheated, because they worked very hard, and I suppose they always believed that some day they'd sit back and enjoy it all. But that wasn't to be, so she feels cheated and alone, and that's where the difficulty is at the moment. My sister is pretty much like me, but a bit easier going. She certainly shows her emotional side more, so she probably showed her grief for a longer period than I did. But she's got her own family; she's got two kids. She's pretty much adjusted.'

'It's certainly Mum that's still—you know. When she was here the other night for my son's birthday—which happened in the same week of Dad's death—she just couldn't help herself by saying, "If Dad had been here it would've been all different". She's still hurting a lot. I think she's adjusting to a new way of life, but she can't help feeling that she's been cheated. If there's been any change in the family, it's brought us closer together. I think I probably see Mum more now. I certainly ring her more, because I'm conscious of her being alone.'

'My faith hasn't changed since Dad died. I don't think it's got any weaker, and I don't think it's got any stronger. It's the same. As a younger person, I used to go church every Sunday. I grew up going to Sunday school, and doing all that. Then I broke away. Some of the things the church gets up to, I don't really agree with. I still consider myself to be Roman Catholic, but I want to do it my own way. I don't think I need to go to church to be lectured and sermonised to have a faith. I think that faith comes from within, and as long as I live a good life in the sense of the way we were taught, I think that's basically all I need to do.'

'These days I only go to church at Christmas, Easter, christenings—and that's about it. I don't relate to the church. I think the church, to some extent, has lost the plot. I don't think they've changed with the times. We've got a parish priest here, who is only in the job because there's no one else to replace him. I don't think that's right. But that's just the way it is. So I think they've lost the plot there. I think religion, or the faith, comes from within. But having said that, my daughter goes to church and Sunday school every Sunday morning, because we still want to bring them up in the faith, and they need the teaching, and we can't give it to them. We'll give them the support, but we can't give the teaching.'

'I do believe there is a spirit. Now, quite where—what you'd call heaven, or what—I don't know. That I haven't really come to grips with. The faith teaches us that the Lord will come down and save everyone, and all this.'

'I believe there has to be something more to our existence than just our physical life here on earth. It just seems a waste if you die and that's it. The concept of that just doesn't seem right. I know we don't have the proof to say that there is this existence after death, but I just can't help feeling that there must be something spiritual. I don't know what form it takes. But perhaps the spirit lives on and somehow looks down, or protects, or guides those who want to be guided, and have that sort of mental telepathy. I don't know what you'd call it. I don't know if that exists, but I just feel it. Something inside me tells me that it does. I can't explain it as being heaven and hell, as in the Bible. I just feel that there is something that the spirit belongs to, or goes to.'

'I don't think that's the traditional Catholic view. It's not exactly as they say. I believe maybe part, or some of it, in a different concept; but it's probably essentially the same.

Obviously, a lot of what was written in the Bible was written to the uneducated masses and it had to be put in a way that everyone understood, so they created analogies. Maybe now, because we are a bit more educated, we see it in a different light; but essentially it means the same thing.'

'Dad wouldn't even go to the cemetery to see his own mother. But one day, three weeks before he died, he did. Why he stopped at the cemetery that day, no one knows. He saw the mausoleum and came home, and to Mum said, "We've got to buy one of these; they're fantastic. You should see it". He was quite adamant that that's the way he wanted to go. And you know, three weeks later: Bang! It's unbelievable.'

'But it is; the mausoleum is just so much better. It's terrible seeing a coffin dropping into the ground; it's just cold and final. The mausoleum is so much more acceptable. Yes, you've had a loss, but you don't feel like you've had such a loss in a way; because there's a concept or feeling that the person is still there.'

'With cremation you're just gone; there doesn't seem to be any emotion in it. The Italian way of crying and all this—and they carry on a little bit—is a way of letting it all out; it helps to cleanse. The Anglo-Saxon way of just being polite keeps the grief still going on. I don't think I could be cremated. I didn't want to go in the ground either; I wasn't sure. But now that I've seen the mausoleum, that's definitely it!'

'I think our friends would probably feel the same as us. I don't think they'd want to be cremated. I mean, we've never discussed it; it's just a sense. It's too final. We had a next-door neighbour here for many years, and her husband died in Sydney. Well, he was cremated and his ashes were scattered over Botany Bay. We couldn't believe that. We knew it was his wish, but she wasn't happy with it afterwards. She felt that there was nowhere she could relate to him after his death, to even take a flower. She was really sorry she did that. So that's why I think the cemetery is very important.'

'We've got other relatives in the concrete vaults. They're terrible because they fill with water. There's no way of stopping it. There is water in the ground and concrete is porous, so you're probably better off to go in the ground anyway. At least it drains away. That's terrible for a lot of Italian people; they have nightmares. That's why the mausoleum is just so much better. That's how they do it overseas. So for the people here who immigrated, it's just back to what they were used to. It's their traditional way of burying people. It's a more expensive option—but not really, if you take into account the amount that's spent on an actual grave and the monument—no: it's not an expensive option.'

'A typical monument on a vault might cost twelve or fifteen thousand dollars, and that's on top of the cost of the vault. I think Dad's crypt was $23 000 and about five or six thousand for the funeral. So it was close to $30 000 for the whole funeral. It's a lot if you think about it in money terms, but I suppose we would like to have the same done for us. We've both got life insurance. We should be covered.'

'Even if I don't drop in to the cemetery, every time I go past or drive anywhere near it, I just can't help but say, "Good day, Dad. How are you going? I hope you're well". The cemetery is a focal point, so it is very important. It is a very special place. I think it's something that should always be preserved. Really, it should be maintained forever and a day: definitely, because it is a history. In a way, it's a living history, because it shows history. Certainly in my lifetime it will have special meaning to me. I don't know about my children, because it's their grandfather and he died when they were very young. They might not have the same feeling as I do, but we're going to follow and then they possibly will. So I think it is a very important place.'

'I don't find the cemetery to be sad or depressing in any way. Just being there brings me closer to my father. It's a focal point that just brings it all together, and it's peaceful. There is a sense of peace there, certainly at the mausoleum. That's peaceful; it really is. It's not as dramatic as seeing the grave. It's just wonderful. I can't speak highly enough of it. It really is fantastic.'

'Straight after the funeral, I probably visited close to once a week, or at least every two weeks. Then after a month or two, it dropped off to once a month. Now, I just go on the anniversary, birthday, and spur of the moment visits, but probably still every one or two months.'

'I don't visit out of any religious obligation, purely out of a feeling that I should see Dad. I normally take one flower, because there's limited space. Sometimes I don't take any, but generally, I try to take one flower at least, if I can fit it in. I don't spend a lot of time there: probably no more than five minutes. I just want to be there and then go; that's all I need to do. My first reaction is to kiss the stone. I just look at Dad's photo and say a few words: that I miss him and I'm still thinking of him, and for him to look after us. I don't say any prayers or anything like that. I feel that's enough. And then, depending on my time, I sometimes do the rounds of the family. But that's more out of respect than anything else, if I've got time. There's my uncle, my grandfather, my grandmother, and my little nephew.'

'I've never done a long visit; I don't see the value in a long visit. Five minutes would be average, unless I meet someone and start talking, but that's not really to do with the visit. I've met, for example, a family that has lost a son, just across from Dad. They're there often, and I think it helps them—not me— but it probably helps them for me to talk to them.'

'I drive to the cemetery sometimes by myself, sometimes with the kids. The kids like coming, because they like their Nonno. But my wife doesn't like going to the cemetery. On Fathers Day, we all go. On his birthday, I would go. It just depends. Fathers Day would be the main day, and not so much his birthday and anniversary day. But sometimes, we just might go for no reason.'

'On Dad's anniversary, I went to the cemetery. I actually rang up to find out what time the gates opened, because I wanted to get there before I went to work. I got there about eight o'clock, but the mausoleum wasn't open yet. From the front of the building there, you can see Dad's plaque, and that was enough for me at the time. I mean, there's no room to put any more flowers. To me, it was just important to go. The fact that I couldn't walk the extra couple of feet didn't really worry me.'

'The important thing is that I saw Dad's photo and said a couple of words. I always tend to say, "Just look after us if you can, if that's the way it works. Look after the family, and make sure that everything goes well". It was important to go. When I left the cemetery, I rang Mum, just to make sure she was all right, because I knew she'd be sort of feeling it a bit.'

'These days, my visits have dropped off a little bit, but I would probably still visit every two months or so. It might be six weeks; it might be eight weeks. Sometimes, if I feel I haven't visited Dad for a while, I just get that urge to go; I can't explain it. And sometimes, when I'm feeling a little low, it helps.'

'I feel that he feels I'm there: that I'm showing respect. I feel that I've got that support: that shoulder—that he gives me strength. I can't explain that, but I feel invigorated a little bit, in the sense that I'm on the right track. I wouldn't have felt this with anyone else, like my grandparents. I would've gone to visit my grandparents just purely through respect. But with my father, it's a bit more. There is more emotion attached to the visit, because it's my father.'

'I think the change is just part of the grieving process. You feel that you need to go because your hurt is still there, but as you start to get your life back together, or back to normality, the pain eases off. I think it's just a natural thing.'

'When I first used to visit, I used to get very tense inside, and maybe draw a tear. Now, I go there and feel good about it. I feel a support that comes from going. It's amazing how it has changed. I think you accept it and make it part of your life: it's happened and you move on.'

'I think it's also got a lot to do with personality and the make up of a person, because my mother still gets very emotional when she goes. But she's the wife; it's a different grief experience. I've got a young family to be concerned about, whereas she's got nothing now. She's got no real responsibility to us; we are all self-sufficient. That's all she's got, whereas we've got other things.'

What Death Is

Leela was born in Sri Lanka 59 years ago. She has one brother and five sisters. She was a teacher by profession, has been married for 34 years, and has two adult children. Leela and her husband continue to observe their Buddhist traditions. 'We came to Australia sixteen years ago to complete my higher studies. My son was about thirteen at the time, and my daughter was seventeen.'

Leela completed her PhD in education at a Victorian university. 'My research was about education, employment and leadership in a colonisation scheme in Sri Lanka. I spent quite a bit of time there, so I maintained contact with my family, and I've been visiting every two years since. I also taught in Australia, but I gave up working last year.' Leela's husband was a policeman in Sri Lanka, and has now also retired after working more recently as a security officer.

'Sri Lanka is a small place compared to Australia. Actually, it's about half the size of Tasmania, but has the same population as Australia. The customs change; like the people who live in the crook of the mountains and those who live in the valley have different customs, though basically everything is the same. The cities are modern and the rural areas are more traditional.'

Leela's 87-year-old mother died just over three months ago, in Sri Lanka. 'She suffered a stroke and lasted for ten days afterwards. I was there for those ten days. I got the call in the morning—early morning—and by 10.30 that night I was there. I thought I was very fortunate to be in Australia, because if I were in any other country, I wouldn't have been able to go so soon. I was really glad.'

'My brother and sisters were all present at the hospital when she passed away. Before this stroke she had high blood pressure, but that's about all she had: no previous strokes or anything.

'My husband's mother died a long time ago. My father also died a long time ago, just before we came over to Australia. When one of my husband's brothers died, he didn't go to Sri Lanka, because he couldn't. I mean, if something happens like that, you can't go every time. It's getting so expensive.'

'When I got the news of my father, we were not living near them. My Dad was living away from me. He just passed away early in the morning. And when I got the message, it was similar to my mother's death in the sense that it happened, the way I got the message, and the time I reached my Dad's place to see him. Although I was overseas at the time of my mother's stroke, I went at very short notice. So we went to see her in hospital.'

'My father didn't suffer. It was just after being asleep in the early morning; and he was still smiling when I left there. But with my mother, she suffered. For ten days she was unconscious, and I saw her suffering. Maybe she didn't feel anything, but I felt it. That was the difference. It's all complex: very difficult to analyse why I feel different.'

'My mother's death actually showed me what death is. My Dad's death didn't have that much of an impact on me—maybe because he didn't suffer, or didn't show any pain or anything. Maybe he did at the last moment; I don't know. But with my mother, I just saw what death did. Now I know that I can go through anything. That's how I feel. I know I can go through any suffering, because she did. I could feel my mother suffer. Maybe it's because I'm a mother too, that I feel that way; I don't know.'

After her mother passed away, Leela stayed with her brother and sisters for about four weeks. 'I think it brought us closer together, but whether it will stay on like that I don't know, because mother was really the link. We still keep in touch. We talk all the time—no more or less—same as before.'

Leela's mother was cremated two days after her death. 'That's not really typical; it just depends. Sometimes, people keep the body for several days until people from overseas come over. It varies; there's no hard and fast rule. My brother and brothers-in-law are the people who contacted the funeral parlour, and they did everything. They took her straight from hospital to the funeral directors, and to the home and the cemetery.'

'Usually, we bring the body home after embalming; so the body was brought in the night. They dress the person in the order that we tell them to, and the body is brought to the house, in the lounge. There's a custom that there must be somebody near the body throughout the night. And we light a lamp throughout the night. We take turns to sit with the body; that's sort of customary in our country.'

'When the people come to see her, they all come; that's fairly customary. On the day of the funeral, the Buddhist priests come, and then there are certain rituals they perform. We offer some cloth to the priests. That is just a symbol to say that you're offering something on behalf of the deceased. And then the priests chant, you know; and then we transfer merit.'

'There's a custom to transfer merit to the deceased person. We just pour some water from a teapot into a cup until the cup spills over. This means—when spirits are awakening—that the merit has gone over to the deceased. It's very symbolic. That's done in the house after the coffin is closed. The coffin is closed and the priests chant. And all this happens before they take the body out of the house.'

'Some people do it outside the house; yes. Normally, it's done in the garden—they do all these rituals there. But we did it inside the house. We leave the doors and windows open in the night, because of incense. That's just to keep the air fresh, you know; there is no spiritual meaning other than to keep the air fresh.'

'We take the body in the coffin to the cemetery and we all walk along just behind the hearse. Then at the cemetery, the coffin is opened, because there may be people just coming into the cemetery to pay their last respects. So the coffin is opened again for those people to pay their respects. It's opened for some time. And then after it is closed, the family and close relatives all take the coffin and then go around the cremator three times. We go around with the coffin, and then finally it goes in. It is actually traditional that we would be cremated in a funeral pyre. We would construct a structure in the cemetery. But nowadays, it's done in a building, but we still take the coffin around it.'

'Traditionally, we construct a pyre; and that's still done in rural areas. For example, my Dad died in his ancestral home in the village, and because the garden was huge, we cremated him inside the garden itself. We made a special pyre, and we piled up wood and covered that, so that was traditional. And then we all looked out the window. The nephew lights up the pyre and approaches it walking backwards. But now it's done more in a crematorium.'

'The funeral pyre is usually in the cemetery. But if you have a large property, then you can do it in any part of your property, as long as all the family members agree. My Dad's funeral was on the property just alongside the house. We really wanted that to happen, because it was my Dad's house—my Dad's, Dad's property. It was very ancestral. The cemetery was close by, but we agreed with my mother to have the pyre alongside the house.'

'Actually, if my mother passed away in her traditional ancestral home, we'd have done the same thing, you know. But she was staying with my sister in the city: in the suburbs. She was looking after her, so the home was there. Everybody was saying, "Why don't you take the body to the village?" But we never did. And mother hadn't made any request either, so it was convenient.'

'The funeral ritual gives you a feeling that you have done whatever is required on behalf of the deceased: that you have transferred merit. You feel that the funeral gives the satisfaction of having done everything possible for the deceased.'

'After the cremation, we have an almsgiving to the priests in the temple. The almsgiving is part of the ritual. Before the cremation we give cloth. After the cremation we give food to the priests and the laity, and we transfer merit to the deceased. Then, after seven days, we also prepare the almsgiving. We invite the priest home and provide him with food. That's how we communicate: by giving alms. And after giving, we transfer merit. We think of our mother and think we transfer merit, because we are doing good. We always say—not a prayer really, but we just make a statement—"May this good pass over to my mother".'

'As soon as a person dies in the family, we don't cook. We shan't cook in that house until the body has been cremated. And we have a lot of friends who would do that here. I mean, here you can practise that if you wish: not like in Sri Lanka where you have to. Even here, the priest goes to the cremato- rium—to the chapel—and the priest does the ceremony in there. The only thing is it's more formal like. But it's the same thing.'

'We have been to a couple of Buddhist funerals here. Once, we only went to the house; we didn't go to the cemetery. But we did to a couple of funerals. It is quite different to funerals at home. Here, you have to go to the undertaker's to see the body, and you don't see what is happening. They don't cremate then and there. They just put the coffin down and cremate it later. You're not there when they light it up. In the urban areas, we're the same now. But we have a custom that the lighting of the pyre is by the son-in-law, or a nephew who lights the fire.'

'I have changed a bit. Any time I think of my mother, you know, it's a very difficult experience; but I'm coping. I think I've become more mature in the way I look at life. I'm sort of ready to accept suffering, and other people's sufferings too. You become much more mature as a person. My mother's death had a real impact on me I think. I feel both more frail and also stronger at times.'

'I think I have a deeper understanding of my religion after my mother's death. In Buddhism, we believe that everything is impermanent: nothing stays the same. I think that my mother's death showed me that. I've always been a believer in the Buddhist doctrine. I mean, the philosophy, or way of life, of Buddhism is very peaceful; and she was a Buddhist. I can't say my belief strengthened; it just remains with me, you know.'

'According to our beliefs, we don't believe there's a soul. We believe in rebirth, and that's why we transfer merit. We think that the person will be reborn, and at least they can gather that merit; because we believe that people are reborn according to the good that they have done. We believe that if you have done bad, or demerit, then you will be born in a place where you can't make use of that merit. But we don't know wherever they are reborn. So anyway, we do the transfer of some merit with the cup. So maybe they benefit: you don't know.'

'I believe that my mother is now in a good place, because I believe that she has done good to deserve a good birth. But I don't know just where she is now. I believe that she has been reborn as a human being. I mean, heaven and hell are both on this earth really. But there may be other worlds. We believe that there are other places, and she would be in the most heavenly place. So I feel my mother must be somewhere in a better place, you know. That's what I believe in.'

'I'm just reflecting and giving merit all the time, because that's our ritual. As a Buddhist, your next life depends on your karma. If you've done good, you will be reborn as a good person. If you have done bad, you might be born as a cripple. But it doesn't mean that that person should be treated any differently. If he does good and merit is transferred, then he can be a normal person. So that's what we do. It's not only for us; we can also transfer merit to a person who's in need of it. But some person might be born in a place where they can't gather merit. For example, as an animal in the animal world you can't gather merit; you have to be born as a human being.'

'I think the way that Buddhists accept death is more due to a religious factor than customs. The priests do some preaching and we soothe our minds, you know. I did feel a great sense of loss with the death of my mother; I still feel it all the time. I've lost my mother, and she's never going to come back. But I reflect on the good things she had done and what I have done to give her merit.'

'We do whatever we could to make her future lives happy. We always feel that if we do something good now, it's because of our Mum; and that gives comfort. Whatever we do, we transfer all the merit to her. It's also a case of keeping her memory alive. And also, we believe what we do is important to our children. What we do to our parents, our children are willing to follow. And they learn to appreciate, and feel gratitude, and send some gratitude to us.'

'In Buddhism, we keep changing all our lives. When you go out, you're not the same person that you were when you came in. Life changes. So we hope our children take note of that, and will grow up with that. We go to sleep firmly believing that if we do good, no harm will come upon ourselves and our children also. What we sow, we reap. Whatever we do to our parents, our children will do to us.'

'We believe that once a person dies, there's nothing there: just ashes. It's just like a piece of bread, you know. There's no soul. Rebirth does not necessarily occur immediately after the death. It could happen much later, you know. There's no specific time. There could be a bit of a spirit, but it's just waiting for rebirth.'

'After a cremation, we collect the ashes and we normally put them into a river. It has to be into flowing water. That's what we did with my mother. Usually, family members get together and do this sometime after the cremation.'

'At the cemetery, there are burials as well as cremations. Some Buddhists are buried and some are cremated. I don't know which ones are buried. I'm not sure of the custom of burial. In our area, the customs are different from other areas. The families from other areas are buried. When a younger person dies, he is usually buried. Younger people tend to be buried, and older people tend to be cremated in accordance with customary traditions, but not everywhere. In some parts of the island, our custom is not there.'

Leela's mother has no specific memorial. 'You can have a memorial if you want. There's no hard and fast rule. It's just an option, you know. But we don't focus on material things, you see. We might just plant a tree. For example, where my Dad was cremated, we just planted a flowering tree where the funeral pyre was lit. Now that tree blooms.'

The Worst Loss

Marion was born in Melbourne 47 years ago. She was the youngest of six children, five of whom were girls. She has not been employed since she was seventeen. 'I was a bookbinder, but I had to leave my job to look after my Mum, because she got sick.'

'Mum raised six children, and most of her grandchildren. Dad was retired. He was a storeman. He worked at a flourmill for 22 years, then he went to a furniture place and was a storeman there until he retired nineteen years ago. None of us ever got on well with Dad, because he was strict. When he used to drink—when we were all younger—he used to belt Mum, and belt us kids. But he mellowed out when he got older.'

'I like the Catholic faith. My Mum was Catholic. My Dad was a Salvo. We didn't go to church, us kids. Dad didn't allow that. So we weren't christened or anything either. I've never been a real churchgoer. I told my Dad I wanted to become a Catholic and he went off his head. You should've heard him: "Roman Catholics—you know I hate them". I said, "Mum was a Catholic, and my sisters all married Catholics. I'm the only one that didn't". He said, "I bloody well hate them". When she got married to him, Dad wouldn't let Mum go to church either.'

Marion has been married to Gerry for nine years now. She has four children and four grandchildren. Gerry fathered her first child 24 years ago.'

'Then we split up. Then I married another guy, and had three children to him. Then we split up. And I got back with Gerry, and then we got married. So our relationship's been 26 years, but we've been married for nine years. Gerry is a machine operator; he doesn't have any other children, only mine.'

Marion's father died five months ago, and her mother, nine months before that. 'Mum was 77. She died five days after her birthday. Dad was also 77 when he died.'

'Mum had dementia, and my father helped prepare me, telling me—you know. She died of a stroke, in the end. She often got worse, and then she'd come good. We always thought she'd get better, you know. The Friday night she died, she didn't get better; she just died. It took a lot of weight off my shoulders, because I was over there nearly every day, you know. It was a relief that she wasn't suffering any more.'

'Eight years Mum had dementia. Over that period of time, it was difficult to communicate and all. I stayed close, you know. I used to have them here. I used to shower her, and—you know. When nurses never came, I'd feed her. I'd do everything. None of my other sisters would do it, because—"We're not touching her"—as if she had germs or something.'

'After Mum died, I got closer with Dad. Yeah: my Dad and I. I was growing close to Dad while Mum was still alive. We were spending every day together, you know. It's a bit hard to sit there and ignore him. No; I'd make his lunch, make his tea, bring his washing home, wash it. I'd do it all from home.'

'Dad died earlier this year from pneumonia and prostate cancer. He'd been ill with the prostate cancer for seven months. The pneumonia just set in. He was in a nursing home and we weren't expecting his death at all. It was quite a shock. Yeah; it was worse than Mother's. I had him home here on Tuesday for lunch and he was happy. I took him back to the nursing home, and he said, "See yah later". I took him inside and I came home.'

'I used to go and see him every day. Then Thursday, he told me he didn't feel too good. So I told the nurse and she got the doctor, and he said, "Oh, he's all right. His prostate's playing up a bit on him, you know". I said, "Yeah, all right". But Friday, about ten to two in the morning, they rang me up and said, "You'd better come down here; your father ain't too good". He died 12.30 that afternoon.'

'With my mother, I hardly cried. At least, not as often as what I did with my father, you know. Because I knew Mum was sick for a long time. And then they said my Dad needed 24-hour care, because I couldn't look after him. I used to go and see him all the time. But it was worse with Dad, you know. I never cried like I did with my Dad. The worst loss was my Dad—yeah. Because he lived here until he went to the nursing home.'

'My grandfather died when I was eleven. He had cancer. I still remember. It was on a Monday—one o'clock in the after-noon—when I saw the undertakers come and take him. I didn't really understand it at the time. But it was different with my mother's death, because she was very sick for eight years.'

Between the deaths of her parents, Marion also experienced two other significant bereavements. 'My children's other grandmother had emphysema, and she choked and died. And my brother-in-law, he died earlier this year. He had lung cancer. He was 53. I was close to my brother-in-law. I used to mind his kids for him and my sister. But she's gone funny, you know. She won the lottery, and doesn't want to talk to us or nothing. And then he died. I didn't go to his funeral or nothing, because I wasn't talking to my sister, and thought I'd better stay away. You know, not cause any problem.'

'The others all live in town, but I don't see them. I don't get on with any of my family. They were all greedy, you know. They try to outdo each other. If one got a new house, the other one had to buy a new house, you know. I couldn't be bothered with that kind of people. You know what I mean? Where you buy a new car, they try and buy one better, to outdo you. That's not my style. You know what I mean? My father never saw none of them after my mother died: not once.'

'Mum's funeral was a requiem mass at the Holy Rosary Church, and then she went to the cemetery. I made the funeral arrangements, and Dad went. Dad and I had it pre-arranged. He thought that him and Mum were getting buried together at the lawn cemetery. When he started to make the arrangements, I said, "No, Dad". He goes: "What? Beg your pardon?" I said, "No. Mum's wishes are that she goes from the house to the Holy Rosary to the cemetery". He said, "Right then". So we did that. Mum's buried: Dad's cremated. Half his ashes are there: half his ashes are here. We made both of the arrangements the same day—prepaid.'

'I said a eulogy for her, and said one for my father. I think we did the right thing. We sent her off the right way. With Mum, the coffin was open the night before, you know. And I went to see her with my husband and the kids. I couldn't see her by myself, because my sisters kept pushing in all the time.'

'With Dad, it was straight to the crematorium. We met there. We had a service at the crematorium chapel: a very short service. It was different to Mum's. It wasn't as long; it's very quick. Mum had rosary the night before, and then she had the church service. Yeah; Mum's was better. But that's not what he wanted. So they each had what they wanted. His ashes have been divided, and half of the ashes are with my Mum: in the grave with Mum. The other half are here at home. None of my sisters were interested in the ashes.'

'My mother-in-law went from home, you know. She went from her backyard, where she'd sit all the time and have coffee with me. They had her service out in the backyard, and then from there to the cemetery. That was nice, yes: simple but nice. They didn't have another service at the cemetery: just had a service at the house. The whole three of them had that: the mother-in-law, the father-in-law, and their daughter fifteen years ago: she had the same. I don't know about my brother-in-law; I didn't go to that. I think he just went from the funeral parlour to the crematorium.'

'I believe there's a God. When my Dad was sick at the hospital that day, I kept telling him to let go. "Let go and go with Mum. Mum's waiting for you." And then in the afternoon he said to me, "Your mother's here. She's got angel wings on". I said, "Yeah; I can see her". He said, "And God's waiting to take her". I said I could see them.'

'It blasted the hell out of me, you know. I couldn't see them, but he could see them. You know what I mean? He must have been going, you know. I said, "Yeah, yeah; I can see it". "No, no; you can't: no". He was telling me to help him find the sky. And I didn't know what he was talking about. "I can't find the sky. Help me find the sky". "What do you want the sky for?" I never knew he was dying. I thought he'd get over that pneumonia.'

'I don't know where my Mum is now: hopefully with her own parents and brother. Where she wanted to be, I hope: up above. I hope she's happy. I just hope where she is she is happy, you know. I don't know about an afterlife. Does anyone know? I guess it's the same with Dad. I think my sisters would rather him be in hell. They didn't even want him in the cemetery with Mum. They tried to get a court order to get him removed. I get short fused and I bite. Just let them try! I don't take nothing from them. Know what I mean?'

Marion says she has developed an interest in embalming since her parents died. 'I just felt like doing an embalming course. I know where the college is, but I have to work two weeks at an undertaker's place first. So I rang up the undertaker who did my mother and father, and they said they'd be willing to give me two weeks there. Some people think that's a bit morbid, you know. But I'd like to help the grieving families and explain to them what I went through. Oh, I hope it could be helpful to other people one day. It might, and it might not. I don't know. I'm not ready for that yet. I'm not going to do the course until next year; after that I should be ready.'

Marion's parents are interred in a family grave in an old monumental section of a suburban cemetery. 'The grave's been there for over sixty years. My grandfather got put in there, and then Mum's Mum when she died, and then Mum last year. So we had it all done up: the marble headstone and all polished, and a picture and all put on there.'

'It gets easier to visit. It's just time, you know. I've been a lot better since I've been seeing a counsellor. He's helped me a real lot, you know. Yeah, I laugh and joke. I'm not morbid all the time. I was worse than what I am now before I went and saw him, you know. He helped me a lot. I just talk about the family, talk about my sisters, you know—what they were like, and how my mother and father were. We'd have a walk around the cemetery, and he'd come to my parents' grave, you know. It was good to sit down and talk.'

'It's really important to me to go to my mother and my father's grave and talk to them. You know: sit there, clean the grave, put fresh flowers there and talk. I spend a couple of hours there, and then go home. There are a few other people— a brother who's dead—that I visit.'

'I'm at ease when I'm at the cemetery; it's a peaceful place. I feel close to my mother and father, and I feel sad because they're not with me any more. I hate to leave there.'

'I visit Mum and Dad's grave every Monday, Wednesday, Friday, and on the weekend, every week. I used to go three times with Dad to visit Mum, and I just kept the tradition going; that's continued through. We used to go three times a week to make sure there was fresh flowers.'

'I just brush the stones back, you know. I keep them all together, and take the vases out and clean them with a rag, put them back and do the headstone. When Dad and I used to go and visit there, I'd put the flowers there and clean the grave.

Then he'd say, "Oh, you can go off there to the mausoleum to have a look while I talk to your mother". So I just left him there, you know, for about fifteen or twenty minutes, and came back and got him.'

'I spend a couple of hours there every time. If some of the flowers are dead, I replace them. I always take more flowers when I go. I don't pray; I just sit and talk to them. I talk to them as a couple, just about life, and how the others are carrying on, you know: about his will and everything. I said, "You're not going to get your last wish, because they're fighting over the will, you know". He left everything to me. Now they're fighting about it. I said, "You're not going to get your last wish". Most of the time I'm there I'm just talking to them.'

'They just wanted to visit Mum without Dad being there. Well, they don't go any more. I can tell if they've been. I'll go three times a week, and I'll go on the weekend. I know what flowers I put there.'

'On a Sunday, my daughter comes: she's seventeen. We leave the car at the kiosk, and we walk down to the grave. You might think we're a bit morbid, but she likes to visit the children's section too, on the way down. And if there's no flowers on one, she'll take some from what we've got, and she'll put it there: yes. "Poor thing: they've got no flowers". The other visits, I'm on my own.'

'I'll keep going. I promised my father I'd keep going for him. It is a bit easier to visit the cemetery now than what it was: not a whole lot easier, but it has got a little bit easier along the way.'

Not a Tear Shed

Peter grew up just north of the Murray River where he was born 54 years ago. He has four brothers and two sisters. During his childhood, Peter's father was a 'practising alcoholic'. 'He gave us a pretty rough time: especially Mum, but also my brothers and sisters and myself. I grew up hating him.'

'After I left home, I began drifting early. My Dad got into Alcoholics Anonymous, and I was getting into trouble. I got down to the Big House, you know. At the age of seventeen, I was introduced to Alcoholics Anonymous, but it wasn't for me. Dad stuck in AA and I continued on. And all my life was drinking and drifting in and out of jobs—just any sort of job—and in and out of jails. Then fifteen years ago, I went to jail for an armed robbery I did on April Fool's Day, and that was my last drink. It was in jail that I got into Alcoholics Anonymous. And when I come out, my Dad and I became pretty good mates. We weren't the ideal father and son; we were just good mates.'

'Alcohol's been in our family all along. Out of five brothers and two sisters, only one brother and one sister are not affected by alcohol. The others are alcohol- and drug-riddled. So it's been a bit of a journey, you know. Today, I'm on a pension, because I had a tumour operation eleven years ago, and I've got no hormones. The tumour could have sent me blind, so they operated on that. But I couldn't hold a job, because I had no energy. So they had to put me on a pension. And after ten years,

I thought I was over it. But last year they discovered I had another one. So I just had another operation a few months ago, and I've got to keep going back to the hospital for another ten years.'

'I'm divorced. I've got two kids: a boy and a girl. But I never see the boy. He lives with his mum, as far as I know. The girl turns 27, next birthday. She was born disabled: with cerebral palsy. Friends who knew me from a kid reared her, because I walked out on the missus years ago. My son is about two years younger, I think. I walked out not long after he was born.'

'I got married in a drunken stupor. I met her in a hotel. It was a bloody rough joint. We got married in the registry office. We lived together for about five years, I think. And then I found out she was pregnant. That's why I did the right thing and I married her. Then the day after we got married, we went back to the hotel, and I didn't see her for a week. I just went on a bloody binge, and I didn't know where I was. That was what I was like in my younger days.'

'I see my daughter pretty often. We go out, and we've got a pretty close relationship. She lives with people, but they're getting on, you know. Well, I couldn't give her what they've given her, you know. She's been around the world and been everywhere. She's got a wonderful life, you know. I get a lot of strength from her. They amaze me, these people in the wheelchairs and everything, they always seem so bloody happy: it's unreal. I can bloody get around OK, and the little things upset me, you know: just the bloody little things.'

'I saw the boy after I came out of jail. He would have been about sixteen or seventeen then. He was in hospital with some infectious disease—herpes or some bloody thing—and I went and saw him. I sent a photo of myself to these people who have got my daughter, and they had handed one on to him. When I walked in, I introduced myself and I said, "Do you know who I am?" And he said, "Yeah; I got a photo not long back".'

'He had this huge tape recorder thing, and it was blaring in the hospital. And I said, "Don't you reckon you ought to turn that down, and think of the other patients and the nurses?" "Oh, f— them", he said. And I couldn't turn around and say, "Well, hey: listen. You'd better knock that off". Because who am I?'

'We had a bit of a yarn, and I said, "Well, you'll be here tomorrow?" And he said, "Yeah". And I said, "Would you like me to come out again tomorrow?" Well, he said, "Oh, you know". I said, "Well, if I don't see you, you know how to get in contact with me if you ever want me".'

'I went back the next day, but he'd gone home. And he never, ever got in contact with me. So I just didn't push the issue. You know, he was still a minor at the time. But I don't believe in pushing myself into his life, you know. You don't do that.'

'I believe there is a God, and I have got a God. I was brought up as a Catholic, but I don't go to church, because I don't believe in religion. Man made religion. And whatever man makes, I reckon he stuffs up anyway. But I have got a God of my understanding, which is Jesus, who made this great heaven and earth. That's my belief. I've got great faith in that, you know.'

'I used to travel all around Australia, before I met my girl-friend and before I got sick again. And I didn't know nothing about cars, or anything like that. I had a beaten up old HQ. And all I knew about cars is that you put petrol in them, and keep up the oil and water, and pump up the tyres, you know. People used to say, "You're mad. What happens if you break down?" I said, "So what?" I said, "Somebody will come along and help me"—which they did.'

'I busted down in the bloody Nullarbor, and I didn't know what was wrong with my car. It just so happened that down the road a little was a road construction gang, and I got talking to the boss. He sent his mechanic back and the mechanic said to me, "Well, it's too crook. Your alternator's stuffed". And I said, "Well, what does that mean?" He said, "That means you can't go nowhere". I thought: "God!" He said, "It just so happens a bloke working on the road construction gang has a HQ with a busted gearbox. For a few dollars, we could swap alternators over, and you're on your way". You know, my higher power looks after me. He's pretty good.'

'Everybody's always been close to God, because God's never lost, you know. Some people say, "I've got to find Him". Well he's never been lost anyway. It's always within you. You know, they say you hand over the reins. Like in AA, we hand our will over to a God of our understanding, you know. And sometimes we take it back.'

'I have a strong faith in God, but the only time I'll go to church or anything is to a funeral or a wedding, because I believe you can pray anywhere you like, and that's fair. I've never liked church, but I've always believed in God. I've never believed in church, because there are priests and God-knows-what making up all sorts of funny little things. I went to a convent at one stage, when I was a little nipper and Mum was having twins in town. And those nuns there were—oh; they were sadists. They were sadists at the time. You know, they'd whack us so much. I reckon they took their frustration out on the kids. Oh, I don't want any of that.'

'Mum always had a sense of humour; she could see the funny side of anything. She was that way. And maybe she got that way by living with Dad all them years when he was on the booze. It was her way of coping. And I inherited that bit of a sense of humour, you know, because I always try and laugh my way through bloody life. Life's too short, you know. Even when I got the eight years with a five-year minimum, the old man said, "You don't look worried". I said, "What's the good of worrying about it? Hell, I've got that; now I'll kick on and just do it". I appealed and had it reduced to six years with a four year minimum, but I copped it on the chin.'

'Well it saved my life, you know. If they hadn't got me when they did—well! I was mad. I was right around the twist, you know. I would've gone on and shot somebody. Coppers were my biggest enemy. Anybody with authority was my enemy. But today, I've turned it all around. I haven't got a single enemy, you know, because it all reflects back on me.'

Ten months ago, Peter's father died at the age of 79.

'About six years ago, he had surgery to remove a cancer. They said they got it all. But they never get cancer. When you've got a cancer, you've always got it. It erupted again, and it wasn't long before he was put in hospital. He only lived there for about two months.'

'I saw him a week before he died, and then the day before he died. I didn't recognise him. You know, I felt like snuffing him out myself, there and then. It's a shocking way to go. All within a week, he just wasted to nothing. He was on bloody morphine, and they couldn't even find any meat or anything to inject, so they had to spray it in his mouth. That's how skinny he was. I mean, he looked like a prisoner of war.'

'When I went in the second time, he couldn't talk; he was sedated. This was a day or two before he died. I took a photo of him. I've got a couple of photos of him: what he was like before and what he was like then. I just said, "Goodbye Dad". And that was it. I was praying for him to go as quickly as possible, because it's shocking. You know, he was a great believer in that euthanasia, and so am I.'

'I was going to send that photo to every bloody politician in Australia and say, "Well, do you want one of your family to go out like this, in pain and Christ-knows-what?" I'd put it to them. That's one thing I didn't want to see: him go out in all that bloody pain. It was just shocking, you know.'

'I felt sorry for him, but I didn't shed a tear at all, because he still gave Mum a hard time even though he'd been sober. He was all self. As I said to my sister once, "He never sobered up; all he did was put down the booze". He didn't live a life of sobriety: one of caring about other people. It was all just: "Me, Me, Me". Even in his will, he had said that he was a widower, and he wasn't. After Mum died, he remarried within three months and picked up a drink, and then it was all his new wife's fault. He caused havoc there. She had to sell the home and get out, and he finished up living with another lady. And now the will's all topsy-turvy. They don't know what's going on. Even though he's six-foot under, he's still causing trouble.'

'I was always close to Mum, but she died eight years ago. I miss her a lot, you know. I can always remember Mum, when her Mum died. She went out to the sleep-out, had a good cry for something like an hour, and then she came back in and was OK. That was over and done with then, and she just got on with life. Mum was like that. And when she passed away—we buried her up by the river and I came back to Melbourne—I was much the same, you know. I went home by myself and I had a good long think about Mum, shed a few tears, and then I got on with life; because I remembered what she said, even though I greatly miss her.'

'I miss my Mum. She had three strokes. The third one killed her. I was working at the time, at the last job I had. As soon as my brother told me she had another stroke, I took off up home with an ex-fiancé. When I was about twenty minutes out of town, I looked across as I was driving, and I said: "She's gone!" And when I got to the hospital, I found out my Mum had died. I asked what time, and it was just about to the second that I had that feeling that she was gone. But after making a few inquiries, it was a blessing that she did go then, because if she had survived her third stroke, she would've only been a vegetable. Mum wouldn't have wanted that.'

'But after Mum died, Dad picked up another drink, and that hurt me a lot. Even though he'd been sober all those years, he was still a mean man. I mean, everything had to revolve around him, you know. If it wasn't going his way, then that was it! Even a week before he died of cancer, when I went in to see him and to say hello from a friend, the old man said to me, "Why don't you and that so-and-so get out of AA and get yourselves a bloody life?" But that's typical of alcoholics. He was as mean as mean. Right up to the last, he was still mean.'

Peter's father was buried at the local bush cemetery, and the funeral did not mean anything special to Peter. 'I think it was just a relief that Dad moved on. I think that's how it was with the whole family, you know. One brother didn't even turn up. As I said before, there wasn't one tear. Most people who went there, in my mind, were just making sure that he was going down, you know. I went along because, you know, it was the thing to do. There was quite a good turnout at his funeral. But you know, there wasn't a tear shed, because everybody knew him. He was just a mean man.'

'It wasn't important to say goodbye to him. I think I said my goodbye the last time I saw him in the hospital. You know, I really wish –. I nearly put a bloody pillow over his head in the hospital. It was just shocking to see a person like that. You know, they'd put an animal down that was suffering that much.'

'He had a pretty good turn up, but not as big as Mum's. Quite a few AA members came along. I think it was just the thing to do up there, you know. It's a small community, and everybody knows everybody else. It might have been a day's outing, or a day to get on the booze at the local pub where they held a reception. And there's always a fight or something afterwards. But I got out early, because I don't drink.'

'I am not sure where my Dad is now. Mum would be in heaven, because she was an angel. But I wouldn't have a clue about the old man; I don't know. He might need me. He might be still drifting. I saw a movie once about a ghost or something, and the guy couldn't leave because he knew he'd been wrongly done by, or something like that. So I don't know. He could be drifting. I wouldn't have a clue. The only thing I'd know for sure, is my Mum's in heaven with my grandparents.'

'The funny thing was, we buried a big mate of mine the day before we buried my Dad. And I felt a hell of a lot of loss cracking me more than I did for Dad, you know. It was funny that. They buried him on top of Mum. One of my brothers said, "I'll go down and dig him up if they put him there".'

'The old man was just terrible, you know. I was having very bad dreams about him after he died. Oh, bloody nightmares they were. I used to have nightmares as a kid. It was always this bloody wolf going to get me. When I got sober I saw a lady who looked into the dreams, and she told me that the wolf was my old man. Then after he died, I started to have the nightmares again about him. I wanted to kill him. And this brother who hated him intensely was going to dig him up. My brother and me ended up fighting. It was just bloody madness.'

Peter considers it was a relief for everybody in the district when his father died. 'When Mum died, we were at the funeral, and his own sister said to my sister, "We're putting the wrong one down here. It should be him".'

'Cemeteries are one of the safest things of all time. I don't mind cemeteries. I like looking at a lot of older graves. I know Mum's soul is not there, but that's where they put her body. I just go in there to say hello: that's all.'

'I would've still been drinking when my grandparents died. I remember once, I called in to see Pop's grave, and I was drinking a bottle. Anyway, I tipped the stubby upside down on his grave. Everybody reckons it was a hell of a joke. You know, Pop would've liked that.'

'The cemetery is a very, very sacred place. It riles me when I hear or read about vandalism in cemeteries, and things like that. That's bad; it is really bad. And when after a certain amount of time they can shift cemeteries—like Vic Market, I think, was built on top of an old cemetery—that's wrong. I wouldn't like anybody going out and ploughing the cemetery up where most of my relations are.'

'I remember years ago, as a kid, when big floodwaters were coming up, and we were filling sandbags. A dark bloke came along, and he said, "You can't dig there. My ancestors are buried there". And we kept digging. And sure enough, there were skulls and bones, and God knows what. At the time, I didn't think anything of it. I took home a couple of skulls, and cleaned them out and had them sitting in my room. But I know today that was the wrong thing to do: a shocking thing to do! We could've gone somewhere else and dug. But at the time, we saw nothing wrong with it. You wouldn't like to do it today. Jesus: you'd cause World War Three! I'll never forget it.'

On the few occasions that he has visited his mother's grave, Peter has been alone. 'I just sit down there and have a little bit of a yarn, and tell her what's going on in my life. I've taken some flowers along. It needs a little bit of grass picked out of the grave. I do that. I'm not a great one for praying, but I talk to Mum. I just tell her how things are going. I think she knows how things are going on anyway. You know, I think they look down and see how we're doing—along with my grandparents up there—but I let her know that I'm still going strong.'

'I don't get up there very often, but my sister visits regularly. She passes through there and says, "G'day, Nell". We all called Mum, 'Nell'. I'm not a great cemetery visitor. Every now and again, when I'm up near home, I'll go and see Mum's grave. My grandparents are buried in the same one, and my godmother is there too. I just call in there and spend a few moments remembering them, you know.'

'I don't have any desire to visit my Dad's grave, but I'll visit out of respect for Mum. They're in the same grave, unless my brother's got to it. But I haven't heard he's been out to dig him up. I'll probably pop in and say hello to Mum, and, "Hello, Dad. How are you doing, wherever you are?" And I'll say hello to the godmother, and grandmother and grandfather. I really miss them.'

'I believe I am where I'm meant to be, you know. And if

I were meant to be up at Mum's grave, well I'd be there. That's the way I look at it. It's not practical to visit very often, but I see Mum every day. I've got a big picture of her in the lounge room, and she's forever in my thoughts. When I'm talking to my sister up the bush, you know we're always having a joke about Nell: what Nell would do with this, or what Nell would do with that. So, she's never out of our thoughts. But if I'm there, and it's appropriate to pull in, then it's meant for me to go in. You need to be where you're at, I reckon.'

'I think she probably understands. But some people might not—like we're all different. Aren't we? Some people go there a hell of a lot. Others don't go at all. And some people just go now and then. We're all made up differently.'

'I haven't shed a tear when I've visited Mum's grave. I've felt the sense of loss, you know. But I've also been happy that I've been there and just told her how I've been kicking along. She wouldn't want me to be grieving all the time. She'd want me to be getting on with life. You know, life's meant to be enjoyed. Instead of going around moping, you have your moment of grief, and then you get on with it. I still miss Mum. I still miss her, for sure. I wish she were still alive today. But I know she's not, and that's it.'

'I was very happy that she saw my seven years of sobriety. She said that she didn't have to look up the law lists any more. She'd be happy if she saw my name there, because she'd know her little boy was in jail and he was getting fed three times a day. That's true. She felt I was safe when I was in jail. I know she'd be happy today that I'm still sober and just doing the right thing. I don't get into trouble today. It's as simple as that.'

Death of a Grandparent

Somewhere to Remember Him

Andrew was born in rural Victoria 25 years ago. He has four brothers and five sisters. 'We are a very close, very big family. We spend a lot of time together, and regularly have over a hundred people at family barbecues.' Andrew now lives with his fiancé in the same town where he is a partner with his father in a local agricultural machinery business.

His 85-year-old maternal grandfather died of heart failure just over a year ago. 'My grandfather lived in town with us, and I saw him about twice a week. They were always coming over for dinner, and we were always going there. He was a motor mechanic, and he helped me through buying cars and those sorts of experiences. Grandfather was pretty special to us. He was also a pretty independent sort of bloke. My grandmother is still alive.'

'In Holland, he was a motor mechanic. He was an ambulance driver during the Second World War. He also fought against the Germans, and was imprisoned for a while. After the war, they migrated to Australia and lived in various locations, and eventually started a motor mechanic business. He retired around the age of 65, and tripped around Australia from then on.'

'He had had a triple bypass. I think he'd had about sixteen attacks altogether, over a period of thirty years. After each incident he was relatively healthy and active, but in the last two weeks, we knew there was not much chance of him going on much longer. He was in hospital for the last three days, and had been in and out over the last couple of weeks. I was away and didn't see him for about a week and a half before his death. I arrived back in town on the train only a couple of hours after his death. So it was a bit disappointing at the time, but we'd certainly spent a lot of time together beforehand.'

'We'd been anticipating it for some time. He'd had a heart attack six months before his death, and I actually thought that he was going to die then. So I suppose it gave me a bit of time to think about it and spend more time with him. That did help: definitely. It wasn't as much a shock to the system as it would be getting that phone call to say that someone's died unexpectedly.'

'There was a requiem mass in the Catholic church. That didn't mean a great deal to me, personally. It meant a lot more to my family: my parents, and especially my grandmother. They are very well-practising Catholics. But it was great to have all the family together in the church. It's also a very peaceful place to sit and contemplate what's gone on, and to hear about his life from people outside the family. The church side was good, but not most important to me.'

'He was buried in the lawn cemetery. We had a viewing the night before, and that was quite interesting and a good opportunity to say goodbye. I spent some time there by myself. It's a pretty hard thing to do when you haven't experienced anything like that before. I think it's quite a difficult decision sometimes, to go to a viewing. But I found it worthwhile.'

'The weekend following the funeral, we all went and cleaned up his house, mowed his lawns, washed his car, and things like that. That was good for everyone, because that's something we'd been doing for some time. It was probably the best way to say goodbye.'

'I've still got two surviving grandparents: my grandmother on my mother's side, and also my grandfather on Dad's side.

Since his death, I've spent a lot more time with the two surviving grandparents learning about their history and just spending some time with them before the inevitable. We talk about their backgrounds; they're pretty interesting. My grandmother will be moving in with my parents soon. She's 83 and living on her own at the moment; it's a bit hard by herself. She also has to live on one pension instead of two, so we tend to help her out a little bit more now.'

'I'm not a churchgoing Catholic, so it hasn't had a major religious impact on me either. My beliefs haven't changed. His death was inevitable. It wasn't something that happened suddenly, and you lose faith. It was more just a passing of life: the end of a cycle, I think.'

'The church was good in its own way, but I don't see him at the cemetery, or anything like that. I see him more or less around town, still at eighty years old. That's more the way I see him, rather than what's left now. I obviously believe in the Christian faith—in that he's gone to heaven—but it doesn't mean a great deal to me at this point in my life. So I see him more in past events.'

'I'm not really sure where I see him, apart from in heaven under a couple of clouds. I haven't got enough faith in that. I just know that he's gone, and lived a great life, and still means a lot to us. I don't have any thoughts of what's happened now. I don't think that I expect to be reunited with him in the future, but I'm not a hundred per cent sure. Well, no one knows for sure. I don't have that sort of faith.'

'One of the most important things about the cemetery is that there's somewhere for the memorial, to remember him by. He's got his place in the ground, or his place in the world, so to speak. His name is always going to be written down and not forgotten, somewhere for the grandchildren and relatives, and people who didn't go to the funeral, to go and visit.'

'It's more important to my grandmother than to anyone else, but I don't think she sees it that way. She's only been out there a couple of times since he died, so that makes it less important to me, I suppose. But I think it's critical that we do remember where our deceased go, and that they do have memorials and plaques to remember them by.'

'We're creating a family heritage at the cemetery. We've actually reserved a fairly large family plot, because of the size of the family. And everyone's got wishes where they want to be buried. He's also surrounded by a lot of his old mates from town, which is a good thing. It definitely creates a heritage. It's got that name there for future generations to go back and look at. I see the cemetery more as a place of remembrance, rather than a sacred place. I also find it very interesting in historical value, more than it being sacred.'

'Within the cemetery, I definitely feel a sense of peace: just peaceful. It's a peaceful sort of quiet place. It's a very beautiful landscape actually: a very nice place to look at. In a certain way, there is a feeling of being close to my grandfather, because I know that he was buried there, but he's certainly not there in spirit. I don't feel at all emotional at the cemetery, apart from the actual burial, when the coffin went down. That was obviously an emotional event.'

'I've been to my grandfather's grave about four times since his burial, but only one of those occasions was by myself. The others were to show relatives who had come to town.'

'Personally, I don't need to go. When I did go by myself, it was about three months after his death. I was just driving past, and I thought it was a good time to go in and have a look at the headstone, which I hadn't seen. It was good to see that he's been memorialised in a nice way. I think I'll probably drop in every now and then, when I'm going past. But I wouldn't make a special trip out there, unless I had something on my mind related to him, which I think is quite unlikely. I've actually been to other funerals at the cemetery since he was buried, but I don't count those as visits. I did see his headstone though, just in passing.'

'On the occasion that I was driving past the cemetery and just decided to call in, I just wandered in and had a look around and just thought about his past. The place is immaculate, so I didn't need to do anything. I certainly wouldn't put flowers there. I don't think that's significant or necessary. I wouldn't have stayed more than five minutes at the most.'

'I think I probably will visit the cemetery every now and then, when I'm driving past and have some spare time or something. Certainly going out there the first time was good to see that everything had progressed the way it's meant to do: like the monument. But I don't think going there is significant in the grieving process, in the sense that some people do. I'd be more than happy to call in if my grandmother wanted to go there, and I'd spend some time there with her. But I wouldn't instigate that sort of thing.'

Family Linchpin

Natasha was born in Adelaide 35 years ago. She was one of three children. Her brother is two years older, and her sister six years younger, than herself. She is married with 'no kids, but one dog'.

'I don't have a religious faith. I did go to Sunday school when I was about five, but my memories of that are vague. I don't even remember what type of church it was. My parents sent us; they didn't take us. We never went to church as a family unit. My husband doesn't have a religion either, but his mother is very strongly Catholic. I think she still goes to church, but his father doesn't. He never went with her.'

'I never liked school: hated it in fact. I finished year eleven, but didn't go any further than that, because of other circumstances. Six months after I left school, I was asked to apply for a job in local government, and, in theory, I have that job today. The authority I now work for grew out of reorganization over the years.'

'I'm the middle child. Of the grandchildren, my brother was the apple of my grandmother's eye. He was the first grandchild and, as it turned out, the only grandson. So I always thought that I was second best, even within our little family unit. When I was five, my mother desperately wanted another child, and she couldn't have one. So my father relented and they adopted my sister. Well, because she was adopted, they gave her everything they thought she needed. That created a huge chasm, with my brother being the golden-haired boy. There wasn't any room left for me. And looking back, I think that's why my father and I had such a very close relationship. He knew that my brother was a bit of a mummy's boy, and a bit of a sook.'

'But I haven't seen or spoken to my Dad in twelve years now. We had a bit of a spat. I'm just like him: stubborn and very obnoxious. Yeah, I'm just like him.'

'The first time I recall my father leaving us, I was eight. Between then and when I left home at nineteen, they just took it in turns: regular. He went and came back, then she went and came back; and they'd patch it up. It was a very stressful time. It's sort of different with my mother, because I know I have never had a close relationship with her, because I always felt that I was the insignificant one. I think that's why I had a closer relationship with my father. My father and I fell out when I was 24 and I'm now 35; it's been a long time. I met my husband that same year, and he's never met my father.'

'My Mum has been remarried for almost three years now. She got married and moved on. I don't see an awful lot of her, which is a shame. I used to see a lot of her before Grandma died, but I don't now. It's quite ironic, because she lives closer to me now than she ever has, other than when I was still at home.'

Natasha's maternal grandmother died in Adelaide almost four years ago, at the age of 79. 'She lived a long way away— about 45 minute's drive—in a public housing trust house. They were the first people to live in that house. When she died, she had been there for forty-odd years.'

'When she was a younger woman, she worked in town at a large emporium and played basketball with the ladies team. You know, neck to knee uniforms: really weird. There are some lovely old black and white photos. They're really good. I enjoy looking through them.'

'Anyway, she met and married my grandfather Jack. Although, he wasn't the first person she was engaged to. She was actually engaged to another bloke, also called Jack. And then—the gallant gentleman that he was—he actually broke off their engagement, because he knew he was dying from TB. Until he did die, they remained firm friends and kept in contact. He died the same year that my mother was born, but he did get to see my Mum as a baby. Anyway, she got married and had two children: my mother and her younger brother. And from those two kids there were five grandchildren.'

'From the time I was a child, up until the age of about fifteen, we would see her often. Every Sunday we went down to Grandma's house for Sunday roast dinner. In her later life, we grew up, left home and established our own houses and partners. In the last six years, I probably saw her once a month.'

'She was quite ill for the last six years of her life, and my mother actually went to live with her to take care of her. She had very severe arthritis from the age of 53: very crippled hands, elbows, knees, hips, and her back. It was a real shame, because she got so frustrated. Her mind was as sharp as anything, but her body just wouldn't do what she wanted it to. I think that, in the end, she just couldn't stand it any more and gave up.'

'Grandma was definitely the linchpin in keeping the family together. She was the head of the house, and she ruled with an iron fist. What she said, we did. And we were happy to do that. Initially, between her death and the funeral, we were at each other. It was almost as if we were vying for that top position: who was the closest to her, who had the best memories and who had the best photographs.'

'When my Grandmother died, I was actually there in the room, as was my mother, my brother, and my husband. We knew she was very ill and that it was her last time in hospital. She had actually developed pneumonia, and my mother and her brother had decided that—well, this is it! They just wanted her to pass away quietly. They didn't want her revived and hanging on for days in pain. So they decided that if she was going to die, it was just to be.'

'I really don't cry a lot. I don't cry at movies, or puppy dogs, or little kids, or things like that. But actually seeing that –. It's really hard to try and describe the emotion I felt, unless you have actually experienced that yourself: knowing that she was going to die.'

'My brother was in the air force at the time. He still is. But he was based in Canberra then. And when she'd slipped into a coma, they let my mother know: "It could be any time now. It could be as quickly as today. It could be tomorrow: two days at best". So she was very anxious to get my brother there: he being the only grandson and the eldest of all the grandchildren. He had a very special relationship with my grandmother.'

'Anyway, he got special compassionate leave, and it was ironic that she hung on for four days. And they had told us, "We know it's awkward, but just keep talking to her. She can hear you". Apparently, your hearing is one of the last senses that goes when you're about to die. And you know, I found myself just sitting there talking to her, telling her that my brother was coming. And when he actually got there, he was only in the room with her half an hour and she died. No one will ever convince me that she did not hang on just to hear his voice. It was absolutely incredible.'

'We all sort of lost it then, but I was more OK. I was really sad that she had actually passed away, but I was more upset for my mother, because for the past six years she was caring daily for her mother. My parents had long been divorced, so I felt a little sorry for my own mother thinking her mother's just died, and she's on her own. OK, she's still got her children, but we're now adults and have moved on. I felt really sad. I almost felt that it was my responsibility to try and fill that void for her.'

'Grandma had been in hospital with several complications. She'd actually had pancreatitis, and she developed pneumonia after that. Everything just failed on her: the liver, and then the kidneys. Everything just started shutting down and turning off. At that stage, because she was so ill, and had been ill off-and-on for several years, and her arthritis, I think she just thought, "Well, I'm here now. I'm not going home any more". When she was very ill and slipped into the coma, we virtually had a 24-hour vigil until she died. Mum and I sat with her for hours on end.'

'When my Grandmother died, my husband and I were standing at the foot of the bed. It was a fairly small room and we could see her breathe. We actually saw that final moment. I remember my mother looking at me and saying, "Well that's it. That's it?" She was looking at me for an answer: "Is it, or not?" But we knew anyway. I remember just stepping back and looking around the room. I was waiting for something to happen. I didn't know what, but I thought as soon as I saw it, I'd know what I was waiting for.'

'You see, two years prior to that, my grandmother was very ill in intensive care, and my husband and I went to see her. She didn't recognise my hubby at all, and she absolutely insisted that I was my mother. Well, she was facing the window and suddenly sat bolt upright. I said, "Oh, my God! What's the matter?" And her eyes were really wide, and she said, "I'm not ready yet, Jack. I'm not coming". Of course, Jack is my grand-father's name, and he would've been dead sixteen years at that time. I knew who Jack is.'

'I got the nurse, who said, "It's probably just all the medica-tion she's on. Maybe she saw a reflection on the window or the television". Well, the television wasn't on. And even after she had recovered from the operation, she relayed that story to me again: that he had come for her and she was just not going; she wasn't ready. I thought, "Well, I'm not going to tell you that he wasn't there. If you saw him, then you saw him". I don't know whether she saw him inside the window or outside the window, but she was adamant that she saw him, and I'm not going to say that she didn't.'

'So, getting back to when she did die, I think I was waiting for Jack. We always called my grandfather Jack. And she always talked about Jack. So I think I was actually waiting for him myself. I don't know whether I expected to see light come into the room or something. I really don't know: or whether she would get up and float off, you know, how they do it in the movies. I don't know, but I was a bit wary.'

'It's amazing you know, during May before she died—she died in October—I was on holidays and I spent two days with her, because I wanted to get out all the photos and start writing down who people were and where they fitted in. I got it all down on paper, and a short time later she passed away. I asked her to tell my mother that when she died, I could have all those family photos. My mum didn't want them. And it turned out that I got all those photos.'

'The only other person I can remember dying was my grandfather: her husband. He died when I was nine. Looking back, I really wished that we had been allowed to attend the funeral, but we weren't.'

'The last time I saw him was two weeks before he actually passed away, and that was in a hospital bed. I have vivid memories of seeing him that last time. The thing that stands out the most is that he had yellow eyes. He was dying from cancer, and we were taken in two weeks prior to his death. And that's the last time I saw him. We were just told, "He's gone now". And that was it.'

'I didn't know that there was a whole funeral process and grieving that went with that. We were just left with the neighbours and my parents went off, and that was that. That was my only other experience, until my grandmother died 22 years later.'

'After she died, Mum asked us if we wanted to have a viewing, and the consensus was: yes. So we all went to the funeral parlour together, and I must say I found that rather strange. I didn't quite know what to expect, but I'm glad I did it. I was really pleased with the way she looked. She looked really well actually, considering that she was rather ill and a tired old lady when she died. I think they did a really good job. And we picked out the clothes and what have you.'

'My youngest cousin told me afterwards that she was absolutely petrified. She didn't want to go in that room by herself. And I asked her why she didn't say something. I would've gone in with her. "No, no", she said, "everybody else went in by themselves, so I thought I just had to be brave enough to go in there by myself". I said, "Oh look, that's really silly. I'd have gone in with you, if that's what you thought you needed".'

'My mother and her brother made the funeral arrangements, and told us five grandchildren that we had to be pallbearers. I didn't want to do it. I was not prepared for that, but thought I really couldn't say no. Because they needed six, they asked my husband as well. I'd never done that before. I had no idea of what to do and where to walk. What if we dropped it? All these things were racing through my mind. I even got a little bit of a giggle fit, walking in as a pallbearer.'

'Mum and my uncle had organised a celebrant who came to my grandmother's house a couple of days earlier. He met with us all to get the eulogy ready, and asked each of us to contribute something to it. And that's when we almost had an all-in brawl. Oh, he was a really lovely man; he really was. I liked him.'

'He went round the room and came to my brother. And that's the only time I've ever seen my brother really crying: absolutely sobbing. I thought, "OK, maybe he is human after all".'

'And the celebrant kept going around the room, and got to my sister. He was just asking us to give a little bit of a story on our individual, personal relationships with my grandmother. But my sister is a bit of a drama queen. She grew up in the theatre. Well, she went on: not about my grandmother, but about her. And that's not why we were there. It was: "I—this", and, "I—that". And, "I'm adopted and Grandma still took me in, and that didn't matter to her", and, "I did this –".'

'I think that if my brother had been any closer to her he would have punched her in the face. Of course, this guy had never met her before and that's all she needed: a complete stranger to put on a show for. I was really annoyed. I actually did punch her in the back half way through her bit, because I just couldn't stand it myself.'

'When it got to me, I was extremely nervous; I don't know why. I just said, "I'm the one in the family who never goes anywhere without a camera". I've got hundreds of photos. I think that stems back from my parents never having any photos of me on my own. There were always hundreds of photos of my brother by himself, and of my sister by herself. But there's none of me by myself; I'm always with either him or her, or both of them. I hated that.'

'And I think that's probably why I've gone the other way. From about fifteen years of age, everywhere I went—family picnics, or even out to dinner—I'd always take the camera and take photos. Grandma really enjoyed getting out her old black-and-white photos to show the family tree. She only had one sister, who died when my grandmother was seventeen. But even her parents, and her parents' brothers and sisters, and our aunties and my grandfather, all had these black and white photos. And I've actually got them myself today.'

'Anyway, we had the funeral and I did cry at the funeral, but nothing like I did at the hospital. I don't know whether I was embarrassed because everybody was there, or whether I just thought I'd already had that sort of initial release, and didn't need anything else. It was pretty weird.'

'From then to now, on the outside, people think I'm really hard and mean. But underneath, I've got feelings the same as the next person; although I must admit, I really try not to show them. I think for me, that stems back to my childhood from when my father would see me and say: "Don't cry. You don't need to cry aloud. You're not hurt. Your leg's not broken. Get up and walk".'

'I was brought up to not show my emotions. My parents were not people to cuddle their children, or tell them they love them regularly. I guess, from then, people perceived me as being hard and almost non-caring. But my husband will tell you differently. He sees the real me without my coat of armour on.'

'I believe the funeral was very helpful. So many little things only meant something to the family. Some were quite funny, and throughout the service, people started to laugh. And I thought, "Well that's really good". The funeral was very important. She was cremated, and that was her wish, because my grandfather had previously been cremated. They had a double plot at the cemetery.'

'I believe that my grandmother is now at the cemetery, where we left her in the ground: and that's it. I don't know about any afterlife: seeing is believing. I guess I'll make up my mind when I'm dead.'

'For me, the cemetery doesn't have any heritage value, but it is a special place. I know that's where they are, and they're safe there. I would like to see it retained. I've got the licence, and it's got another 21 years on it. I'll get that renewed again at the end of that time, and maybe thereafter for another 25, if I'm still here.'

'My mother asked me to go with her to the memorial park office to organise the plaque. And we almost had a brawl in their reception area, because I wanted to say one thing and she wanted to say something else. I relented because I didn't want to get anybody upset, but I tried to tell her.'

'We took my grandfather's plaque off, and had a big double one placed instead, with both of their names and their dates, and then us. I said to Mum, "No; I don't need my name on it. It's not about me; it's about them. Let's just say something about them that would tell people more about who they were, not who we are. That is really insignificant". We were just arguing in the reception area.'

'Both of my cousins—my mother's brother's girls: the youngest two grand-daughters—had just had babies. They both had a son in June, and of course, Grandma passed away in October. Well, that made her a great-grandmother. Didn't it? My uncle insisted that those boys' names went on the plaque before they ever knew her. They don't care. I was really angry. He insisted that their names be put on it; and they are. I didn't feel that I needed to have my name on it. It wasn't about me. OK, I was one of her grandchildren. But so what? She had five: she could've had fifty. Who cares? I just thought it needed to be a bit more about her, and her life.'

'I haven't told my mother this, but I might actually change it. Wouldn't my Grandma die?'

'When I'm at the cemetery, I feel close to my Grandmother, because that's where she is. For the initial twelve months, I needed to go there and leave flowers and talk to her. I think that helped me in my own personal grieving process. But I used to have terrible arguments with the others, because they never went. Even if I rang them up and said I was going, and I'd offer to pick them up, they wouldn't want to come for the drive: "Too busy!" I get so angry with them.'

'I last went there on Mothers Day. I must say this year I've been a bit slack. I keep saying, "I must get there". It takes me over an hour to get there; but that's no excuse. I'm a firm believer that you should visit regularly. I get so annoyed with the rest of the family, because the bastards never go. I don't know why they made such a fuss about having a memorial if they're never going to look at the bloody thing.'

'I've been really slack this year; I've probably been three times. I went on Mothers Day, her birthday, and in March, when I was on holidays. But for the first two and a half years, I went once a month; it was a routine. I felt I had to; I needed to do that. I just felt that it was the right thing to do. That's what people do when they lose family; they go and visit them. You don't just stop thinking about them. That's one of the reasons I couldn't understand why everybody's name had to be on the bloody plaque, and no one goes to visit. I felt really angry. Even my mother probably only goes twice a year: Mothers Day and her birthday.'

'When I do go, I sit there and talk. I sit down on the grave. I always buy flowers. There's just a bronze plaque; the cremated remains are in the lawn and the bronze plaque is on the concrete plinth.'

'One time—I got so annoyed—my mother actually took bloody plastic flowers there. I chucked them away and told her I didn't see them; they must have blown away or something. She knows that I go regularly, and I knew that she put them there. After about twelve months, they'd been really weather beaten and they looked awful; I didn't want to look at them. I thought, "No, Grandma deserves better than that". So I tossed them out. And the next time I heard from her, she said, "Oh, have you been up to the cemetery?" I said, "Yes". "Did you see my flowers?" "No, they weren't there; they must have blown away".'

'I normally visit by myself. My husband's probably been with me a dozen of those times during that four years. He hasn't been this year. I usually stay about half an hour. I get there and chuck out the old flowers and put the new ones in, and get the water and just wipe over the plaque, and just sit there and chat. Although I must say, the last time I went, I was in and out, because it was raining and I was getting wet. On a good day, I would sit on the grass and—you know. I mean, that's where the remains are, right in front of you. I have actually put my hand on the grass while I'm talking to her, knowing that the remains are directly underneath there.'

'I talk to her about the past and what's going on in my life: a bit of an update on what's happening, and what all the others are doing, because I know they don't visit. I remember telling her when my younger cousin had her second child: a little girl. I remember telling her that she looks like this, she's nothing like that; and it's a shame that you weren't here. You know, just a bit of a gossip session really: one way.'

'I felt really relieved the last time I went, because I felt so guilty that I hadn't been for a while. That was a Saturday and I had so many things to do that day, just running around. I got my hair cut, and I had to go and do the grocery shopping; I had to ring and catch up with a friend, and I had to drop in on my cousins and pick something up. I also had to fit in a trip to the cemetery, which is on the other side of town from me.'

'And I do really remember that day feeling, "I've got to get there. This is not one of the things that I can just put off. I can put off one of the others, but this isn't one of them". And when I did get there, I recall feeling relieved. I felt better within myself for doing that. And as it turned out, I managed to fit in all the other things anyway; but I was almost a little bit panicky, you know. "I really have to get there today. It's her birthday; I can't not go". But I think I was just putting the pressure on myself a little bit.'

'I feel I have less of a need to visit now than I did earlier, but I'll still go. It won't be as often as it was in the first two and a half to three years, but I will always go. I just couldn't feel comfortable within myself not doing that. I think she'd be hurt. I don't go as often as I would like, because of other things in my life. Something has to give way. Because it's on the other side of town, it takes me over an hour to get there. If it only took me ten minutes, I'd go every week or so.'

'I'm not someone who goes there and cries. I will always go there, and I will always talk to her. My visits have never been a very emotional experience. I think that's my own personal failing. As I said, I'm not a crier at the movies, or kids, or puppy dogs: no. I knew that I'd done my crying at the hospital, and at the funeral. It's over now. I've done that; now move on. I never actually sat there and had a bit of a cry. I've always been sitting there talking to her. Is that a bad thing? It's just who I am! I don't cry.'